	F	S
A		
~~A~~		

$$F_A + S_A = 1$$
$$F_{\bar{A}} + S_{\bar{A}} = 1$$

$$C > B\left(1 - \left(F_A + S_A\right)\right)$$

$$F_{\bar{A}} + S_{\bar{A}} \leq 1$$

—Least reason to act is world in which all probs equal .5

FREE RIDING

Richard Tuck

Free Riding

HARVARD UNIVERSITY PRESS
Cambridge, Massachusetts, and London, England   2008

Library of Congress Cataloging-in-Publication Data

Tuck, Richard, 1949–
  Free riding / Richard Tuck.
    p. cm.
  Includes bibliographical references and index.
  ISBN-13: 978-0-674-02834-0 (alk. paper)
  1. Social choice.   2. Social interaction.   3. Cooperation.
4. Self-interest.   I. Title.

  HB846.8.T78 2008
  302'.13—dc22   2007043819

Contents

Preface

This book has been an inordinately long time in writing. I first became interested in the question of free riding, or the puzzle of co-operation in large groups—as I subsequently realised—not long after Mancur Olson's book *The Logic of Collective Action* had been published in 1965. It was a puzzle which we discussed as undergraduates and graduate students at Cambridge in the late 1960s and early 1970s, though I don't think any of us were aware at the time of quite how recent the puzzle was (this is, of course, a familiar kind of ignorance on the part of students); to the participants in those discussions, particularly John Skorupski, John Barber, John Urry and Ben Wint, I owe the greatest thanks. The relationship between the puzzle and the sorites occurred to me somewhat later, partly as a result of discussions about the topic with Margaret Goddard, Jeremy Butterfield, Philip Pettit and Ross Harrison; my essay 'Is there a free-rider problem, and if so, what is it?', which appeared in a collection edited by Ross Harrison in 1979,[1] grew out of those discussions, and Philip Pettit and I have continued ever since to think and talk about the issue—until, as he generously said of me in his 1986 article 'Free Riding and Foul Dealing', 'I am unclear what is his property, what mine'.[2] I discovered subsequently that the sorites had come to be on a number of other people's minds in the late 1970s, both as a problem in epistemology and as something linked in a teasing way to the free-rider problem. Other projects then occupied my time, but I remained interested in the question, and returned to it at intervals; during this period, I found the challenge put to what I thought by Bernard Williams the most

1. Tuck, 'Is there a free-rider problem, and if so, what is it?', in *Rational Action: Studies in Philosophy and Social Science*, ed. Ross Harrison (Cambridge: Cambridge University Press, 1979), pp. 147–156.
2. Pettit, 'Free Riding and Foul Dealing', *Journal of Philosophy* 83 (1986): 361.

stimulating incentive to further reflection, and like everyone who had anything to do with him, I owe him an enormous amount. I was also helped
considerably by Martin Hollis, someone else whose death left a permanent
hole in British intellectual life. After moving to Harvard in 1996, I found
myself in the ideal environment to return to these issues; among the many
colleagues, students and friends who have helped me since then I should
single out Jim Alt, Michael Aronson, Eric Beerbohm, Charles Beitz, Alex
Broadbent, Daniela Cammack, John Ferejohn, Ben Friedman, David
Grewal, Istvan Hont, Bob and Ellen Kaplan, Michael Kramer, Helène
Landemore, David Lyons, Jane Mansbridge, Pratap Mehta, Eric Nelson,
Emma Rothschild, Martin Sandbu, Michael Sandel, Andrea Sangiovanni,
Amartya Sen, Ken Shepsle, Peter Spiegler, Anna Stilz, Dagfinnur Svein-
bjornsson and the anonymous readers for Harvard University Press. I would
especially like to thank the Centre for History and Economics at Cambridge
for supporting a term's leave from teaching in order to work on this book,
and for help and encouragement in very many ways.

Introduction: Olson's Problem

This book has a modest objective, which can be described as follows. When people collaborate in various ways—when large numbers of them share the burden of physical labour in order to erect a structure, or share the burden of funding for complex modern social services, or take over the streets in a revolutionary uprising, or turn out to vote into office a candidate of their political party—each one of them will usually believe that he is accomplishing something by what he does. Or, more accurately, each of them would *once* have believed this, since a striking feature of much modern teaching about political life is that it instructs its audience that beliefs of this kind are mistaken. Individual actions in settings like this (so it is argued) do not have the efficacy which people used to think they did; since any one of the participants could normally drop out of the enterprise without significantly affecting the outcome, the individual's contribution does not by itself have an instrumental point. It does not necessarily follow, on this view, that people should not combine in large groups to bring about collective goods (though some people have indeed concluded this), but it does follow that they cannot do so simply by thinking of themselves as possessing any individual causal efficacy. Instead (on one account) they should be compelled by some external structure of coercion to perform acts which from their individual perspective are pointless, or (on another account) they should think of what they are doing as fulfilling a duty to perform a certain action irrespective of its consequences, or (on yet another account) they should think of themselves as 'we', and thus locate agency at a level where it reacquires efficacy, or (on another) they should look on their action as 'expressing' values or loyalties. The objective of this book is simply to defend the ancient intuition that actions of this kind do have an instrumental point as individual actions, though (as we shall see) it turns out that in the process

1

we will have to think again about some of the most fundamental and puzzling features of instrumental behaviour.

I said that this objective is modest, because I do not necessarily want to use this argument to call into question any claims about the character of rational action itself. It has been commonly said that if these cases of collective action cannot be understood in terms of instrumentality, then we should not restrict the notion of rationality to instrumental action. I agree that we should not think of rational action as purely instrumental, but I do not believe that how we think about collective action ought to decide the issue; there are many reasons independent of the puzzles of collective action for supposing that a narrow account of rationality in terms of pure instrumentality does not make sense.[1] On the other hand, it would be a mistake to conclude from this that if we have a wide definition of rationality, and if individual actions in collaborative situations will fall into the category of rational action irrespective of whether they possess instrumentality, then we do not need to concern ourselves with the question of their causal efficacy. Each of the alternative views I outlined above has real consequences for the agents, including, among other things, the creation of new and possibly unnecessary coercive institutions, or psychological pressure on agents to act only if they think of themselves as part of a pre-defined group, or the turning of such things as voting into a kind of theatre of politics and weakening their relationship to the actual exercise of power. Indeed, all of these consequences can be seen in modern politics, and it may well be that they have flowed precisely from the teachings about collective action which we are going to consider in this book.

The one immodest feature of the book involves modern economics. As we shall see from the historical section (Part II), the origin of a great deal of the teaching about the inefficacy of individual collaborative actions lies in a particular tradition of economic theory which has come to be dominant at the beginning of this century. This is not just of theoretical interest, for one of the central pillars of modern economics, the notion of perfect competition, rests precisely on the claim that it is irrational in instrumental terms to contribute to a collective enterprise where one's contribution makes no appreciable difference to the outcome. The apparent naturalness of this claim led economists in the twentieth century simply to assume that it was uncontest-

---

1. See, for example, the discussion in Chapter 5 of Robert Nozick's *The Nature of Rationality* (Princeton, N.J.: Princeton University Press, 1993).

able and to build complex structures of thought upon it; and while they would be untroubled by the claim that theirs is a narrow definition of rationality (for most practising economists fully recognise this, and acknowledge that they are working within an artificially restricted domain), they would be troubled by the argument that even within their definition the prime assumption about perfect competition does not make sense.[2] Part of the point of the historical parts of the book is actually to call into question the naturalness of the assumption, by showing that most economists and political philosophers did not share it (on a large scale) until the 1930s, and that it seemed far from 'natural' to most thinking people in human history.

The best statement of the argument which we are considering came at the beginning of its widespread use in modern political science, in the 1965 book by Mancur Olson, *The Logic of Collective Action*. Olson expressly took the standard account of competition in modern economics, which he drew from the work of Edward Chamberlin in the 1930s (which we shall examine in Chapter Five), and simply extended it to social actions of all kinds.[3] What was essentially the same idea had, as Olson acknowledged, been put forward in a more limited context six years earlier by Richard Musgrave in *The Theory of Public Finance*, complete with the same reliance on Chamberlin.[4] Musgrave was concerned with 'public goods', a term which in 1959 still meant strictly goods provided to a population as a whole through a political process, such as defence, justice or free education, and he too argued that where large numbers of people were involved, they could not provide public goods through voluntary contribution, whereas small numbers might be able to. The distinction between large and small groups was at the heart of this idea; as we shall see, there had previously been a number of writers who were sceptical about the possibility of uncoerced collaboration, but it was

2. A notable exception to this generalisation is the important article by George Stigler, 'Perfect Competition, Historically Contemplated', *Journal of Political Economy* 65 (1957): 1–17.

3. Olson, *The Logic of Collective Action: Public Goods and the Theory of Groups* (Cambridge, Mass: Harvard University Press, 1965); see in particular pp. 9–10. It is worth noting that precisely at the same time James Buchanan had the same idea; see his 'Ethical Rules, Expected Values, and Large Numbers', *Ethics* 76 (1965): 1–13, esp. pp. 8–11. He acknowledges acquaintance with Olson's then unpublished work on p. 13 n. 8; Olson does the same with Buchanan's in *The Logic of Collective Action*, p. 38.

4. Richard A. Musgrave, *The Theory of Public Finance: A Study in Public Economy* (New York: McGraw-Hill, 1959), pp. 79–80. See Chapter Five below for an account of the background to Musgrave's work.

the special feature of Musgrave's, Olson's and James Buchanan's work that they stressed the theoretical importance of group size.

As I said, they did so simply by generalising the account of competition which was standard in their generation of economists. According to that account there are three types of competition in a developed market economy, 'monopoly', 'oligopoly' and 'perfect competition'. A monopolist is an agent (a single individual, a single corporation, or a successful but informal cartel) who controls the entire production of a particular commodity for a particular market. Consequently, he is able to raise or lower the price of the commodity by releasing as much or as little of it onto the market as he chooses, until he has maximised his profits. Oligopolists are—as the name implies—a few producers acting independently of one another. Because their market shares are relatively large, their decisions about how much of the commodity to bring to market also affect the price, but they lack complete individual control over the causal process. One producer can cut his price but then be undercut by another and be forced to respond in some way. Nevertheless, some degree of strategic calculation about market prices is possible for oligopolists as long as their shares in the whole industry are relatively large, since their decisions have a determinate effect on their competitors; the actual outcome is usually supposed to vary greatly with the kind of strategic assumptions employed and to be to that extent indeterminate, though under certain assumptions a degree of collaboration or collusion is entirely rational. 'Perfect' competition occurs when each producer produces so little, relative to the overall production of the industry, that he can have no individual influence on the market price: whatever his own decisions about levels of output and so on, he can take the price at which the commodity is sold as given by external forces. It is perfect competition which has played a central role in the formulation of modern general equilibrium theory. The standard example of a perfectly competitive industry in modern textbooks is the production of grain, and particularly the North American grain market, with its multitude of relatively small farmers; as we shall see, this choice of example is an extremely significant one from a historical point of view.[5]

Olson made a similar threefold division in the provision of collective goods—that is, goods which, once provided, can be enjoyed by all the group,

---

5. I have used the control of price as the distinguishing characteristic of these three types of competition, but there are, of course, other possible manipulations of the market open to monopolists and oligopolists and closed to perfect competitors. Price control is, however, the most familiar example, and the original example in the early literature. I deal with the history of discussions about the grain market in Chapter Five below.

whether they have contributed to the provision of those goods or not (as in the examples from which I began).

> In a small group in which a member gets such a large fraction of the total benefit that he would be better off if he paid the entire cost himself, rather than go without the good, there is some presumption that the collective good will be provided. In a group in which no one member got such a large benefit from the collective good that he had an interest in providing it even if he had to pay all of the cost, but in which the individual was still so important in terms of the whole group that his contribution or lack of contribution to the group objective had a noticeable effect on the costs or benefits of others in the group, the result is indeterminate. By contrast, in a large group in which no single individual's contribution makes a perceptible difference to the group as a whole, or the burden or benefit of any single member of the group, it is certain that a collective good will *not* be provided unless there is coercion or some outside inducements that will lead the members of the large group to act in their common interest. (p. 44)

This last remark was at the heart of Olson's argument: *coercion*, on his account, was justified only in these cases, where the fact that any one person's contribution was negligible rendered the whole enterprise impossible without an external apparatus of compulsion. People in these instances have to be forced to do what is undeniably in their own interests, and it is the paradoxical appearance of this claim which has continued to attract comment and discussion.

Although Olson, and many people after him, talked sometimes as if the *absolute size* of the group were what mattered, just as it was the *number* of producers who mattered in the standard economic theory, he made perfectly clear that, strictly speaking, this is not so (any more than it is, strictly, in the theory of competition).

> The standard for determining whether a group will have the capacity to act, without coercion or outside inducements, in its group interest is (as it should be) the same for market and non-market groups: it depends on whether the individual actions of any one or more members in a group are noticeable to any other individuals in the group. This is most obviously, but not exclusively, a function of the number in the group. (p. 45)

He coined the term 'latent group' to describe a group whose members contribute negligibly to the collective outcome, irrespective of whether the group is large or small in number (p. 50).[6] It is, however, a usage which has not widely been followed, and he himself often continued to refer casually to 'large' groups, as I also shall do; but it must always be remembered that size is not in itself the critical issue. Some very large groups, either in a market or in a wider social setting, will have members who behave like oligopolists. It is not difficult to find examples; a particularly instructive case (though not, it should be said, one used by Olson) would be provided by a large group of handloom weavers, who are in a perfectly competitive market under existing levels of technology—none of them, even by working all the hours in the day, can produce enough to alter unilaterally the price of cloth. But once the possibility of mechanised weaving becomes known to the group, each of them is in the position that if he is the first person to move to a machine, he can make enough cloth to alter the market price and enjoy an increase in his profits. They are now in an oligopoly, and yet the *number* of participants in the industry has not changed. (What has changed is the supply curve for each weaver.) As we know from the history of Luddism, such a change can easily take place in an industry, and the behaviour of the producers caught up in the situation will be that of oligopolists: they will try to prevent each other from moving to the new production levels, or they will try to be first in the race and make enough money to weather the subsequent storm of bankruptcies, and so on—all the moves which oligopolists characteristically make, and which, as Olson emphasised, are consequent upon their awareness that they can mutually affect one another.

Another important and interesting example where size is irrelevant, though one which Olson himself handled somewhat awkwardly, might be thought to be a large group of people who have decided to act *unanimously*. If the agreement of every participant is required to construct a collaborative enterprise, then however small any one person's contribution is relative to the whole, his refusal to make it has a direct and dramatic effect on the others. All kinds of bargaining strategies will then open up, along the lines that we shall be looking at in Chapters One and Two, and while the participants

6. In Olson's terminology, the first kind of group in the tripartite scheme mentioned above, where 'a member gets such a large fraction of the total benefit that he would be better off if he paid the entire cost himself' (that is, the equivalent of monopoly), is a 'privileged' group; the second kind, where 'the individual was still so important in terms of the whole group that his contribution or lack of contribution to the group objective had a noticeable effect on the costs or benefits of others in the group' (that is, oligopoly), is an 'intermediate' group; and the third kind is a 'latent' group.

may not get the outcome which ideally they would have wanted, some kind of co-operative activity is likely to emerge at the end of the bargaining process. Three years before Olson published *The Logic of Collective Action*, James Buchanan and Gordon Tullock had published their well-known book *The Calculus of Consent*, in which they argued just this, and claimed that a principle of unanimity would permit co-operation in areas where otherwise it must fail.[7] Olson, however, was notably reluctant to accept this argument; he recorded that

> one friendly critic has suggested that even a large pre-existing organization could continue providing a collective good simply by conducting a kind of plebiscite among its members, with the understanding that if there were not a unanimous or nearly unanimous pledge to contribute towards providing the collective good, this good would no longer be provided. This argument, if I understand it correctly, is mistaken . . . [I]f a pledge were required of every single member, or if for any other reason any one member could decide whether or not the group would get a collective good, this one member could deprive all of the others in the group of great gains. He would therefore be in a position to bargain for bribes. But since any other members of the group might gain just as much from the same holdout strategy, there is no likelihood that the collective good would be provided. (p. 45)[8]

But as Buchanan and Tullock had already pointed out, this conclusion does not follow: there is no reason to suppose that bargaining of this kind will lead to *no* collective action, since *ex hypothesi* it will be in everyone's interest to make *some* collaborative arrangement, even if it is one which benefits the holdout more than the other participants.

There *is* a problem about a unanimity rule in this context, however, and it may be that Olson intuitively grasped this. The point of unanimity, according to Buchanan and Tullock, is that it 'makes collective decision-making voluntary'; they contrasted it in this respect with, for example, majority voting, in which 'the minority of voters are forced to accede to actions which they cannot prevent and for which they cannot claim compensation for damages resulting'.[9] But in fact unanimity is a form of coercion. To see this, consider the situation faced by the people confronted by a holdout. They

7. Buchanan and Tullock, *The Calculus of Consent* (Ann Arbor: University of Michigan Press, 1962), esp. pp. 85–116.

8. With a reference to Buchanan and Tullock.

9. Buchanan and Tullock, *The Calculus of Consent*, pp 89–90.

might reasonably take the view that they could all clearly do much better by making their own arrangements and disregarding the veto of the other person; this would particularly be the case if the other person's material contribution (as distinct from his veto) had a negligible effect on the collective good. The holdout would enjoy the benefits without contributing (since we are, of course, supposing that the public good is non-excludable), but that would not make any difference to the rest, who could construct a better form of collaboration without him. But the constitutional structure in which they are operating obliges them not to do so and thereby forces them to act in ways which are patently inferior (for them) to what they would otherwise choose to do. There is no significant difference between coercion of this kind and the sort of coercion which Olson had in mind when he talked about (for example) the union closed shop as a coercive mechanism designed to prevent defection from the co-operative enterprise, despite the fact that Olson treated a unanimity rule as the antithesis of the closed shop (pp. 89–91). So Olson's reluctance to treat as one of his 'latent' groups a situation where a large number of contributors operate under a unanimity rule may have been justified, but not because the contributors would fail to collaborate; rather, because they would not be doing so *freely.*

Olson was emphatic about something else of great importance to our discussion, namely, that his theory was applicable to rational agents *whatever their goals,* and irrespective of whether they were self-interested in a narrow sense of the term or not. The concept of the latent group, he argued,

does *not* necessarily assume the selfish, profit-maximizing behavior that economists usually find in the marketplace. The concept of the large or latent group offered here holds true whether behavior is selfish or unselfish, so long as it is strictly speaking 'rational.' Even if the member of a large group were to neglect his own interests entirely, he still would not rationally contribute toward the provision of any collective or public good, since his own contribution would not be perceptible. A farmer who placed the interests of other farmers above his own would not necessarily restrict his production to raise farm prices, since he would know that his sacrifice would not bring a noticeable benefit to anyone. Such a rational farmer, however unselfish, would not make such a futile and pointless sacrifice, but he would allocate his philanthropy in order to have a perceptible effect on someone. Selfless behavior that has no perceptible effect is sometimes not even considered praiseworthy. A man who tried to hold back a flood with a pail would probably be considered more of a crank than a saint, even by those he was trying to help. It is no doubt possible infinitesimally to lower the level of a river in flood with a pail, just as it is possible for a single farmer infinitesimally to raise prices by limiting his production, but in both cases the effect is imperceptible, and those who sacrifice themselves in the interest of imperceptible improvements may not even receive the praise normally due selfless behavior. (p. 64)

In arguing this, Olson was simply aligning himself with a standard claim in twentieth-century economics, that its theories apply to rational altruists as much as to rational egotists; what is important is the connection between means and ends, not the ends themselves. This is taken for granted in much writing on the subject, but we shall see that there is a major difference in this area between the rationality of the egotist and the rationality of the altruist, a difference which (the second part of this book makes clear) corresponds to quite distinct literatures in political theory. Moral philosophers working in the utilitarian tradition had faced the problem of negligible contributions by altruistic individuals to collective enterprises long before Olson, and they had come in general to quite different conclusions—and rightly so.

These passages in Olson, as I said, still represent the best summary of the modern theory. Olson himself applied his theory to trades unions (Chapter 3), the state itself (Chapter 4) and pressure groups in a modern democracy (Chapters 5 and 6). He also touched on what became one of the prime examples for his type of argument, voting in an Anglo-American first-past-the-post system, remarking that

though most people feel they would be better off if their party were in power, they recognize that if their party is going to win, it will as likely win without them, and they will get the same benefits in any case . . . [T]he average person will not be willing to make a significant sacrifice for the party he favors, since a victory for his party provides a collective good. (pp. 163–164)

He was, however, a little hesitant about treating voting as a clear-cut case for his analysis, and argued that in practice many voters will feel that the sacrifice involved in voting is so small that it is not outweighed by the very small chance of influencing the outcome. His reluctance in this area may have been the result of an awareness that the facts of voting do not fit his argument (for surprisingly many people vote in political systems which lay no penalty on not voting), but it may also reflect an instinct that voting is different from his other cases, though he gave no indication of why that might be so.

Nevertheless, since Olson's time it has become a commonplace that his argument covers voting,[10] and this was already implied by one of Olson's precursors in using standard economic theory to cover political action, Anthony Downs. Downs's *An Economic Theory of Democracy* (1957) has probably had as much influence on modern political science as *The Logic of Collective Action* itself; in it, Downs attempted to interpret party behaviour in a modern democracy as a strategy intended to secure as many votes as possible in the equivalent of a competitive market, and voting as a means to 'purchase' the political outcomes which the voter desired.[11] Virtually at the end of the book, Downs raised a problem about his model: in a normal modern election, 'hundreds, thousands, or even millions of other citizens are also eligible to vote; so each man's ballot is only one drop in a vast sea. The probability that his vote will decide the election, given the votes of all others, is extremely small, though not zero'. Accordingly, there was no good reason for a citizen in normal circumstances to vote at all.[12] Downs did not spell out

10. See, for example, Morris P. Fiorina, 'The Voting Decision: Instrumental and Expressive Aspects', *Journal of Politics* 38 (1976): 392.

11. Downs, *An Economic Theory of Democracy* (New York: Harper, 1957). Downs was unclear about whether his voters were acting for egotistic or altruistic reasons—that is, whether they believed that they would personally benefit from a particular party's victory or whether they thought that such a victory would benefit other people in the community. When defining what he called 'the meaning of rationality in the model', he was emphatic (like Olson) that economic rationality 'refers solely to a man who moves towards his goals in a way which, to the best of his knowledge, uses the least possible input of scarce resources per unit of valued output', and that even an ascetic could be 'rational' in this sense (p. 5). But later he remarked that the axiom which is 'crucial to all the rest of our model' is that 'every individual, though rational, is also selfish . . . Thus, whenever we speak of rational behavior, we always mean rational behavior directed primarily towards selfish ends' (p. 27). His own resolution of the voting problem was that people get 'satisfaction' from sustaining democracy; even apart from its vulnerability to his own argument (something which has often been pointed out, for example by Fiorina in the article cited in n. 10), this view renders the distinction between selfishness and altruism hard to maintain, since 'satisfaction' in the standard economists' account simply means securing a particular goal, which may itself be entirely altruistic in character.

12. Ibid., p. 244. He also talked about a vote under normal circumstances having 'almost no chance of influencing the outcome' (p. 245). As we shall see in Chapter Two, these may not be equivalent ways of expressing the idea.

precisely what he meant by 'deciding the election', and it is clear that he did not think it was necessary to do so: he was relying on the claim that unless I believe that the election will be determined by one vote (in the simplest two-candidate cases, either there will be a tie, in which case one vote has prevented one of the candidates from winning, or a candidate wins by one vote), I have no instrumental reason to cast my ballot. He was also relying on the fact that in a large-number electorate, my vote will have very little chance of being the determining vote (this is the point at which Downs's argument seemed later to be a version of Olson's). Downs tried to save his general theory from this apparently devastating objection with the argument that the rational voter will vote even when he thinks that there is a very small chance that his vote will be decisive, if he puts a very high value on averting the collapse of democracy, but this argument has usually failed to convince his readers. After all, if many other people vote, democracy is secure, and if I am the only citizen to vote, democracy is doomed anyway, so either way (apparently) I should not vote, as long as there are any appreciable costs for me involved in the process. This obviously resembles Olson's argument, with either the election of a particular candidate or the preservation of the democratic system being the common good and a single vote being the negligible contribution towards it. Judged by Olson's test, which was (it will be remembered) to ask whether an individual's action made a noticeable difference to the other members of the group, any particular vote is on the face of it most unlikely to pass muster.

The negligibility of a particular contribution to the common good was thus at the absolute heart of Olson's argument, and it is this which is going to concern us in the rest of this book. But it is important to observe that Olson himself did not fully recognise the far-reaching difficulties into which he was potentially getting himself. I will simply sketch the difficulties here, as they are discussed in greater detail later, but they will indicate some of the issues we shall be concerned with. As we saw, Olson believed that for a latent group, 'a collective good will *not* be provided unless there is coercion or some outside inducements that will lead the members of the large group to act in their common interest'. He meant by this, we should be clear, something stronger than the familiar weak claim (with which it would be hard to quarrel) that one should not always rely on voluntary contributions to provide common benefits. David Hume, for example, whose views in this area I shall broadly be endorsing (and who was in fact the opponent of Olsonian kinds of reasoning, despite the fact that he has often been called in aid by Olson's followers, and indeed by

Olson himself),[13] took the common-sense view that although it might make instrumental sense to contribute, people often do not act rationally, and mechanisms of enforcement such as the state are desirable to get them to do so. This is theoretically quite different from Olson's position, since the striking feature of Olson's argument is precisely the claim that non-contribution without enforcement is not a *failure* of reason but an *exercise* of it.

Olson believed this, as we have seen, because (on an analogy with perfect competition) any particular contribution to the common project makes no appreciable difference to the outcome and it is therefore irrational for me to make the contribution. The problem with his solution, however, is that if this is so, then on the face of it *enforcing* any particular contribution to the common project can make no appreciable difference in itself and is therefore (by the same reasoning) an irrational action for the enforcement agency to take. One might of course say that there *is* a non-negligible benefit from forcing a particular prospective defector to contribute, though not from his contribution itself, since if his defection is not prevented, there will be some kind of incentive to other people to defect. But there is no reason to suppose that this is going to be true in most cases. For example, the incentive is presumably provided by the knowledge that in a particular instance the rule has not been enforced, and one case of non-enforcement which is insignificant in other respects is unlikely to lead the other members of the group to conclude that the coercive mechanism has suddenly rusted up. After all, most of us worry about being punished for breaking the law while living in societies with very high levels of non-enforcement. Enforcement in a particular case will have a significant cost—the enforcer's time, at the very least, and presumably also some cost to each member of the society through the expense of the agency—and it will not in *that* instance deliver a significant

13. Olson, *The Logic of Collective Action*, p. 33 n. 53 records Olson's debt to John Rawls, who had been interested in free-rider problems at least since his 'Justice as Fairness' article (*Philosophical Review* 67 [1958]: 164–194) and arguably since his famous 'Two Concepts of Rules' (*Philosophical Review* 64 [1955]: 3–32), for drawing his attention to Hume's well-known remarks in the *Treatise of Human Nature* about draining a meadow, though Olson observed correctly that 'Hume's argument is however somewhat different from my own'. The idea that Hume's views were the same as Olson's appears to have entered the mainstream with an article by Norman Frohlich and Joe A. Oppenheimer, 'I Get By with a Little Help from My Friends', *World Politics* 23 (1970): 104–120. See also Russell Hardin, *Collective Action* (Baltimore: Johns Hopkins University Press, 1982), p. 40, and Michael Taylor, *The Possibility of Cooperation* (Cambridge: Cambridge University Press, 1987), pp. 159–160. I discuss Hume's view in detail in the historical section of this book.

benefit; so why should we require the members of the enforcement agency to act? We cannot, of course, on Olson's premises introduce at this point such notions as fairness, since if they were given weight in the first place, an enforcement agency would not be necessary in the sense that Olson supposed—though it might well be necessary in the weaker, Humean sense.

Oddly enough, Olson himself made just this point in his general discussion of the theoretical issue involved in his idea.

> Some critics may argue that the rational person will, indeed, support a large organization, like a lobbying organization, that works in his interest, because he knows that if he does not, others will not do so either, and then the organization will fail, and he will be without the benefit that the organization could have provided. This argument shows the need for the analogy with the perfectly competitive market. For it would be quite as reasonable to argue that prices will never fall below the levels a monopoly would have charged in a perfectly competitive market, because if one firm increased its output, other firms would also, and the price would fall; but each firm could foresee this, so it would not start a chain of price-destroying increases in output. In fact it does not work out this way in a competitive market; nor in a large organization. When the number of firms involved is large, no one will notice the effect on price if one firm increases its output, and so no one will change his plans because of it. Similarly, in a large organization, the loss of one dues payer will not noticeably increase the burden for any other dues player, and so a rational person would not believe that if he were to withdraw from an organization he would drive others to do so. (p. 12)

Or drive others to *stop* him from withdrawing, by the same argument.

We can see the difficulties which arise more clearly with the theory, perhaps, if we drop the idea of a separate agency and imagine individuals committing themselves to contribute to the common good on condition that other members of the group do likewise (analogous to the model in Thomas Hobbes for the transition from the state of nature to civil society, though as we shall see, Hobbes's theory is in fact dealing with quite different issues from these modern ideas about collaboration). Each individual could follow up his commitment with some personal mechanism for ensuring that he sticks to the commitment if the conditions are met, such as the devices that people employ to force themselves to give up smoking (or Ulysses employed against the Sirens), so there is no difficulty in principle about ensuring that the commitments once made will be honoured. The difficulty lies rather in specifying the conditions under which the individual will bind himself to participate. In Hobbes, it is famously a universal agreement: civil union is

> made by Covenant of every man with every man, in such manner, as if every man should say to every man, *I Authorise and give up my Right of Governing my selfe, to this Man, or to this Assembly of men, on this condition, that thou give up thy Right to him, and Authorise all his Actions in like manner.*[14]

But outside the special circumstances of Hobbes's political theory, a *universal* conditional agreement of this kind does not make sense. It cannot be that I bind myself in a large group to contribute on condition that *everyone* does likewise, since then one defection is sufficient to destroy the whole enterprise. As I said, we all live perfectly happily and responsibly in states where compliance with the law is very far from universal (a point which Hume also made, and which is connected to his much looser and more reasonable view of these matters).

Instead, the common-sense condition has to be something like 'I agree to contribute if *enough* other members do so', and here we encounter the deep difficulties implicit in Olson's argument. Is 'enough' going to be a specifiable number? If it is, is it an arbitrary figure, or does it represent a genuine threshold below which contribution is pointless, since there will not be sufficient contributions to construct a common good which is better for each of the contributors than holding on to their money, time or effort would have been? If it is an arbitrary figure, then the same objection applies as in the case of universal compliance—why should one defection mean that an enterprise fails when even with that defection it could have succeeded? If it is a genuine threshold, then the negligibility condition has been violated: there is at least one action—the action which pushes the group over the threshold—which is not negligible and which makes a real difference to all the members of the group, including the relevant contributor. Once the negligibility condition has been violated, on Olson's argument, strategic interaction becomes possible and the analogy with perfect competition breaks down.

As I said, this is a sketch of the difficulties, and in particular I do not at the moment want to go into the question of how the negligibility assumption *can* be true for each member of the group (something which people often deny when presented with the argument outlined above). But it is enough

14. Hobbes, *Leviathan,* ed. Richard Tuck (Cambridge: Cambridge University Press, 1991), p. 120.

to show that putting negligibility at the centre of an argument about collective action can have far-reaching consequences, well beyond Olson's initial intentions. The truth is that Olson, like others who have seen coercion as an answer to the puzzle, smuggled in through the back door an assumption that collaboration is natural, and that the insignificant is significant, just as long as the arena for collaboration is organising the effective coercion of the members of the group. But if we should be swayed by the negligible character of our contribution, then we should be swayed at every stage of the argument, and no collaboration becomes possible.

I have divided this book into two parts. In the first part, I look at the theoretical assumptions underlying the Olsonian argument and distinguish the various versions of the argument, which have often been confused; I then consider what may be the appropriate way to think about the causal relationship between an individual's action and a collective or aggregate outcome. Part I ends with an extended discussion of the implications of negligibility, for both our judgements (that is, our descriptions of things) and our actions. The second part is concerned with the history of ideas about collaboration, in order to establish the point which I made at the beginning of this Introduction that Olson's argument, and the arguments of the economists on whom he drew, were remarkably recent: very few real instances can be found of this kind of theory much before the 1930s! Of course, there are some precursors, as there are to any novelty, but on examination they virtually always turn out to have lacked some vital feature of the modern approach. This history is theoretically important, as well as interesting in its own right, as one of the pillars of the modern view has often been thought to be its obviousness: the idea that we should not collaborate in these circumstances is not supposed to be a subtle or complex one. And yet until the 1930s the opposite would have been true, and the idea that we should *not* collaborate where the outcome would clearly be beneficial to all of us would have seemed very far-fetched. Philosophical discussion concentrated on the question of the circumstances in which we might be required to sacrifice our own interests on behalf of *other* people, and not on whether we ought to be required to do so on behalf of *ourselves*. Seen from a long perspective, the past seventy or eighty years have been a very unusual period, in which a rather paradoxical account of human rationality has been adopted as the norm; if we abandon it, we will find that eighteenth- and nineteenth-century theorists are often better guides for us than their twentieth-century successors have proved to be.

PART I

Philosophy

CHAPTER ONE

The Prisoners' Dilemma

Olson's argument must be carefully distinguished from various similar arguments about the difficulty of collaborative activity. He himself did not always need to do so, and it sometimes comes as a surprise to current readers of his book that—for example—he nowhere used the term 'free rider' to describe the member of a latent group who does not contribute to the common project, nor did he discuss his ideas in terms of the familiar notion of the 'prisoners' dilemma'. Both these features of modern discussions did, however, emerge right at the beginning of the discussion of Olson's problem, in the article by James Buchanan which I mentioned in a footnote on page 3. Buchanan spelt out the relevance of large groups to the 'free-rider' problem in public finance theory, and drew attention to a similarity between this argument and the prisoners' dilemma, though he was also well aware of the important difference between them. The problem, he wrote,

> is similar to, although not identical with, that which is commonly discussed in games theory as the 'prisoners' dilemma'. . . . The difference between the prisoners' dilemma and the large-group ethical dilemma discussed here lies in the fact that, as ordinarily presented, the former remains a small-group phenomenon. The results emerge because of the absence of communication between the prisoners and because of their mutual distrust. The large-number dilemma is a more serious one because no additional communication or repetition of choices can effectively modify the results.[1]

1. James Buchanan, 'Ethical Rules, Expected Values, and Large Numbers', *Ethics* 76 (1965): 8.

But many subsequent writers have been much less sensitive to the dissimilarities between the various arguments.[2] In the next three chapters I want to distinguish between the different arguments with which Olson's problem has been confused, so that we can be clear about what was distinctive in his theory and—among other things—how recent it was.

The central issue we are considering, we should remind ourselves, is whether it is rational to defect from a collaborative enterprise when one's contribution to it is negligible, but not rational (or at least not necessarily so) when it is not. Olson's claim, and the claim of the economists from whom he derived his ideas, was that many small-scale situations offer good reasons for the participants to collaborate, even when there is no direct and immediate benefit to them from doing so; strategic considerations, or questions of long-run as against short-run benefits, can lead people to contribute to collective goods when their contribution can make an appreciable difference to the outcome. This is never going to be the case (they believed) where the contribution is very small in comparison with the size of the enterprise. The particular cases in which they were interested were initially collaborations between producers in an industry—formal or informal cartels—but the theory was straightforwardly generalisable to other forms of collaboration, as Olson realised.

It is important to stress that the theory put forward by Olson and Buchanan was not in general a sceptical one about social co-operation: unlike a number of earlier writers,[3] as Buchanan's remark quoted above illustrates,

2. Among the principal works which treat Olson's problem as an instance of the prisoners' dilemma are Michael Taylor, *Anarchy and Cooperation* (London: Wiley, 1976), and Russell Hardin, *Collective Action* (Baltimore: Johns Hopkins University Press, 1982). Hardin was able to do so in part because he simply asserted, with no textual support, that Olson meant by a latent group anything which is not 'privileged' (p. 20; for this terminology, see Introduction, n. 6). That is, he squeezed Olson's argument into a form where (in Olson's terms) oligopoly is the paradigm for non-co-operation rather than perfect competition, and therefore Olson's problem automatically becomes the prisoners' dilemma. He then expressed some puzzlement that Olson had apparently elsewhere divided latent groups into 'intermediate' and 'latent' (pp. 39–40). The identity of the two puzzles is often now taken for granted, for example by Per Molander in 'The Prevalence of Free Riding', *Journal of Conflict Resolution* 36 (1992): 756: 'the dilemma, normally labelled the free-rider problem or the prisoner's dilemma . . .'.

3. William J. Baumol is a good example. In the first edition of *Welfare Economics and the Theory of the State* (Cambridge, Mass.: Harvard University Press, 1952), a 'somewhat revised' version of his Ph.D. thesis submitted in 1949 at the London School of Economics under the supervision of Robbins), he gathered many examples of situations where individuals might fail to collaborate in group activities even though their interest lay in successful

they believed that small groups could in principle solve co-ordination problems even where the immediate interests of the participants might pull in the opposite direction. Instead, they were exercised by what they took to be the impossibility of such a solution in the case of a large group,[4] even where (as Buchanan said) communication among the members of the group was permitted. The difference between the two situations, for them, turned on the *causal efficacy* of an individual action: my action might be said to have contributed towards a beneficial outcome for myself if the action had a determinate effect, in the sense that without it the outcome would have been significantly different. This might be because my action directly brought about some benefit for me, but it might also be (for example) because it had a determinate effect on some other person, and his response represented the benefit for me. But (they believed) negligible contributions could never have causal efficacy of either a direct or an indirect kind assigned to them; their negligibility consisted precisely in their being so insignificant that nothing of consequence could be affected by them. This was the point made in the long passage about incentives which I quoted from Olson in the Introduction:

> When the number of firms involved is large, no one will notice the effect on price if one firm increases its output, and so no one will change his plans because of it. Similarly, in a large organization, the loss of one dues payer will not noticeably increase the burden for any other dues player, and so a rational person would not believe that if he were to withdraw from an organization he would drive others to do so.

To understand the point which Olson and Buchanan were making, as I have said, we should consider the arguments with which their claim is often confused. There are two in particular which deserve close attention: the first

---

collaboration, but he never clearly distinguished between cases where the individuals' actions directly affected one another (and therefore strategic interactions were possible) and 'Olsonian' cases where they did not. One of his main examples (Chapter 8) was international relations, but the relative size of countries is such that they seldom by their actions produce negligible effects on their neighbours. He was also willing to use Augustin Cournot's account of duopoly as an example of the failure of collaboration, though at the same time he acknowledged the difficulties in doing so (p. 152 n. 2, 2d ed., 1965; I discuss Cournot's ideas in Chapter Five). It is significant that Russell Hardin took the view that Baumol broadly anticipated Olson (*The Logic of Collective Action*, p. 21); this makes good sense, given Hardin's belief that Olson's problem and the prisoners' dilemma are the same problem.

   4. By 'large', of course, I mean *relatively* large—an Olsonian latent group.

is the prisoners' dilemma; the second is the kind of argument which Anthony Downs put forward about voting. As we have seen, Olson and Buchanan recognised both these arguments as being similar to their own but were cautious about accepting either of them as identical to their idea— rightly, in my opinion. Many readers may be surprised to find me claiming that voting is not an instance of an Olsonian puzzle, given that (as I have already remarked) there is a widespread belief among political scientists that it is a prime example of the irrationality of participation in a large-scale enterprise; but we shall see that individual actions in the kind of common enterprise which a voting system exemplifies can in fact have real causal efficacy. I shall deal with voting in Chapter Two, while in this chapter I shall consider the prisoners' dilemma.

There is no difficulty about showing that the causal efficacy of the participants' actions is a key feature of a standard prisoners' dilemma. The puzzle in its standard modern form appeared around 1950[5] and was widely used only after it featured in R. Duncan Luce and Howard Raiffa's *Games and Decisions* in 1957,[6] so it was a relatively recent idea when Buchanan referred to it. The basic shape of the puzzle, on the other hand, may be extremely old, and even its formal analysis (though not in game-theoretic terms) goes back to the early nineteenth century, since it is essentially the economists' puzzle of duopoly or oligopoly. It was precisely their familiarity with the arguments about oligopoly which led Olson and Buchanan to be wary about the resemblance between their idea and the prisoners' dilemma. In the game-theoretic version of the puzzle, two criminals have been captured by the police and are kept in separate cells. Each one is then offered a deal: if he makes a full confession, implicating his partner, and that confession is instrumental in convicting the partner, he will be given a reward and set free.

5. It is believed to have been invented by Merrill Flood and Melvin Dresher and to have been named, and linked to the story of the prisoners, by the pioneering game theorist A. W. Tucker of Princeton at a seminar in the Psychology Department at Stanford University in that year. Tucker, however, never published a discussion of the puzzle (a circumstance oddly similar to that of another famous puzzle in decision theory, the Newcomb Problem, which, to compound the oddity, can itself plausibly be seen as a version of the prisoners' dilemma; see David Lewis's 'Prisoners' Dilemma Is a Newcomb Problem', *Philosophy and Public Affairs* 8 (1979): 235–240, reprinted in his *Philosophical Papers* (New York: Oxford University Press, 1986), II, pp. 299–304. For the 1950 seminar, see George Norman and Manfredi La Manna, *The New Industrial Economics* (Leicester: Edward Elgar, 1992), p. 43 n. 4, and for the role of Flood and Dresher, see Hardin, *Collective Action*, p. 24 n. 16.

6. Luce and Raiffa, *Games and Decisions* (New York: Wiley, 1957), pp. 94–102.

Arab

	Confess	Keep Silent
Confess	ii, 2	iv, 1
Keep Silent	i, 4	iii, 3

Roman

Figure 1.1

If he refuses to confess but his partner implicates him, he will receive a heavy sentence (say ten years). If he confesses but the confession does not help the police because his partner confesses at the same time, he receives a light sentence (say one year). If both the criminals keep silent, the police have to let them go. So each criminal is faced with four possible outcomes; in ascending order of preference, they are (1) a heavy sentence; (2) a light sentence; (3) freedom; (4) freedom and a reward.

The criminals can then think about what the best response for each of them would be to any particular policy followed by the other, and we can arrange these outcomes in a familiar game-theoretic matrix. To make the matrix clearer, and to avoid introducing what are often confusing questions about interpersonal comparisons of utility between the prisoners, I have chosen to use roman numerals to denote the outcomes for one prisoner and arabic numerals for the other, and to label the prisoners accordingly (see Figure 1.1).[7]

The 'dilemma', as is well known, then arises from the fact that in this situation, whatever the other criminal does, it is in each criminal's interest to confess (in game-theoretic terminology, the 'dominant' choice is to confess and the 'dominated' choice is to keep silent). If the Roman keeps silent, the Arab does better by confessing than by keeping silent (4 is better for him than 3); if the Roman confesses, the Arab still does better by confessing than by keeping silent (2 is better than 1). The same is true *pari passu* for the Ro-

---

7. So the Roman, in the conventional terminology, is the row man.

man. So both the Roman and the Arab will confess, but both would have been better off if they had both kept silent. So what is 'rational' for each of them to do individually (assuming that to follow the dominant strategy is to act rationally) turns out to be what economists call Pareto suboptimal for them—each of them would do better if both of them acted 'irrationally'.

An important feature of this single episode, which game theorists have termed 'the one-shot game', is that although neither criminal's decision depends on what the other criminal chooses to do, it is still the case that each criminal's actions have a real and appreciable effect on the other criminal's utility. If the Roman chooses to confess rather than keep silent, then whatever the Arab has chosen to do, the Arab's utility is affected by the Roman's decision. The matrix is constructed in such a way that given any particular choice by one of the criminals, the other criminal's action is both necessary and sufficient to bring about the outcomes for each of them. If this were not so, then there would, of course, be no dilemma, at least not of the kind captured by this matrix. What we might have instead would be a matrix like the one in Figure 1.2, in which it is straightforwardly sensible for each player to confess.

Because the prisoners' dilemma does not have this structure, many people have observed that it makes sense for a player in it to retaliate in various ways to the other player's actions, once the possibility of playing more than one round in the game has been raised. There is now a large literature examining the possible strategies which can arise in repeated games of this sort. An obvious one, which is the subject of a whole book by Robert

| | Arab | |
	Confess	Keep Silent
Confess	ii, 2	ii, 1
Keep Silent	i, 2	i, 1

(Roman)

Figure 1.2

Axelrod,[8] is 'tit for tat': if you defect from our common enterprise and make me suffer, next time round I will defect and make you suffer, and so on until we end up co-operating. This is also in effect what has been suggested by modern economists as the correct strategy for firms under oligopolistic conditions.[9] Of course, if we know the games are going to end at a determinate point, tit for tat ceases to make sense as a strategy as the last round approaches, though precisely where it ceases has been a matter for debate. Strictly speaking, prior knowledge of where the sequence of games will end ought to dictate non-co-operation in every round. If I know that the sequence ends at round 100, at 99 I will know that a defection in 100 will not be punished, and therefore I should defect at 100. You will reason likewise. Consequently, I know that you are going to defect at 100 anyway; my action at 99 will have no effect on what you do, and my decision at 99 will accordingly not be motivated by a desire to prevent you from punishing me. Therefore I will defect at 99; so will you. And so on, back to the first round.

But the situation in this determinate repeated game is still different from that in the one-shot game, because my strategy depends on my estimate of what my opponent will do. In a one-shot game—this is, after all, a key feature of it—it does not matter to me whether you choose to co-operate or to defect, since defection is my own dominant strategy. In contrast, it may well be—as Luce and Raiffa, writing in the early days of game theory, recognised—that players would not actually follow backward inductive reasoning of this kind in a repeated game; a long but determinate series of rounds might instead invite what Luce and Raiffa called a kind of 'game teaching', in which at the beginning the players manifest their intention to punish defection by offering co-operation and then withdrawing it for some rounds if their opponent does not co-operate. If each player has grounds for expecting that his opponent will play in this way, he will himself have a reason to do so. At some point the players will decide that the end is close enough to abandon this strategy and move to full non-co-operation, but it will be hard to say precisely where that point will be. As long as there is a chance that my opponent is not fully committed to backward inductive reasoning from the last round, it makes sense to try to guide him into co-operation. (This is also the conclusion reached by Russell

8. Axelrod, *The Evolution of Cooperation* (New York: Basic Books, 1984).
9. See, for example, James W. Friedman, *Oligopoly Theory* (Cambridge: Cambridge University Press, 1983), pp. 124–132.

Hardin.)[10] Moreover, it is agreed by everyone who has considered the matter that if the end of the iterated games is *not* known in advance, strategies such as tit for tat make perfectly good sense indefinitely—and this is normally the case in real-life versions of the prisoners' dilemma, such as oligopoly. But—to repeat the point—underlying all these discussions is the assumption that there is a good reason for employing some kind of strategy against an individual opponent, because that opponent is in turn capable of significantly affecting one's own utility, and this is precisely what is denied in the original Olsonian argument. It is this absence of mutual effect which also, as we saw in the Introduction, undermines Olson's own solution to the free-rider puzzle, which might otherwise have been on the same lines as Axelrod's: the absence of mutual effect precludes the implementation of effective coercive mechanisms unless we introduce some extraneous principle which might have been sufficient to justify collaboration in the first place.

Although mutual effect is most obvious in a two-person version of the prisoners' dilemma, there is no reason in principle why a dilemma of this shape cannot be constructed with any number of players. I say 'this shape', as one has to be cautious how one extends the two-person version to an *n*-person version; different assumptions about what is salient in the two-person version lead to different formulations of an *n*-person version. Thomas Schelling gave good advice in a well-known article of 1973, when he observed that in the classic prisoners' dilemma,

> [t]he influence of one individual's choice on the other's payoff we can call the *externality*. Then the effect of his own choice on his own payoff can in parallel be called the *internality*. We then describe prisoner's dilemma as the situation in which each person has a uniform (dominant) internality and a uniform (dominant) externality, the internality and the externality are opposed rather than coincident, and the externality outweighs the internality.
>
> The situation is fairly simple to define. But when we turn to the three-person or multiperson version, the two-person definition is ambiguous. 'The other' equals 'all others' when there are but two; with more than two,

---

10. Hardin, *Collective Action*, pp. 146–149. Hardin also notes the similarity between this situation and the well-known 'Hanged Man' or 'surprise examination' paradox. Timothy Williamson, 'Inexact Knowledge', *Mind* 101 (1992): 217–242, provides arguments for the failure of backward induction based on his general theory of inexact knowledge. For a recent, somewhat different way of putting the same point, see John Geanakoplos, 'The Hangman's Paradox and Newcomb's Paradox as Psychological Games', Cowles Foundation Discussion Paper 1128, 1996.

there are in-between possibilities. We have to elaborate the definition in a way that catches the spirit of prisoner's dilemma, and see whether we then have something distinctive enough to go by a proper name.[11]

His suggestion about how to catch the spirit of the two-person version, which remains the best attempt to do so, went as follows.

There are two main definitional questions. (1) Are the externalities mono-tonic—is an individual always better off, the more there are among the oth-ers who play their dominated strategies? (2) Does the individual's own pref-erence remain constant no matter how many among the others choose one way or the other—does he have a fully dominant choice? Tentatively an-swering, for purposes of definition, yes to these two questions . . . a *uniform multiperson prisoner's dilemma* . . . can be defined as a situation in which:

(1) There are n individuals, each with the same binary choice and the same payoffs.

(2) Each has a dominant choice, a 'best choice' whatever the others do. (And the same choice is dominant for everybody.)

(3) Whichever choice an individual makes, his dominant or his dominated, any individual is better off, the more there are among the others who make their dominated choices.

(4) There is some number k, greater than 1, such that, if individuals num-bering k or more make dominated choices and the rest do not, those who make dominated choices are better off than if they had all made dominant choices, but, if they number less than k, this is not true. (The uniformity of participants makes k independent of the particular indi-viduals making dominated choices.)[12]

Schelling thus took non-negligible mutual effects to be an essential part of the 'spirit' of the prisoners' dilemma: this is captured in his condition that

11. Schelling, 'Hockey Helmets, Concealed Weapons, and Daylight Saving: A Study of Binary Choices with Externalities', *Journal of Conflict Resolution* 17 (1973): 385–386.

12. Ibid., p. 386. This last condition expresses the idea that a public good may benefit more people than are necessary to bring it into existence; as Schelling said later, k 'repre-sents the minimum size of any coalition that can gain by making the dominated choice. If k is equal to n, the only worthwhile coalition—the only enforceable contract that is profit-able for all who sign—is the coalition of the whole. Where k is less than n, it is the mini-mum number that, though resentful of free riders, can be profitable for those who join (though more profitable for those who stay out)' (p. 387).

externalities are monotonic, since in Olson's problem it is at some point a matter of indifference to me whether any other individual plays his part in the collaborative enterprise (this, after all, is what it means for his contribution to be negligible). By the same token, the existence of a determinate point when the loss of one individual renders the enterprise no longer a prisoners' dilemma (Schelling's k) presupposes that one individual's contribution makes a real and appreciable difference to the other participants. Consequently, an Olsonian latent group is not an example of an n-person prisoners' dilemma, at least as it was defined by Schelling. A Schelling-type n-person prisoners' dilemma is in principle soluble by repeated play, like the two-person version; but as we have seen, that cannot be true of Olson's problem.

One might, of course, simply stipulate (as Hardin, again, has done) that an Olsonian latent group is a limiting case of an n-person prisoners' dilemma— that as the relative effect of each participant's actions gets smaller, the situation tends to become closer to the Olsonian picture. Obviously in some sense this is right, but the key point is that many distinctive features of the prisoners' dilemma disappear at the point at which the agents concerned begin to treat their effect on one another as negligible. In the economic tradition from which Olson drew, this point was taken to represent a step change in the behaviour of the group,[13] precisely because one cannot (so to speak) gradually recognise that one has a negligible effect. (We shall see later why the language of a step change may not in fact be suitable for analysing these situations, without its being the case that there is a gradual transition from a prisoners' dilemma to an Olsonian problem.) More importantly, perhaps, the difference between Olson's problem and the small-number prisoners' dilemma means that we cannot learn very much about the characteristics of the former simply by studying the latter. Olson was well aware of this, and it was indeed one of the points of his study.

There has been a vast amount of research into the small group in recent years,[14] much of it based on the idea that the results of (experimentally

---

13. For example, Edward Hasting Chamberlin, *The Theory of Monopolistic Competition,* 5th ed. (Cambridge, Mass.: Harvard University Press, 1947), p. 48. For further discussion of this point, see below, p. 200.

14. Olson gave a number of examples, including Kurt Lewin's *Field Theory in Social Change* (New York: Harper, 1951), and Sidney Verba's *Small Groups and Political Behavior* (Princeton, N.J.: Princeton University Press, 1961).

convenient) research on small groups can be made directly applicable to larger groups merely by multiplying these results by a scale factor. Some social psychologists, sociologists and political scientists assume that the small group is so much like the large group, in matters other than size, that it must behave according to somewhat similar laws. But if the distinctions drawn here among the 'privileged' group, the 'intermediate' group, and the 'latent' group have any meaning, this assumption is unwarranted, at least so long as the groups have a common, collective interest. For the small, privileged group can expect that its collective needs will probably be met one way or another, and the fairly small (or intermediate) group has a fair chance that voluntary action will solve its collective problems, but the large, latent group cannot act in accordance with its common interests so long as the members of the group are free to further their individual interests. (pp. 57–58)

At a time when there is, for example, extensive interest in experimental instances of small-number prisoners' dilemmas as a way of learning something about political science, Olson's warning still seems timely.

An additional point of some importance is that whereas Olson and Buchanan (and Downs) asserted that their argument was applicable to both altruists and non-altruists, this is not true of small groups with potential strategic interactions. Clearly, many kinds of altruists will not be troubled by a prisoners' dilemma; a pair of utilitarians, for example, would simply choose the utilitarianly optimal outcome (often, though not invariably, collaboration).[15] In the Roman/Arab example above, if we assume interpersonal comparisons and a common scale, both prisoners keeping silent is straightforwardly the preferred outcome for each participant if they are utilitarians. Olson and Buchanan were justified in saying that their argument was applicable to altruists precisely because they envisaged circumstances in which there would be no causal effect on the outcome of any particular action, and therefore no reason even for an altruist (at least of a utilitarian type—I exclude altruists who are primarily concerned with justice) to be interested in collaborating. Under other circumstances, one's general moral position will make a powerful difference to one's behaviour, as might be expected.

15. See Donald H. Regan, *Utilitarianism and Co-operation* (Oxford: Oxford University Press, 1980), pp 62–63.

CHAPTER TWO

Voting and Other Thresholds

As I said in the Introduction, many modern political scientists have supposed that voting is a prime example of an Olsonian problem: what is the instrumental point of voting in a normal election, when the chances of one's vote making any real difference in a large electorate are apparently negligible? As Anthony Downs said, '[E]ach man's ballot is only one drop in a vast sea'. No one vote has any causal relationship to the outcome of the election unless the election is so close that the winning candidate wins by one vote. So the reason for voting cannot be the causal or instrumental character of the act with respect to the outcome but must instead be some feature of the activity which makes sense irrespective of the electoral result. In this chapter, I want to consider this claim in more detail, and to argue that the point of voting has been widely misunderstood. Voting can in fact be seen as a particularly clear example of a certain kind of instrumentally rational collaborative action, and if we properly distinguish between this kind of practice and a genuinely Olsonian situation, we will see much more deeply into what Olson had in mind.

Though Downs remains the best-known figure to have argued that there is no straightforward point to voting, he was not the first. Significantly, the argument seems not to have occurred to any of the many writers on democratic politics in the eighteenth and nineteenth centuries (any more, it should be said, than Olson's idea did; see Chapter Four). In particular, one looks in vain for any proper discussion of the problem in the great mid-nineteenth-century works on voting systems, such as Thomas Hare's *Treatise on the Election of Representatives, Parliamentary or Municipal* (1859), in which he urged the adoption of a complex system of proportional representation.[1] But by the middle of the twentieth century it was taken to be obvious: thus Jonathan Harrison, in a 1953 article dealing with what later came to be termed 'rule' versus 'act' utilitarianism (see Chapter Six), could say casually that

[t]here are some actions which we think we have a duty to refrain from doing, even though they themselves produce no harmful consequences, because such actions would produce harmful consequences if the performance of them became the general rule. I think I have a duty to vote for that person whose party I think would govern the nation best, although I do not think that the addition of my vote to the total number of votes which are cast for him is going to make any difference to the result of the election, simply because I realise that, if all his other supporters were to do as I do, and fail to go to the polls, the man would not be elected.[2]

Harrison's remark came in the context of a discussion of 'duty', that is, of a non-self-interested account of participation in electoral activity, while Downs

1. The closest Hare comes to it is his discussion of the extra value possessed (under the existing system) by potential swing votes, a value expressed in the distribution of bribes (*Treatise on the Election of Representatives, Parliamentary or Municipal* [London: Longmans, 1859], pp. 128–129). John Mill read Hare closely and sympathised with his views; see his *Representative Government*, Chapter 7. Neither Hare nor Mill, however, supposed that there was any good reason that an individual voter might not go to the polls. One—partial and late—exception to this generalisation is the American writer John R. Commons in his book *Proportional Representation* (New York: Crowell, 1896). After describing the low turnout in recent elections, Commons remarked that 'up to the present time the greater part of the agitation for better government consists in bitterly criticizing the intelligent voters who stay at home, and beseeching them to meet their political duties. It is assumed that their only reasons are bad weather, dirty politics, business engagements, and lack of public spirit. Indeed, such reasons come to the surface; but even when these classes are aroused, as at the present time, and ready to do their share of work, no one can fail to see that they are cowed and silenced by the utter helplessness and the hopelessness of their cause' (p. 155). But as his subsequent discussion of proportional representation shows, Commons did not think that the negligibility of a single vote was particularly important, compared with such things as the drawing of district boundaries and the existence of primaries.

2. Harrison, 'Utilitarianism, Universalization, and Our Duty to Be Just', *Proceedings of the Aristotelian Society* 53 (1952–1953): 107. This example became a commonplace in the rule-utilitarian debate; see, for example, A. K. Stout, 'Suppose Everybody Did the Same?', *Australasian Journal of Philosophy* 32 (1954): 16. It then proved central to David Lyons's discussion (see below).

was, of course, primarily concerned with his own model of self-interested participation, in which voters behaved like consumers in a competitive market. But Downs (as I observed in the Introduction) also asserted, like Olson, that his general argument applied to altruistic conduct, insofar as the conduct was instrumental—that is, intended to secure an outcome which was desired for non-self-interested reasons. Harrison's argument was accordingly a straightforward precursor of Downs's, though unlike Downs, Harrison concluded that the voter would have to recast his reasons in terms of a non-instrumental, or at least not straightforwardly instrumental, principle. Downs was unaware of Harrison's article, and in general the discussions among political scientists and moral philosophers about this issue have run along different tracks, in part precisely because there may be an instrumental reason for altruists to participate in voting which is not available (to the same degree) to non-altruists.

Political scientists since Downs have broadly accepted his argument, and have accordingly expended a great deal of effort on suggestions about alternative ways of thinking about voting, in which the vote is not seen as a straightforward attempt on the part of the voter to bring about a desired outcome in the election. One feature of the discussion has been a recognition that (despite the low turnout in very recent elections) on the whole a surprisingly large number of people still vote in countries which do not have legal penalties for not voting.[3] So enforcement mechanisms, contrary to what Olson might have expected, have played little or no part in the discussion. Instead, theorists have largely concentrated on the thought that voters must be receiving some intrinsic satisfaction from the act of voting, independent of the vote's practical efficacy in bringing about a result. The general idea was expressed most clearly first by William H. Riker and Peter C. Ordeshook in 1968: they proposed that a citizen's reasons to vote should be regarded in large part as having to do with the utility which the voter gets from voting 'as a self-contained act' with 'effects for which the magnitude is independent of the individual's contribution to the [electoral] outcome'.[4] Voters would still take into account the probability of making an actual difference to the outcome by their vote, but in most situations this probability would

3. Two that do are Belgium and Australia.

4. Riker and Ordeshook, 'A Theory of the Calculus of Voting', *American Political Science Review* 62 (1968): 27.

be so small as to play little or no part in their final calculation;[5] the predominant element in their decision would be the intrinsic satisfactions of the act itself. Riker and Ordeshook listed as possible examples of these intrinsic qualities 'satisfaction from compliance with the ethic of voting', 'satisfaction from affirming allegiance to the political system', 'satisfaction from affirming a partisan preference', 'the satisfaction of deciding, going to the polls, etc.', and 'the satisfaction of affirming one's efficacy in the political system,'[6] and all these examples have been explored in detail by subsequent writers. Since Morris Fiorina's 1976 paper (see n. 5), it has been customary to describe these kinds of intrinsic reasons as 'expressive', in contrast to Downs's 'instrumental' reasons. This is not an entirely satisfactory term, since on an ordinary understanding of what is involved in expressive behaviour, such things as 'the satisfaction of deciding', or even 'the satisfaction of compliance with the ethic of voting', would not count strictly as expressive;[7] but it will do as a technical expression to cover the range of reasons which treat the vote as non-*electorally* instrumental. It is a broad range, including among other things Harrison's 'duty' to vote, which is of course—when recast in the language of positivist political science—precisely 'the satisfaction of compliance with the ethics of voting'.

But this kind of theory has often been questioned, partly on the grounds that once theories of this kind incorporate expressive as well as instrumental reasons in their models they have lost their distinctiveness as theories, and partly on the grounds that voters appear strongly to believe that there is *some* instrumental quality in their vote.[8] Indeed, it would be reasonable to suppose that even if the act of voting does express something like civic alle-

---

5. John Aldrich ('Rational Choice and Turnout', *American Journal of Political Science* 37 [1993]: 251) described this as an 'expansion' of Downs's claim that there would be a point to voting if one believed that one thereby preserved democratic institutions, but there is, of course, a vital difference—Downs was still thinking (implausibly, as we saw in the Introduction) that one's vote could actually bring about an outcome, while Riker and Ordeshook were genuinely thinking in terms of some other principle. The difference had been clearly stated by Morris Fiorina in his 1976 paper 'The Voting Decision: Instrumental and Expressive Aspects', *Journal of Politics* 38: 392–393; this paper is substantially a more sophisticated version of Riker and Ordeshook.

6. Riker and Ordeshook, 'A Theory of the Calculus of Voting', p. 28.

7. As Fiorina observed; see 'The Voting Decision', p. 393 n. 12.

8. Both these points were made by Brian Barry in *Sociologists, Economists and Democracy* (London: Collier-Macmillan, 1970), the former on p. 20 and the latter on p. 30.

giance, it does so precisely because it is widely thought to have some civic *point*, that is, to have some instrumental or causal relationship to the choice of a candidate or a plebiscitary proposal. This difficulty is particularly obvious in the case of Riker and Ordeshook's last suggestion, 'the satisfaction of affirming one's efficacy in the political system'. They lamely appended to this the observation that 'the theory of democracy asserts that individuals and voting are meaningful and for most people the only chance to fulfill this role is at the voting booth',[9] but on their own account the theory of democracy must in this respect be false. This is a particularly good illustration of the general difficulty with positivist political science, pointed to by such writers as Charles Taylor: the 'scientist's' theory is the same kind of reasoning that the people whose activities are the object of the 'scientific' inquiry use to make sense of their own lives, and it ought therefore to be incorporated into their own mental activity and—in this case—if true, to undermine their existing beliefs. The same difficulty was faced in the most far-reaching attempt to develop this part of Riker and Ordeshook's manifesto, Alexander Schuessler's *A Logic of Expressive Choice*. Schuessler developed a systematic account of turnout precisely on the presupposition that 'what matters is not so much my actual instrumental contribution to the collective outcome, but my ability to claim to others, as well as to myself, to have been responsible for the outcome', but he too supposed that this must be a *false* claim, since (he believed) no voter can actually bring about the desired outcome. Instead, he asserted that claims of responsibility are simply the most familiar and important means of affirming an attachment to or identity with a political project—'the *idiom* is still an instrumental one, as the claim is about determining an outcome. However, the *mechanism*, as I will argue, is one of expressive attachment'.[10]

These problems dog any attempt to develop an expressive theory of voting, even if—as rarely happens—the theory would be satisfactory in its own terms. For example, John Ferejohn and Morris Fiorina argued in a joint paper in the mid-1970s that we should think of voters as exercised by anxiety about the appalling consequences (to them) if they did not vote and their preferred candidate lost by one vote. To insure against this outcome, they

9. Riker and Ordeshook, 'A Theory of the Calculus of Voting', p. 28.

10. Schuessler, *A Logic of Expressive Choice* (Princeton, N.J.: Princeton University Press, 2000), p. 16 and n. 3. For another extended discussion of voting as expressive, see Andrew Brennan and Loren Lomasky, *Democracy and Decision* (Cambridge: Cambridge University Press, 1993).

claimed, rational voters would be willing to pay the small cost of casting their vote—a strategy they termed 'minimax regret'.[11] This is an expressive theory in the sense that Fiorina used the term, since although the voters are not expressing either to other voters or to themselves an allegiance or identity, their vote is not an attempt to bring about an electoral outcome. Though not included on Riker and Ordeshook's list (which was never intended to be comprehensive)[12], mimimax regret clearly has a family resemblance to the other 'satisfactions' they outlined, since it too construes voting as designed to bring about a particular psychological state in the voter which is strictly irrespective of the result of the election—in this case, the psychological state of freedom from this form of regret. As long as I vote, on Ferejohn and Fiorina's view, I will receive the psychological benefit of knowing that I will be secure from regret, just as I will receive the psychological benefit of knowing that I have done my duty, expressed my allegiance to party or to democratic process, or experienced any other 'satisfaction' on the Riker and Ordeshook list. Ferejohn and Fiorina also failed to give any very good explanation of why a voter should be so concerned with this particular satisfaction.

When they circulated their paper in manuscript, they encountered a host of critics, who voiced their objections in the subsequent issue of the *American Political Science Review,* mostly making the natural point that minimax regret seemed to be a very unreasonable procedure, given the vanishingly small chance of the calamity against which voters were supposed to be insuring and given the relatively minor character of the disaster in most real electoral situations (short of something like a profound constitutional transformation).[13] Why did ordinary standards of rational choice under uncertainty not apply, according to which there would be little point in buying insurance in such a situation? Ferejohn and Fiorina in their reply simply

11. John A. Ferejohn and Morris P. Fiorina, 'The Paradox of Not Voting: A Decision Theoretic Analysis', *American Political Science Review* 68 (1974): 525–536.

12. 'Doubtless there are other satisfactions that do not occur to us at the moment'; 'A Theory of the Calculus of Voting', p. 28.

13. See in particular Nathaniel Beck, 'The Paradox of Minimax Regret', *American Political Science Review* 69 (1975): 918, and Stephen V. Stephens, 'The Paradox of Not Voting: Comment', ibid., pp. 914–915. Other comments in this issue of the journal were Lawrence S. Mayer and I. J. Good, 'Is Minimax Regret Applicable to Voting Decisions?', pp. 916–917; Gerald S. Strom, 'On the Apparent Paradox of Participation: A New Proposal', pp. 908–913; Gordon Tullock, 'The Paradox of Not Voting for Oneself', p. 919; and R. E. Goodin and K. W. S. Roberts, 'The Ethical Voter', pp. 926–928.

claimed that their model gave better predictions of turnout than any other models on offer, tacitly accepting that it was hard to see how the minimax strategy they suggested made much sense as a normative principle of rationality.[14]

Other satisfactions added to the Riker and Ordeshook list since 1968 include one proposed by John Aldrich in his 1993 paper 'Rational Choice and Turnout' (see n. 5): he observed that because both the costs and the benefits of voting are very low, we should not expect much calculation about the instrumental efficacy of their votes on the part of most citizens, and should suppose that small extraneous features of elections (such as bake sales at the polls) might make a big difference to people's decision to vote.[15] Again, this is only an expressive theory in the technical sense, but it still fits into Riker and Ordeshook's category, since the bake sale is simply another direct satisfaction involved in or associated with the *act* of voting and has nothing to do with the vote's contribution to a desired electoral outcome.

The assumption behind all these suggestions is, of course, that (in Harrison's words) 'the addition of my vote to the total number of votes' does not 'makes any difference to the result', or (as Riker and Ordeshook put it) that there is a very low probability 'that the citizen will, by voting, bring about the benefit' which he desires as a result of the election.[16] This is taken to be the same as saying that my vote will not be 'decisive' (Downs) or 'pivotal' (the usual modern term), that is, that the result of the election will not turn on my vote. But these are not the same thing: in an election of the usual kind, it is perfectly reasonable to say that my vote may bring about the result even if it is not pivotal. Moreover, insofar as there is a problem about voting, it is not—or at least not straightforwardly—the consequence of my vote's being 'one drop in a vast sea'; the numbers involved are not particularly significant. I say this because the essential feature of an election (unlike genuine Olsonian cases, such as those we shall be considering in the next chapter) is that embedded in it must be a determinate threshold at which a candidate is elected, or at which his election is guaranteed.[17] Because of this,

---

14. John A. Ferejohn and Morris P. Fiorina, 'Closeness Counts Only in Horseshoes and Dancing', *American Political Science Review* 69 (1975): 920–925.

15. This essay is also a very useful survey of the literature.

16. 'A Theory of the Calculus of Voting', p. 25.

17. The distinction is between the actual number of votes which give the candidate victory in a particular election—in the Anglo-American system, one more vote than his nearest rival actually receives—and the number of votes which one can say beforehand will guarantee victory, that is to say, a majority of the names on the electoral register.

it is possible in principle to engage in strategic interaction with the other voters along lines which resemble those discussed in Chapter One, and which preclude voting from being an example of Olson's problem; it is also possible to think of one's vote as possessing a causal efficacy even though it is not pivotal.

The importance of what he termed the 'threshold effect' was first made clear by David Lyons in his path-breaking *Forms and Limits of Utilitarianism*,[18] though his insight was ignored among political scientists, primarily because he was concerned not with Downs but with Harrison and his critics, and with the general problem of utilitarianism. Voting had been used by Harrison as an example in a general argument that what he called 'modified' utilitarianism was the correct way to think about utilitarian moral choices.[19] Whereas, he believed, earlier utilitarians had normally supposed that the utility principle requires us to perform the *particular action* whose likely consequences we believe to be better for the general good (however specified) than any alternative, 'modified' utilitarians should instead choose between *general practices* on the basis of their probable aggregate utility. In saying this, he was one of a number of philosophers in the 1950s who believed that moral judgements should primarily be made about practices or sets of actions. Some, like John Rawls, thought that in general the practices about which the judgements were to be made would be real social institutions with explicit systems of rules, such as a penal system,[20] whereas Harrison thought that they were—so to speak—constructed in an ad hoc fashion by asking oneself what would happen if everyone performed a particular type of action. The principal reason these philosophers put forward for supposing that practices rather than actions should be the objects of moral scrutiny was precisely that otherwise, actions such as voting would be impossible to justify in consequentialist terms, and they took this to be a *reductio ad absurdum* of the earlier utilitarian position. (It should be said in passing that it was a misunderstanding of the history of utilitarianism to think that its classical

18. Lyons, *Forms and Limits of Utilitarianism* (Oxford: Oxford University Press, 1965).

19. The terms 'modified' and 'unmodified' utilitarianism which Harrison used were replaced in the literature first by 'restricted' and 'extreme' utilitarianism, coined by J. J. C. Smart in 1956 as part of his defence of the 'extreme' type ('Extreme and Restricted Utilitarianism', *Philosophical Quarterly* 6: 344–354), and then by the terms 'rule' and 'act' utilitarianism, introduced by Richard Brandt in his *Ethical Theory* (Englewood Cliffs, N.J.: Prentice-Hall, 1959). Brandt's terminology came to be preferred even by Smart himself; see his 'Extreme Utilitarianism: A Reply to M. A. Kaplan', *Ethics* 71 (1961): 133–134.

20. John Rawls, 'Two Concepts of Rules', *Philosophical Review* 64 (1955): 3–32.

writers, such as Jeremy Bentham, John Austin or even J. S. Mill, had endorsed the position attributed to them in the 1950s, a misunderstanding which Rawls himself, though not many other writers of the period, fully recognised.[21] See Chapter Four for a discussion of this historical question.) After Harrison, voting became one of the standard examples in the literature; it was accompanied by serious activities such as punishing and promise-keeping, and by less serious ones such as watering one's garden in a drought or—a topic especially dear to philosophers in Oxford and Cambridge colleges—walking on an ornamental lawn.

The central criticism of this movement, made right from its beginnings, was that the utility principle (in whatever form) implies at the very least a moral commitment to maximise the utility of actual people, since otherwise the principle lacks any plausible grounding in human interests. But the utility of actual people might often be increased by breaking the rules of a practice, so why should we not do so? In the voting case, given that on any particular occasion I would benefit myself by not going to the polls (through the rain, a long walk, and so on) and would not inflict any harm on anyone else (since *ex hypothesi* my vote will make no difference to the outcome), utilitarian reasoning must still require me to abstain from voting. If that is a *reductio ad absurdum,* so much the worse not for act utilitarianism but for utilitarianism as a whole. This is a powerful argument, and it may be what led Rawls to abandon his earlier position and move on to the non-utilitarian theory enshrined in *A Theory of Justice.* But loyal utilitarians wished to counter this argument, and in the process they were led to focus closely on the causal status of actions in these kinds of situations and to raise the question of whether it is actually correct to say that an act such as voting 'makes no difference' to the outcome. The most powerful analysis came eventually from Lyons; he was not personally a utilitarian (see his last chapter, in which he puts forward a theory close to the mature idea of Rawls, who had been the chair of his Ph.D. committee at Harvard), but he was keen to show that act utilitarianism had been misunderstood and that one did not need to construct a form of rule utilitarianism in order to rule out the self-defeating implications of a concentration on individual acts.

Lyons believed that in many cases where there is a determinate threshold at which one can say that a benefit has been achieved—and voting is par excellence such a case—*each* action which is intended to produce the benefit

21. See the long note in ibid., pp. 18–22 n. 21.

can reasonably be regarded as bringing it about. A full description of the causal character of such an action, treating it as an individual action but taking into account the context in which it is performed, will attribute to it the property of causing the desired outcome; act utilitarianism (at least in some areas—and Lyons, though cautious about the scope of his principle, may nevertheless have overestimated the number of situations where there is an easily determined threshold) then itself covers the cases which rule utilitarianism was invented to deal with. Lyons's presentation of this argument was not entirely satisfactory, but it is possible to recast it on a more secure basis and preserve his basic insight.

He began by making the fundamental point that embedded in many collective and collaborative practices where there is a threshold must be a subset of actions which have a causal efficacy over the outcome which the other actions lack; the efficacious actions contribute to the crossing of the threshold, but the rest are surplus and unnecessary. In the case of voting, this can be seen most clearly in the case of a roll-call vote; a particularly good real-life example (not used by Lyons) would be the method of voting used in the Roman Republic, though I shall disregard the fact that the Romans voted by tribes.[22] When Ultimus casts his vote for, say, Tiberius Gracchus as tribune, Gracchus is thereby elected, since precisely the necessary majority of the voters less one have already voted for him. Any votes after that point have no influence on the result, and (except for considerations such as the *size* of

22. The republic had a series of complex and interesting voting systems. The most important assembly, the *comitia plebis tributa* or *concilium plebis,* operated as follows: the citizen body (which in Caesar's day numbered close to a million voters) was divided into thirty-five tribes *(tribus),* and a candidate for office or a proposed law had to have a simple majority of the tribes. Voters were called to the tribunal (a platform at the end of the space where the *comitia* met) to cast their ballot tribe by tribe, the order of the tribes being decided by lot at the beginning of the vote, and the results for each tribe were declared before the next tribe voted. Each voter dropped his ballot into an urn placed on the tribunal. Once the candidate or the law had secured a majority of tribes, the voting stopped. In many elections there were several offices to be filled (for example, ten tribunes), and in these cases the voting continued in order to decide between the remaining candidates, with each one being declared elected and removed from the poll at the point at which he secured a majority. One of the many striking features of this system was that it avoided Condorcet cycles, which are always a hazard in multi-candidate elections, though of course at the cost of sometimes not electing a candidate who would have received more votes than the one who was elected (there's always some cost to eliminating Condorcet effects). Presumably the Romans worked this out through trial and error. See E. S. Stavely, *Greek and Roman Voting and Elections* (London: Thames and Hudson, 1972).

the victory) there is no reason that anyone else should step up to the tribunal. So when Ultimus goes up to the tribunal, he knows that his vote will bring about Gracchus's election, and looking back on the process he can say that his vote caused Gracchus's election. But by the same token his predecessors at the tribunal, Primus, Secundus, Tertius, and so on, can also say that, given Ultimus's vote, *their* votes caused Gracchus's election. It is true that these other votes are necessary conditions for it to be the case that Ultimus determined the result, and similarly Ultimus's vote, together with Secundus's, Tertius's, and so on, is a necessary condition for it to be the case that Primus determined the result; but we are perfectly familiar with the idea that some action or event causes an outcome, conditional upon other actions or events occurring or having occurred. A good comparison would be with a boat which can be lifted if six people pick it up but not if five try to do so: when six (and we will presume at the moment only six) people do so, each one of them is causally responsible for lifting the boat, conditional upon the other five's also lifting.

It should be stressed that each vote for Gracchus carries what we may call full causal weight in bringing about the result. In these kinds of cases, people sometimes talk as if each contribution represents only a fraction of the causal power necessary to create the result, so that in the case of the boat each person would contribute one sixth to the outcome. Even Lyons slipped into this way of talking, remarking that 'the first k favourable votes can be regarded as equally efficacious, as composing a causally homogeneous class each member of which can be ascribed $1/k$th the threshold effect'.[23] It is true that each person lifting the boat dislodges one sixth of its weight, but nevertheless each action (assuming the other actions are performed) wholly causes the boat to be lifted. Each vote adds only one to the total, but nevertheless each vote causes the outcome. As I said, we are familiar with the idea that the causal antecedents of an event include a whole series of previous occurrences, each one of which was necessary in order for it to be *that* series which caused the event. But we do not feel the need to quantify the degree to which any one occurrence in this sequence 'caused' the outcome (nor could we conceivably do so even if we wanted to): each one of the occur-

---

23. Lyons, *Forms and Limits of Utilitarianism*, p. 85—though see his different remarks on the next page.

rences did so, given the other ones. This is the view which has been taken in both civil and common law.[24]

This fact—that each vote carries the full causal responsibility for bringing about the result—has also sometimes led to confusion about assigning utility values to actions. In a debate about Lyons in the 1970s between Harry S. Silverstein and Jan Narveson,[25] it was presumed by both parties that one can assign a measure of utility to an action equivalent to the utility of the consequences which it brings about. If one can do this, it is clear that the claim that each contributory action in these situations has full causal weight leads to paradoxical results. Suppose that Gracchus's election represents utility of 100 (on some scale) for the Roman Republic; if one assigns utility to actions in this way, each vote on the analysis I am suggesting would then represent 100 utiles, and the total of the whole election (presuming a million voters, the number at least in Caesar's day) would be 50,000,200 utiles![26] Narveson thought this was clearly false, being the 'magical' creation of extra utility, and he fell back on the idea that we should assign a proportion of the

24. For civil law, see the argument in the *Digest* XLVII tit. 2 leg. 21 § 9, in which it is claimed that if two or more men have stolen a beam which one of them alone could not carry off, each of them is entirely responsible for the theft. (See also Hugo Grotius, *The Rights of War and Peace*, III.10.4.) For common law, see, for example, H. L. A. Hart and Tony Honoré, *Causation in the Law*, 2nd ed. (Oxford: Oxford University Press, 1985), p. 351. J. S. Mill made the same point, using voting as his example: '[W]hen the decision of a legislative assembly has been determined by the casting vote of the chairman, we sometimes say that this one person was the cause of all the effects which resulted from the enactment. Yet we do not really suppose that his single vote contributed more to the result than that of any other person who voted in the affirmative' (*A System of Logic*, III.v.3). It is also the conclusion to which Derek Parfit came (*Reasons and Persons* [Oxford: Oxford University Press, 1984], pp. 68–69), though since he was also still committed to the idea that we each cause an aliquot share of the outcome, he expressed the thought by saying that in these situations I cause *both* my share of the outcome (for instance, one sixth of the boat's being lifted) *and* my companions' shares (since they could not accomplish their part without me). But if this is true, then the notion of shares *in the outcome* does not make sense, since on the final accounting each one of us has (as Parfit recognises) brought about the whole result.

25. Harry S. Silverstein, 'Simple and General Utilitarianism', *Philosophical Review* 83 (1974): 339–363; Jan Narveson, 'Utilitarianism, Group Actions, and Coordination or, Must the Utilitarian be a Buridan's Ass'? *Noûs* 10 (1976): 173–194; and Harry S. Silverstein, 'Utilitarianism and Group Coordination', *Noûs* 13 (1979): 335–360.

26. Five hundred thousand and one voters are causally responsible for Gracchus's election out of the electorate of one million; each of these votes is worth 100 utiles, and the original 100 utiles for the republic should presumably be added.

full causal weight to each action,[27] so that each vote would represent 100/500,001 utiles. Silverstein argued against this that there was no difficulty, since one would not expect the utility of a group to be the sum of utilities possessed by different kinds of entity:

> Collective properties of groups are not in general linear functions of individual properties of the groups' members; to suppose otherwise is simply to commit the fallacy of division (and/or composition). One can hardly be accused of belief in 'magic' if one affirms that rats in New York are numerous but denies that any individual rat is numerous.[28]

But neither response to Lyons seems reasonable. We talk about the utility of *actions* only in a derivative sense: to say that an action has utility is to say no more than that it brings about a certain amount of utility. Utility inheres in *people,* not actions; this can be seen clearly if we revert to the original language of utilitarianism and talk about *pleasure* instead of utility. If this were not so, we would find ourselves in a hopeless paradox even where collective causation was not an issue. After all, we might say that the single act of Caesar in crossing the Rubicon represented utility of, say, 200 for the republic, but we would believe this because we thought that benefits (crudely, appealing psychological states, but less crudely, whatever we want to count as a benefit) were provided by his action for the citizens of the republic which we can estimate at 200 utiles. (We can include in this, of course, any benefits inherent in the action itself independent of its wider causal status—such things as Caesar's own satisfaction at the decisiveness of his act and so forth.) Do we count his action as 200 utiles and what it brought about as another 200 utiles, making 400 utiles produced on that day in 49 B.C.? Clearly not: we recognise that the utilities we sum when calculating the utility of an action must not themselves include the 'utility' we ascribe to the action once we've done the sum, since otherwise we would be double-counting. So by the same token we are perfectly free to say that each vote for Gracchus 'has utility' of 100, without being tempted illegitimately to sum these derivative utilities. Perhaps the best way of registering the distinction in ordinary discourse is to use (as we often do, and indeed as I have just done) the language of representation: we can say that an action 'represents' a utility of 200 without concluding that it *possesses* such utility, precisely because the notion

---

27. Narveson, 'Utilitarianism, Group Actions, and Coordination', p. 187.
28. Silverstein, 'Utilitarianism and Group Coordination', p. 341.

of representation implies that the thing represented is different from its representative. In this sense, the 'utility of an action' is indeed a different kind of entity from the utility the action brings about, though not (it might be noted) for the reason suggested by Silverstein, since it has nothing to do with the relationship between a group and its members. In matters of utility, at least, a group simply *is* a sum of its individual members, as there are no bearers of utility other than individual human beings.

In the example I have been considering so far, we are presuming that voting stops at the point at which a majority is achieved (as in the Roman case), and that each one of the votes up to that point is causally responsible for the result. As Lyons recognised, in practice elections of this kind are rare; but the point of the example is that in any election, even if more votes are cast than are necessary to secure a candidate's election, there must be a subset of votes which carry causal responsibility for the outcome, simply by virtue of there being a determinate threshold at which the candidate is elected. We can look at the threshold embedded in a conventional election in various ways, but a particularly vivid example is provided by a British parliamentary election, in which the votes are marked on ballot slips and put into boxes. When the polls close, the boxes are emptied and teams of people count the votes, placing them in separate piles for each candidate. Though the people counting the votes may not know it (since they do not consolidate their figures until the end of the process), at some point in the course of the evening one candidate's piles of ballot papers add up to the precise figure necessary for a majority, and those ballot papers have therefore by themselves accomplished the task of electing him. The extra votes which the teams continue to count will be redundant (though they might be important for securing some other outcome, such as the size of the majority).[29] There may be a recount, in which the ballot slips are counted again and no doubt to some extent in a different order, but that merely shows that the first majority set of ballots did not succeed in electing the candidate; the set which first reaches the majority in the second count will then do so, or in the third count, or in however many counts are necessary to satisfy the returning officer and the candidates that a proper count has been made.[30]

29. Assuming that what I say in Chapter Three is true.

30. It is worth observing, for the benefit of readers unfamiliar with this system, that elections apparently decided by a very small number of votes invariably attract recounts, and the figures almost always come out differently on each count. So any prudent candidate and his supporters would plan for well over a simple majority, even if they believed that it is only rational to vote if your vote 'makes a difference'.

We can be confident that there must have been what I will call an 'efficacious set' buried in the piles of ballot papers, but we obviously cannot usually point to the piles of votes on the town hall tables which brought about
the result and separate them from the piles of votes which did not. But we
can still know some things about the set, including most importantly its size
and the chance that our own ballot paper was part of it (assuming that we
voted for the winning candidate). If, say, in an election 10,000 votes were
cast for Candidate A and 3,999 for Candidate B, the efficacious set must
have consisted of 4,000 of the 10,000 votes cast for A, and there is therefore
a 2 in 5 chance that our ballot was part of it. The smaller the majority, the
larger the probability that our vote was part of the efficacious set, but even
with a sizable majority (as in this example), the probability is still quite
high that the efficacious set contained our ballot and that our vote thereby
brought about the result. This is true, it should be said, of the British (and
American) voting system, where the efficacious set in a contest is always the
set of votes sufficient to give the winning candidate a majority over the next
most popular candidate, even where there are many candidates—if A gets
10,000, B gets 5,999, and C gets 5,998, the efficacious set is 6,000 of A's
votes. Under proportional representation (PR) the position is more compli-
cated, and it may be quite hard to talk about the properties of an efficacious
set; in my view, this greater complication and lack of transparency is in itself
a substantial—though not necessarily decisive—argument against PR.

The fact that there is a determinate threshold embedded in the election in
this manner, with each vote in the efficacious set having true causal efficacy
in bringing about the result, has a number of implications. The first and most
general one is that any analysis of voting which presumes that no individual
vote has causal power over the result unless it is pivotal is mistaken; voting
is not a good example of a genuinely Olsonian problem in which individual
contributions to a collective good have in themselves no causal relationship
to the outcome. Only the cases which we shall consider in the next chapter,
in which there may be examples of true negligibility, really give rise to
Olson's problem; any case where there is a threshold at which there is an appreciable change as a consequence of adding or subtracting one increment
will not count as an example of his problem.

Second, precisely because there are a determinate threshold and a large
set of actions which have causal power over the outcome, a variety of strategies becomes possible which would not make sense in conditions of true

negligibility. Most obviously, voters can in principle co-ordinate their actions in such a way that they eliminate any wasted votes. Lyons was not especially interested in this ('in the ideal case we can disregard special conditions and voter interactions')[31], since he was principally concerned with trying to show that even without such co-ordination there might still be a good reason to cast a ballot. But it had already been suggested by J. J. C. Smart in a response to Harrison (a suggestion which Lyons presumably had in mind when he wrote, though he did not specifically mention it). Smart did not expressly deal with threshold effects, but he nevertheless observed that a society of utilitarians could perfectly well coordinate its actions in such a way that the utilitarianly optimal number of people participated in a co-operative venture of this kind. The particular instance he addressed was the question of whether I should water my garden in a drought; he remarked that in a society of 'extreme' or act utilitarians, it would be reasonable for them to estimate the optimum number of people who could water their gardens,[32] and each person should ideally (by using some chance device, such as throwing dice successively) give himself a very small probability (which in practice might approximate to zero) of watering his garden, such that the total number watering their gardens would be the optimum. As he observed, '[T]his would be to adopt what in the theory of games is called "a mixed strategy",' a method which is often proposed for situations of this kind.[33]

31. Lyons, *Forms and Limits of Utilitarianism*, p. 85.

32. That is, the number above which any further diminution of the general water supply represents a total disbenefit to the community greater than the benefit to any individual of watering his garden.

33. Smart, 'Extreme Utilitarianism,", p. 133. This argument does not appear in the first version of Smart's 'Extreme and Restricted Utilitarianism' in *Philosophical Quarterly* 6 (1956), though he did consider there (p. 352) the possibility of using game theory in this context, responding to the use of the watering example by Stout, 'Suppose Everybody Did the Same?', who was in turn responding to Harrison. It appears in a revised version of 'Extreme and Restricted Utilitarianism' reprinted in Samuel Gorovitz, ed., *Utilitarianism [by] John Stuart Mill with Critical Essays* (Indianapolis: Bobbs-Merrill, 1971), pp. 195–203), though no indication is given there that the article had been revised. It also appears in Smart's *An Outline of a System of Utilitarian Ethics* (Melbourne: Melbourne University Press, 1961), pp. 42–44, and he repeated the argument in his contribution to J. J. C. Smart and Bernard Williams, *Utilitarianism For and Against* (Cambridge: Cambridge University Press, 1973), pp. 57–61, linking it there to the Lewis-Schelling idea of a convention.

Smart was thinking about utilitarians, who would treat each person's utility as equivalent to their own, and would not prefer that someone other than themselves bore the costs required by the collaborative activity. But even self-interested agents could use a similar strategy, though, unlike utilitarians, they would be faced by the additional problem of securing compliance—for example, everyone who wished for a particular candidate to be elected might employ a mixed strategy, but any one person whose randomising device chose him to vote would have an incentive to make it known that he was not going to, in the hope that someone else would be forced to take his place to prevent the numbers of voters turning out from falling below the predetermined and desirable level. In other words, the presence of a threshold might lead self-interested agents to play the well-known chicken game. This has been extensively studied in recent times, notably by Michael Taylor and Hugh Ward, as part of their interest in what they have called 'lumpy' or 'step' goods, that is, goods which display threshold effects.[34] Suppose each voter in the Roman example knows that there is at least one other potential voter (call him Proximus) who is known to support Gracchus and who would vote for him if it were necessary—that is, if one out of the set Primus . . . Ultimus did not vote. Given the structure of the election, in which there is a clear threshold—Gracchus is declared elected when precisely the necessary majority of votes has been cast for him—there is an incentive for each voter (assuming that the act of voting is to some degree burdensome) to induce Proximus to vote in his stead; Proximus will do the same. As the analogy with the chicken game illustrates, this is not a prisoners' dilemma: it is better for each player that he should be the one who votes at the last moment than that no one should vote, though it is also better for each of them that the other

34. See Taylor and Ward, 'Chickens, Whales, and Lumpy Goods', *Political Studies* 30 (1982): 350–370; Michael Taylor, *The Possibility of Cooperation* (Cambridge: Cambridge University Press, 1987), pp. 40–45; Hugh Ward, 'Three Men in a Boat, Two Must Row: An Analysis of a Three-Person Chicken Supergame', *Journal of Conflict Resolution* 34 (1990): 371–400; and Hugh Ward, 'Game Theory and the Politics of the Global Commons', *Journal of Conflict Resolution* 37 (1993): 203–235. See also Russell Hardin, *Collective Action* (Baltimore: Johns Hopkins University Press, 1982), pp. 55–66. Chicken is, of course, the game in which drivers race towards one another on a narrow road and dare one another to swerve at the last minute. Neither wants to be humiliated, but they want to be killed even less.

Ultimus

	Vote	Not Vote
Vote	ii, 2	ii, 3
Not Vote	iii, 2	i, 1

Proximus

Figure 2.1

votes and he does not. (Compare Figure 2.1 with the matrices in Chapter One).[35]

And unlike the prisoners' dilemma, this kind of situation usually elicits some type of co-operative behaviour, though there is a wide variety of possible instances; the theory of conventions developed by David Lewis out of Thomas Schelling's work is appropriate here, as in the end all the parties have an interest in co-ordinating their actions in such as way as to ensure

---

35. I have assumed no resentment on the part of the voters that they vote while the other does not—that is, their payoff for 'vote' is the same, irrespective of the other's action. If one builds resentment in, one still does not get a prisoners' dilemma; the matrix is then

Ultimus

	Vote	Not Vote
Vote	iii, 3	ii, 4
Not Vote	iv, 2	i, 1

Proximus

Figure 2.2

that the requisite number of people in the end turn out to vote.[36] A mixed strategy along the lines suggested by Smart has also featured in modern discussions of chicken;[37] Ward has discussed other strategies, including variants in which there are complex pre-game interactions. The general principle, however, is that it is in the interests of the participants to construct some set of conventions which will allow them collectively to cross the relevant threshold, and that this would not be the case were there to be a genuine instance of Olson's problem—for, as we saw in the Introduction, there is (on his account) no reason for anyone to stick to a convention of this sort where his contribution makes no difference to the outcome.

As far as the general analysis of free riding goes, the important distinction is then between collective enterprises which incorporate thresholds of some kind and those which do not. The former will usually in principle lend themselves to the construction of a suitable convention, so it is among the latter that we must look for clear instances of a free-rider problem. This will be the object of my next chapter. But before turning to that issue, I want tentatively to consider an additional possibility, that the existence of a threshold within a practice such as an election gives us a reason to participate, even if a convention is *not* in place to eliminate wasted votes or their equivalents. I should emphasise that if this does not turn out to be possible, the existence of a threshold still precludes free riding, since the participants will be able to construct a suitable self-sustaining convention; but most discussions of voting have taken place against a background assumption that no such conventions will be in place, as of course they usually are not in real-life elections, and it is worth asking what it is rational for a voter to do under these circumstances—and by the same token what it may be rational to do in many other collective enterprises.

It is certainly true that there is a problem about voting when there is no convention among voters to turn out just the required threshold number, but it is surprisingly hard to specify accurately just what the problem is. Lyons, for example, gave what were in effect two separate accounts of what

36. See David Lewis, *Convention: A Philosophical Study* (Cambridge, Mass.: Harvard University Press, 1969), and Thomas Schelling, *The Strategy of Conflict* (Cambridge, Mass.: Harvard University Press, 1960).

37. See, for example, Gary Bornstein, David Budescu, and Shmuel Zamir, 'Co-operation in Intergroup, N-Person, and Two-Person Games of Chicken', *Journal of Conflict Resolution* 41 (1997): 384–406.

is involved in an ordinary election, and neither of them was wholly convincing. One was that

> all the *m* favourable votes [that is, the number of votes cast for the winning candidate] may most reasonably be viewed as composing a causally homogeneous class. For it does not seem possible to distinguish, among the *m* favourable votes simultaneously cast in these ideal conditions,[38] some *k* that do (as opposed to some *m* − *k* that do not) actually contribute to the production of the passage-threshold effect. We would have no way of deciding which particular acts have threshold-related effects and which do not, since the circumstances we have supposed guarantee, in effect, a uniform condition of voting. Thus all the acts within the general practice (the *m* favourable votes) are here alike and must be treated alike, despite the fact that fewer favourable votes would have been sufficient for passage.[39]

Though this is the argument upon which Lyons himself apparently put most weight, it is an odd way of looking at the situation. If there is no way in practice of distinguishing between votes which were causally efficacious and those which were not, why do we have to conclude that they were all efficacious, rather than that none of them were? Lyons may have assumed that it depends on the predominant character of the votes; but in a two-person election in which one candidate has such a huge majority over his opponent that the most of the favourable votes must have fallen in the *m* − *k* class, the predominant character of the votes is that they were causally inefficacious, and we would have to conclude on Lyons's argument that *none* of the favourable votes brought about the result.

Lyons's second answer (though he did not fully distinguish it from his first) was not merely that all the favourable votes should be *treated as if* they contributed to the result, but that they actually *did* do so.

> It is essential not to confuse two things: (1) the fact that *k* favourable votes would have been sufficient, and therefore that, if only *k* favourable votes had been cast, the threshold effects would be ascribable only to them, with (2) the claim that, under these circumstances, some of the *m* favourable votes do not actually contribute to the threshold effects. If it takes six men to push a car up a hill and, not knowing this, eight lend a hand and do the

---

38. He specified these conditions as 'that each voter decides independently, is unaware of the intentions of others, is not under party discipline, and so on'. In other words, he excluded strategic interactions.

39. Lyons, *Forms and Limits of Utilitarianism*, p. 87.

job, what are we to say? If all actually pushed, and pushed equally hard, and delivered equal forces, are we to say that only some of them actually contributed to the effects because fewer *could* have done the job?[40]

But this is a misleading analogy. If eight people push the car, each person pushes one eighth of the weight; if each person expended that amount of effort and no more, then eight of them would be needed to move the car (as in my boat-lifting example above). The expenditure of that amount of effort by each of a subgroup of six people would not in this instance have been enough to shift it. The fact that if eight people had not been present, six people could have moved the car by expending *more* effort does not make any subset of six people causally responsible for lifting it when eight people were actually taking part and each of them was expending effort equivalent to only one eighth the weight of the car, any more than if half a firing squad shot into the air, they would still be taken to be causally responsible for the death of the victim on the grounds that they *could* have aimed straight if the other members of the squad had not done so. So it is indeed reasonable to say that all the participants in the activity of pushing a car are responsible for the outcome, even though not all of them are needed, in the sense that some of them could have accomplished the same result by behaving differently. But voting is not like lifting, since we cannot alter the amount of (so to speak) electoral effort we put into the operation. The fact that all the men who push a car up a hill are causally responsible for moving it, whatever the numbers who are lending a hand, does not in itself tell us anything about the causal efficacy of voting.[41]

Nevertheless, Lyons was correct in his instinct that the existence of a threshold effect within the practice of voting is critical to our understanding of the activity even where there is no prior convention to restrict the numbers voting to precisely the threshold number. The right way to think about the voting problem, on the account I am putting forward, is actually that voting is a particularly good example of what is commonly termed 'redundant' causation, where an action causes an outcome, but if the action had not taken place, the outcome would still have been brought about by some

40. Ibid., p. 89.

41. See Allan Gibbard, *Utilitarianism and Coordination* (New York: Garland, 1990), for a thorough critique of Lyons's argument for uniformity in this class of actions, though Gibbard assumes that the car example is indeed like the voting example, with redundant actions on the part of some of the group. Gibbard's argument against Lyons rests on the claim that 'a consequence of an act is something which would happen if the act were performed and would not happen if it were not performed' (p. 81), and as we shall see presently, that assumption is false (though it may be that Lyons himself shared it).

other cause. Alvin Goldman, in an article of 1999, was (I think) the first person clearly to state this,[42] though there is a gesture towards it in Derek Parfit's *Reasons and Persons,* of 1984. What follows is broadly along the same lines as Goldman's account, though I differ slightly from him over the analysis of redundant causation and over the question of why a voter might wish to be part of an efficacious set.

Redundant causation has proved to be a notorious problem for analysis in terms of the currently most popular theory of causation, which treats causal relationships as possessing a counter-factual character—in the simplest form of the relationship, if the action or event which counts as the 'cause' had not occurred, then the 'effect' would not have occurred. One of the principal differences between Lyons's account of voting and that of the political scientists is on precisely this issue (though neither has spelt it out clearly), for a 'pivotal' or 'decisive' vote is one which counter-factually brings about the result, while the member of an efficacious set may not do so. But the difficulty of analysing redundant causation in counter-factual terms, it has generally been accepted, does not mean that it is not causation—it means, rather, that the counter-factual approach is inadequate.

The efficacious set is, as it were, selected from a larger number of ballot papers, any of which could have done the job, and whose capacity to do so is guaranteed, since they are already in existence. The equivalent in a roll-call vote (where the issues tend to be clearer) would be a situation where there is no question of chicken: that is, where the roll call continues after the candidate has been elected, and where there are good grounds for supposing that at least some people are going to continue to cast their votes for the winning candidate. So when Ultimus steps up to the tribunal, he is very confident that were he not to do so, Proximus would take his place: he knows that he has caused Gracchus's election by his action, but he also knows that if he had not voted, Gracchus would still have been elected, for Proximus was going to do just that. Ultimus's action 'pre-empted' Proximus's. But this does not mean that he did not cause the result. To leave aside any possible difficulties with the voting case, we can see this clearly in the case of a policeman who shoots and kills a bank robber, and does so a split second before one of his colleagues would have done. The first policeman caused the robber's death—if his action did not do so, what did? But if this policeman had not fired, the robber would still have been killed.

---

42. Alvin I. Goldman, 'Why Citizens Should Vote: A Causal Responsibility Approach', *Social Philosophy and Policy* 16, 2 (1999): 201–217.

One response from those who wish to preserve simple counter-factuality is to say that the policeman did not cause the *same* event that his colleague would have caused—the particular story of the bullet's path, the time of the robber's death, and all the actual material features of the robber's death are specific to that policeman's act, and they are part of the description of the event.[43] But that way out has been rejected by almost everyone, for obvious reasons: if true, it would, for example, mean that we could never postpone an event (since it would not be the same event at a different time, let alone with all the other slight changes which would arise), and that we would not be able to say that the second policeman wished to cause the same event (the robber's death) as the first policeman, despite the fact that they were both there to do precisely that.[44] What we might term the same episode in world history can encompass very many separable events: the robber died, he died in that bank, he died in that bank at that time of day, he died in that bank at that time of day wearing a red shirt, and so on. The causal story we tell about one of these events will not be the same story we tell about another (the fact that his laundry had lost his other shirts is part of the explanation of the last of these events, but not of the first), and the events we are interested in will generally be a rather restricted set—in this instance, I take it, we are not very interested in the event that the robber died (for we all have to), but we are interested in something like the event that he died in the bank at more or less that time, and it is that event whose causes we are concerned with.[45] In the case of voting, it is clear that we are interested in

43. See J. L. Mackie, *The Cement of the Universe* (Oxford: Oxford University Press, 1974), pp. 45–46.

44. See David Lewis's discussion in 'Causation', in his *Philosophical Papers* (Oxford: Oxford University Press, 1986), II, pp. 195–199, and the remarks against Mackie in the second edition of Hart and Honoré's *Causation in the Law,* pp. xli–xlii.

45. See Lewis, 'Events', in *Philosophical Papers,* II, p. 255 ff; 'Causation', pp. 197–198. In saying this, I do not want to commit myself necessarily to the proposition that what is caused *is* an event; L. A. Paul, for example, has argued that the causal relationship is between properties, not events, partly because such an analysis can handle pre-emption rather well ('Aspect Causation', in *Causation and Counterfactuals,* ed. John Collins, Ned Hall, and L. A. Paul [Cambridge, Mass.: MIT Press, 2004], pp. 205–224; pre-emption, pp. 216–218), while Hugh Mellor has long championed the idea that the causal relationship is between facts (see *The Facts of Causation* [London: Routledge, 1995] and 'For Facts as Causes and Effects', in *Causation and Counterfactuals,* pp. 309–323). See also Jonathan Bennett, *Events and Their Names* (Indianapolis: Hackett, 1988), pp. 139–142. But the particular attempt to get round our intuitions about pre-emption which I am considering depends on the idea that causes and effects are events, and is therefore vulnerable to the observation that even if they are events, the same event may have a pre-emptive *and* a pre-empted cause.

the bare fact that Gracchus is elected, and not in the precise details of the circumstances;[46] and there can be no question but that from this perspective the same event that Ultimus caused would also have been brought about by Proximus.

So simple counter-factual analyses of this kind do not work, something conceded by Lewis himself. Whether more elaborate ones will do so is not something which particularly concerns us at the moment, since all such attempts have in common the fact that they leave our intuitions about pre-emptive causation more or less unmolested. Lewis, for example, came to propose that an event or action possesses 'causal influence' if we can say that counter-factually varying it in some way will result in significantly more change in the effect than would be generated by varying any other event. Thus if the first policeman had shot the robber in the heart and not the head, the circumstances of the robber's death would have been materially different; this is not true if the trajectory of the second policeman's shot were similarly altered, since the second policeman's shot did not kill the robber. So there is still some element of counter-factuality in the ascription of a pre-emptive cause.[47] This may not be entirely convincing, and many people would say at the moment that we simply lack a fully convincing analysis of causation.[48] But from the point of view of my wider enquiry, what matters is that pre-emptive causation is as well-established a phenomenon as anything else which a theory of causation has to deal with, and short of abandoning the notion of 'cause' altogether (something which some political scientists

---

46. On the account I have given of the embedded efficacious set, we could not even know those details; the only thing we could know would be that some set was sufficient to bring it about that the candidate was elected, and not the detailed circumstances—the particular ballot papers, the identity of the scrutineers, and so on.

47. See Lewis, 'Causation as Influence', in *Causation and Counterfactuals,* pp. 75–106; but see Paul's comments in 'Aspect Causation', ibid., pp. 216–219. Lewis originally proposed a relationship of 'quasi-dependence' to cope with pre-emption ('Causation', pp. 206–207), in which a cause brought about an effect pre-emptively if the process involved was sufficiently similar to a clearly counter-factual causal relationship, but he abandoned this idea in his later work.

48. See, for example, the editors of *Causation and Counterfactuals,* John Collins, Ned Hall, and L. A. Paul, 'Counterfactuals and Causation: History, Problems, and Prospects', ibid., pp. 1–57 (inter alia a useful summary of the literature), and Jonathan Schaffer, 'Trumping Preemption', ibid., pp. 59–73. Certainly Lewis's revised account would be quite hard to fit to the idea of an embedded efficacious set of ballot papers, where there would seem to be no material difference if we suppose one efficacious set brought about the result rather than another.

have indeed suggested), we have to accommodate our theories to it.[49] (It should be added, though, that it would be especially hard to analyse rational human action without the notion of a cause, since the essence of instrumental action is, after all, that what we do is a *means* to an *end*, that is, *causes* it.) If the simple counter-factual analysis does not yield a full account of causation, then a vote can have causal power over the result of the election even though there is no counter-factual account according to which the election would have gone differently without the vote.

Cases of pre-emption, including voting, thus have the interesting feature from the point of view of decision theory that I know that by performing an action I will bring about the outcome—that is, my action will have an instrumental point—but I also know that the outcome will occur if I do not act. How in general are we to think about such situations? One might argue that as far as human decision-making is concerned, it is rational only to perform actions which are necessary to the desired outcome,[50] but that pre-emptive actions can often fall into that category. In particular, we might suppose that people often value bringing about an outcome as well as valuing the outcome itself, and they might then rationally choose to pre-empt someone else whose action would have brought about the same result. For example (to extend my boat-raising case), suppose that the boat is a lifeboat launched manually in a small fishing village. When the alarm is sounded, volunteers rush to the harbour, but only six people will be chosen to launch the boat (maybe it is too small for more people to be able to get round it). Each person in the village knows that more than six people invariably turn up at the harbour. Why should any particular person run to help with the boat? A plausible response is, 'Because I want to be one of the people who is

49. For a good discussion of the way the law does so, see Hart and Honoré, *Causation in the Law,* pp. 123–125 and 248–252. They make the point that 'different legal systems, from the Romans to our own, have been vexed by these anomalies which in a sense represent the breakdown of our ordinary causal concepts' (p. 125), but they recognise that the law cannot accommodate itself to those concepts without doing grave violence to its general purposes—and I would claim that politics and economics must follow suit.

50. In other words, one would adopt a causal decision theory of the kind outlined in Lewis's 'Causal Decision Theory', *Philosophical Papers,* II, pp. 305–339. Gibbard's theory is an example of a causal decision theory which is explicitly counter-factual in character (see n. 34 above, and Allan Gibbard and William Harper, 'Counterfactuals and Two Kinds of Expected Utility', in C. A. Hooker, J. J. Leach, and E. F. McClennen, eds, *Foundations and Applications of Decision Theory* [Dordrecht: D. Reidel, 1978], I, pp. 125–162). Below, I give some reasons for being hesitant about adopting a counter-factual causal decision theory.

responsible for the lives saved by the boat—I will feel that I have accomplished something worthwhile by helping in this way'. This view has an expressive element, since it involves a general sense of the value of being a certain kind of person, and to this extent it continues to operate within a general theory which requires counter-factual causal efficacy for an action to be rationally chosen. It is still the case that there is a particular desired outcome which will not occur unless I act, though the desired outcome is now not merely 'saving the sailors' but 'my being responsible for saving the sailors'. However, the value inheres precisely in actually being effective and launching the boat, and not merely in registering solidarity with the lifeboat men in some other fashion. It is this element, that the 'expression' requires causal efficacy for it to be significant, that the expressivists such as Riker and Ordeshook or Schuessler neglected, because they were committed to the idea that the causal relations must be narrowly counter-factual in character—that, so to speak, counter-factuality must go all the way down.

In this example, I am interested in helping other people, the drowning sailors, and motives of this sort have indeed hitherto been discussed by theorists (mostly economists) writing about the concept of so-called imperfect altruism or (in the better terminology of Robert Goodin) 'agency altruism'.[51] According to this view, which was put particularly clearly by Kenneth Arrow and Thomas Nagel in a symposium in 1972,[52] a 'pure' altruist is interested only in the provision of a particular public good and does not care whether it is provided through his own action or through that of someone else; an 'impure' or 'agency' altruist gets a 'warm glow' (Andreoni's term) from his participation in the provision. The utility of the impure altruist is

---

51. See James Andreoni, 'Giving with Impure Altruism: Applications to Charity and Ricardian Equivalence', *Journal of Political Economy* 97 (1989): 1447–1458, and 'Impure Altruism and Donations to Public Goods: A Theory of Warm-Glow Giving', *Economic Journal* 100 (1990): 464–477; Robert Goodin, *Reasons for Welfare* (Princeton, N.J.: Princeton University Press, 1988), pp. 155–157; Gary Becker, 'A Theory of Social Interaction', *Journal of Political Economy* 82 (1974): 1063–1093. The term 'agency altruism' comes from Goodin; see, for example, Nancy Flobre and Robert Goodin, 'Revealing Altruism', *Review of Social Economy* 62 (2004): 1–25. See also the discussion on agency in Amartya Sen, *On Ethics and Economics* (Oxford: Blackwell, 1987), pp. 40–45, and the papers of Arrow and Nagel mentioned in n. 53.

52. Kenneth J. Arrow, 'Gifts and Exchanges', in *Altruism, Morality, and Economic Theory,* ed. Edmund S. Phelps (New York: Russell Sage Foundation, 1975), pp. 17–18; Thomas Nagel, '*Comment*', ibid., p. 65. Arrow's paper was also published in *Philosophy and Public Affairs* 1 (1972): 343–362.

then a function of both the public good and his own pleasure in participating in the collective activity. Pure altruists, on this view, will have no good reason to contribute to a public good if someone else is likely to do so (and if they reckon that the disutility of the contribution to the other person is equal to or less than the disutility they would themselves suffer), whereas impure altruists will, since they get utility from the act of participating itself. But in fact the importance of agency goes beyond the domain of altruistic actions: it is quite possible to value agency in the same way even where *someone else's* interests are not at stake. If I can get a 'warm glow' from agency in altruistic actions, then by the same token I can get one from self-interested actions—if agency *as such* matters to me, then it must matter irrespective of the altruistic character of the action. And indeed it is not unreasonable to take satisfaction in actively bringing about a benefit for oneself, rather than in merely passively receiving it.[53] Concern with agency would then be a special case of the concern with 'process' or what Sen has termed 'comprehensive' outcomes, rather than 'culmination' outcomes, 'outcomes *given* the acts of choice'.[54]

We might nevertheless distinguish between certain kinds of altruistic conduct and self-interested behaviour. Goodin observed apropos of the idea of 'pure' altruism that 'it depicts as charitable paradigmatically someone who not only would *let* others help instead, but, on balance, would *prefer* that others help instead. But that is just not what it is to *care* about someone else'.[55] Strictly speaking this is not so, as the pure altruist would be indifferent between an outcome brought about by his own action and one brought about by someone else, but Goodin's general point still stands, that there is something puzzling about caring about another person's welfare but not caring about whether or not one's *own* action makes any difference to it. In situations where I could bring about a benefit for someone else (as in the lifeboat case), and where the alternative state of affairs if I chose not to do so would involve another person's providing the benefit and my enjoying some self-interested satisfaction (such as sitting at home on a stormy night), then it might be reasonable to say that I could not plausibly claim to care

53. See Sen's suggestive remarks in n. 15, p. 44 of *On Ethics and Economics*.

54. Amartya Sen, 'Maximization and the Act of Choice', in Sen, *Rationality and Freedom* (Cambridge, Mass.: Harvard University Press, 2002), pp. 158–205. Sen links this to voting (p. 165), though not quite in the way I am suggesting.

55. Goodin, *Reasons for Welfare*, p. 157. He went on to observe that actual patterns of charitable giving suggest strongly that people do care about their own agency.

about the sailors unless I chose to go down to the beach. In the case of purely self-interested actions, while it remains true that we would feel a kind of puzzlement about someone who claimed to care about an outcome but did not care about his own role in bringing it about, the decision to (for example) stay at home rather than go the polls (where voting is taken to be a self-regarding act) is not similarly puzzling. If I choose to abstain from going to the polls, I am still deciding to act in order to bring about an outcome—but the action which I wish to claim agency over is staying at home, on the assumption that someone else will elect my candidate. (We might say that if I do go to the polls, it is on the—equally justifiable—assumption that I will not be needed at home to stop the house from burning down.) So viewed from this perspective, it is not unreasonable to say that there may be a good reason to perform a pre-emptive altruistic act (where the choice is between one altruistic act and one or more self-interested ones; clearly, competing altruistic demands are more like competing self-interested ones), but not necessarily a good reason to perform a pre-emptive self-interested one where the competing action is also self-interested. It should be emphasised that the reason for acting altruistically in these circumstances is not to save someone else trouble—in the case of the lifeboat, the major disbenefit to the people concerned is leaving their warm homes, and everyone standing on the beach has already done that, while in the voting case similarly everyone has already cast his vote. The reason is simply to save the lives of the sailors, this being a project which I care about, and which I can accomplish through my own efforts.

I remarked earlier that a response of this kind, involving the notion of a desire to claim causal agency over an outcome, stays within a broadly counter-factual view of decision-making. Given the prevalence of that view, this may be all that needs to be said to explain choice in situations of redundant causation, and what I have to say next is accordingly not critical to my general argument; but it must be conceded that there is something unsatisfactory about this kind of response. When the first policeman fires, he does not do so after considering whether or not his companion will do likewise and whether he himself wishes to claim agency over the outcome; he does so *because he wants to shoot the robber,* and because he knows that he has at that moment the power to do so. In other words, the most plausible account of his action is that he knows that among the many outcomes which his action would (in the circumstances) be sufficient to bring about is one which he prefers to all the others, and he chooses it accordingly. Similarly, our normal idea of moral responsibility—of someone's being liable for credit or blame for an action—does not seem in any marked degree to differentiate between acts which are necessary and acts which are sufficient to bring about the outcome in question: it is enough that someone performs the action. For example, it could not be a defence in court that my intentional action—say, shooting someone—pre-empted the action of someone else, and it could not even diminish in any way the severity of a sentence.[56] And in the same way, it does not diminish the praise which I would receive for performing a meritorious act, that had I not done it, someone else would have done. (And though for me to say so might be a familiar way of expressing modesty about my own achievement—'It was nothing special'—no one would expect an utterance of this kind to be taken seriously, and the praise or reward to be promptly reduced accordingly.) The question of the likely alternative simply does not arise in the evaluation of the action.

Though it is rather unfashionable at the moment, there is a general theory of causation according to which this is perfectly reasonable, and one should not expect people to be interested in anything other than causal sufficiency. This is the theory famously advanced by John Stuart Mill in *A System of Logic,* and (broadly) adopted by H. L. A. Hart and Tony Honoré as being closest in spirit to the implicit theory of causation present in our legal system. Mill argued that 'the cause, philosophically speaking, is the sum total of the conditions, positive and negative taken together; the whole of the contingencies of every description, which being realized, the consequent invariably follows'.[57] He meant by this, it is clear from his subsequent discussion, that we should strictly speaking term a 'cause' any antecedent condition to an event whose occurrence, given the other conditions in place, was 'invariably' associated with the outcome, and in whose absence the other conditions would not be so associated. (Mill's whole project was intended to avoid using the idea of 'necessity', the doctrine of which, he remarked, 'weighed on my existence like an incubus'.)[58] The idea is that if we have conditions A and B and C, any two of them will not be invariably associated with D, but all three will be. It should be stressed that this does not mean that D *requires* A + B +

56. See the discussions in Hart and Honoré, *Causation in the Law,* pp. 122–125, 235–236.

57. Mill, *A System of Logic,* III.v.3.

58. This is a quotation from his *Autobiography,* in John Stuart Mill, *Collected Works,* eds. John M. Robson and Jack Stillinger (Toronto: University of Toronto Press, 1981), I, p. 175. For a discussion of his view of necessity, see R. F. McRae's introduction to *A System of Logic* in Mill's *Collected Works* (Toronto: University of Toronto Press, 1973), VII, pp. xxxii–xxxiii.

C: Mill wrote explicitly about the 'plurality of causes', or—in our terminology—redundant causation, making the point that A + B + E might also be invariably associated with D.[59] This has often been misunderstood. Mackie, for example, defined what he called 'strong' causal sufficiency as (in effect) the claim that if we have A and B, then the non-occurrence of D entails the non-occurrence of C;[60] but Mill was clear that the only form of necessity which he would admit into his theory was the proposition that a particular set of conditions defined in this way would entail a particular outcome, and not that they were necessary for it.[61]

There are problems in specifying the elements of a minimally sufficient set of conditions,[62] but as we have seen, there are major problems about all theories of causation, and it is not clear that Mill's is more vulnerable than Mackie's or Lewis's. It also has the major merit, as Hart and Honoré recognised, of being closest to the best-worked-out account of the role causation plays in human decision-making, the one that is embodied in two thousand years of legal argument with substantial penalties looming over the participants if they make mistakes. If we accept Mill's theory, then it follows that a causal decision theory could not be counter-factual in character, since causal relations are solely relations of sufficiency. Accordingly, rational choices (if we accept that causation matters to our decisions) must include decisions based simply on our knowledge of our action's sufficiency to bring about the outcome.

This does not, of course, preclude a rather low-level notion of 'necessity' from playing some part in our decisions; it might obviously be a good reason for doing something that I am probably the only person able to do it. But on a Millian account this is not the *only* good instrumental reason for doing something, and it is certainly not the case that I should restrict the domain within which I make choices to those outcomes which only I can bring about—this would be a fantastic and quite unrealistic account of delibera-

59. Mill, *A System of Logic*, III.x.

60. Mackie, *Cement of the Universe*, pp. 39–40; though it should be said that he defined the other conditions or 'circumstances' on p. 31 in such a way that they included the absence of any other possible event which would cause D, and thereby made his strong causal sufficiency trivially true. Mill's 'negative conditions' only included the absence of *checks* on the causal efficacy of the positive conditions, thereby allowing a space for redundant causation.

61. For a good discussion of Mill's theory, see John Skorupski, *John Stuart Mill* (London: Routledge, 1989), pp. 175–202.

62. See Lewis's remarks in 'Causation as Influence', p. 77.

tion. Nor is it even the case that my being the only person able to bring about an outcome means that I should perform that action in preference to an alternative where my action is merely sufficient: it might well be that I consider the outcome in the second case to be much more important than the outcome in the first case. For example, I am taking my dog for a walk on the beach, and I see a swimmer in distress. Someone else on the beach has also seen the swimmer. Only I can make sure that my dog does not run away and get into trouble, while if I do not help the swimmer, the other person will do so. But it is unlikely that I would decide that the best course of action for me must therefore be to hold tightly on to the dog's leash and not go to the help of the drowning man. Similarly, the fact that by voting I can probably bring about my desired result (if enough like-minded people vote) is in itself, and without extraneous considerations of the value of agency, an adequate reason to go to the polls (though it may not be, nor should it be, an *overriding* reason—that depends on how strongly I feel about the importance of the election, and how pressing the alternatives open to me are).

I said, 'if enough like-minded people vote', and the last point to discuss on this topic is the question of whether it is rational to vote irrespective of the numbers that I expect to do so. On my account, it is rational to vote (all other things being equal) only if I believe that there are likely to be enough votes for my candidate for *my* vote to be part of a causally efficacious set. (Other things, of course, may not be equal—for example, I may want to achieve some end other than electing someone, such as registering that there is at least one Communist voter in Kensington.) In other words, I think that it is precisely in the situation where it looks on the standard modern view as if my vote is unnecessary that I have a good reason to vote. The same is true of the lifeboat: if I am very confident that no one else will turn up (perhaps I know they're all at a rock concert), I have no *instrumental* reason for going down to the beach, though I may want to register that unlike the rest of the village, I think about the lifeboat. Political scientists have talked about a 'bandwagon effect' and have been rather puzzled by it. There is no question but that it exists; a particularly well documented example is provided by Larry Bartels's work on presidential primaries in the United States.[63] But on the standard account of instrumental action, it is not at all clear why a rational voter should join a bandwagon. Bartels talked about the

63. Larry Bartels, *Presidential Primaries and the Dynamics of Public Choice* (Princeton, N.J.: Princeton University Press, 1988).

desire of a voter not to 'waste' his vote and therefore to vote as part of a prospectively victorious group, but he could not give a clear account of how this could count as rational.[64] But if I am correct, it is a natural part of instrumental politics and needs no special explanation. It does not follow that very safe constituencies should always produce high turnouts—first, the safety of the constituency may render the whole business of politics rather dull (that is, alter the value I put on having my candidate elected), and second, as we have seen, the chances of my vote's being in an efficacious set are the ratio of the overall vote for my candidate to the vote for the most successful losing candidate, and when that ratio gets *very* big, I might reasonably conclude that it is not worth going to the polls.

It will be remembered that Olson took the view that no collaborative action was worthwhile (in the absence of a coercive mechanism or some other inducement), because

> selfless behavior that has no perceptible effect is sometimes not even considered praiseworthy. A man who tried to hold back a flood with a pail would probably be considered more of a crank than a saint, even by those he was trying to help. It is no doubt possible infinitesimally to lower the level of a river in flood with a pail, just as it is possible for a single farmer infinitesimally to raise prices by limiting his production, but in both cases the effect is imperceptible, and those who sacrifice themselves in the interest of imperceptible improvements may not even receive the praise normally due selfless behavior.[65]

But this can be true even though collaboration makes sense, precisely because it can be reasonable to contribute when enough other people do but not when they do not—the crank trying *by himself* to lower the river with a pail has (if my argument has been correct) a quite different causal relationship to the desired outcome from that possessed by the individual member of a bucket chain, where there are enough people taking part for their collective efforts to be successful in reducing the water level.

The fact that my action depends on enough other people behaving in a similar way also indicates that the right way to think about these kinds of

---

64. A point made particularly strongly by Schuessler in his *A Logic of Expressive Choice*, pp. 114–115. He regards bandwagons as a prime example of why an expressive theory of his kind is needed.

65. Olson, *The Logic of Collective Action* (Cambridge, Mass.: Harvard University Press, 1971), p. 64.

collaborative activity is in fact in terms of Schelling-Lewis conventions, even if we are not part of a group which has committed itself in some way to precisely the right number turning up. We all have an interest (if my argument is correct) in each other's turning up in sufficiently large numbers for our individual actions to count towards the securing of our common goal, without its being the case that the number has to be *exactly* the minimum necessary: as long as it is big enough, there is likely to be a point to *my* action. So the convention now has to be construed not as co-ordinating us so that we get precisely the correct number, but as co-ordinating us so that each of us has a good chance of being responsible for the outcome. This kind of co-ordination is pre-eminently the object of conventions, which (as Schelling and Lewis observed) can develop without any formal interaction between the participants, simply on the basis of a perceived community of interest and the recognition of certain naturally salient features of the situation. Once the convention is in place, we have a straightforward reason to persist in our collaboration and not to defect. This latter point should perhaps be stressed, as it is sometimes overlooked: the key issue for Olson was that *irrespective* of whether other people contribute, we have no reason to do so. On my interpretation, this is not so. Either we have put in place an exact co-ordination, of the Smart kind, knowing that we are faced with a threshold, or we have put in place a rather less exact co-ordination, knowing that thereby each of us has a reasonable opportunity to bring about the desired result. Either way, if there are enough other contributors, we have a reason to contribute; and given that we have prior knowledge that that will be the case, we all have a reason to construct a convention, as it will be not be prone to defection.

In the next chapter I shall deal with the important question of what *counts* as 'enough'. I also suspect that the commonplace response to a proposal to defect—'What if everyone did that?'—is not the vulgarly Kantian view it has often been taken to be, but rather a way of drawing our attention to the fact that enough other people are contributing and that we therefore have a good reason to do likewise. But I shall have more to say on this particular issue later.

CHAPTER THREE

Negligibility

We have now seen that Olson was entirely justified in having reservations about including as an example of his problem either the prisoners' dilemma or voting. More generally, we have confirmed his—and Buchanan's—sense that wherever strategic interaction is possible among the participants in a collaborative enterprise, we will not find a clear case of Olson's problem; and in particular we have seen in the previous chapter that even in large-scale enterprises, free riding will not necessarily occur if there is a determinate threshold at which the relevant benefit is secured. Does that exhaust the possible cases, with the consequence that Olson (and with him, most twentieth-century economists) was straightforwardly mistaken about his puzzle? I think he *was* mistaken, but not straightforwardly: the mistake was at a very deep level. Olson was, after all, well aware that the kinds of cases we have been considering fell outside the scope of his argument. What he believed, as we saw in the Introduction, was that there is an important and quite pervasive set of cases in economic and social life where *no* determinate threshold will be encountered, and where it makes perfectly good sense to say that any one contribution to the communal enterprise is genuinely what he normally termed 'imperceptible' (for example, pp. 44 and 64) or not 'noticeable' (for example, p. 50), or what I have termed 'negligible'.

Olson simply assumed the existence of such cases, following the tradition among theorists of perfect competition. But it was not at all unreasonable for him to do so—there are many situations where on the face of it there is in actuality no determinate threshold. Despite the fact that Lyons wished to assimilate it to the voting case, walking on the grass is a classic example: it is clear that the eventual accumulation of crossings by people wears down turf in a visible and aesthetically unpleasant way, but it is equally clear that no *individual* crossing makes a perceptible difference—a difference, that is, which is perceptible *in the same sense* that the eventual damage is perceptible. This is a critical point, as obviously at some micro level we could detect the effects of a single crossing (enumerate the broken blades of grass, say), but those effects are not perceptible in the coarser sense that we use when we say that the *overall damage* is noticeable. But from the point of view of assessing the action, it is this coarser sense which is relevant, since it is this damage which we care about (who cares about some microscopically damaged grass?). To see this, consider what we would say about the last person in a series of people crossing the grass. He can perfectly correctly say that *his* crossing makes no difference, in the sense that it cannot add to any visual damage already inflicted on the lawn. The damage is either done, in which case there is no point in worrying about an additional walker, or it is not done, in which case by definition his action cannot bring it about, since we cannot tell in terms of perceptible damage whether someone has crossed the grass or not. As he is the last person, we cannot even say straightforwardly that his action contributes in some way to the accumulation of crossings which together ruin the lawn. But if this is true of the last person, it will be true of any member of the set of people crossing the grass that, assuming the actions of the other people to take place, his own action makes no difference. (This is the counterpart to the causal efficacy possessed by everyone *given the actions of the others* in a threshold case—in this instance, there is causal *inefficacy*, given the actions of the others.) So we have a classic instance of Olson's problem, and Lyons's solution will not work, since there is as a matter of *fact* no relevant threshold, unlike voting.[1]

Any genuine Olsonian problem has this feature, that there is a discrepancy between how we evaluate the outcome and how we can discriminate between contributions to it. Let us take his most important case, a trades union. Olson argued that

---

1. Philip Pettit, in his important paper 'Free Riding and Foul Dealing', *Journal of Philosophy* 83 (1986): 361–379, has also stressed that genuine free riding is not soluble by strategic interaction, though he has also observed that there are cases which resemble free riding (what he calls 'foul dealing') where a single defection from a common enterprise can render at least one other participant actually worse off, and that these cases are accordingly soluble by strategic behaviour. The example he uses is a Hobbesian commonwealth, in which a defector acquires the means of power over other people which all had renounced on their exit from the state of nature. See Chapter Four for some doubts about this characterisation of Hobbes's argument, but Pettit's general point still stands, and is an important corrective, for example, to Russell Hardin's use of the prisoners' dilemma model to solve all collective action problems.

[a] labor union works primarily to get higher wages, better working conditions, legislation favorable to workers, and the like; these things by their
very nature ordinarily cannot be withheld from any particular worker in
the group represented by the union . . . It follows that most of the achievements of a union, even if they were more impressive than the staunchest
unionist claims, could offer the rational worker no incentive to join; his individual efforts would not have a noticeable effect on the outcome, and
whether he supported the union or not he would still get the benefits of its
achievements. (p. 76)

The thought here is that something like successful lobbying in a legislature
to get favourable legislation passed, though it needs funds from the union,
or the capacity to lay on demonstrations of workers outside the legislative
building, needs no *precise* or *particular* sum of money or number of demonstrators. It would be very surprising if 1,000 demonstrators could secure
their object and 999 could not; mostly (in a fashion strictly analogous to the
grass case) the efficacy of a demonstration consists in its *visible* mass and
menacing aspect, and one participant more or less can make no difference to
that. Similarly, if the union's budget is in the millions (as may well happen
with a large union), a single member's contributions will be negligible; given
the scale of the enterprises with which the union is concerned, its success in
securing its objectives cannot reasonably turn on whether it has $1,000,000
or $1,000,050 in its coffers. But the union's ability to mount a demonstra-
tion or to enjoy a decent treasury involves the accumulation of contributions which are discernible and numerable, and for each one of which it
is reasonable to say, as in the grass case, that it makes no difference to *this*
outcome—though it might, of course, make a considerable difference in
another setting. The contribution of a trades unionist *would* have causal
efficacy in the context of his personal expenditure, whether of an altruistic
or a self-interested kind (better to spend the money by giving it to a beggar
than to the union if we are altruists, better to spend it on a good meal if we
are self-interested).

All this seems to be true, but there is always a certain air of paradox about
it. Some people have responded to this paradoxical quality by denying that
there can be instances of true negligibility at all—which, if correct, would
immediately render Olson's argument false, and convert most cases of large-
scale social collaboration into instances of a Lyons-style threshold effect.
Brian Barry, for example, exploded as follows on reading Olson's claim that

'even if the member of a large group were to neglect his own interests entirely, he still would not rationally contribute towards the provision of any collective or public good, since his own contribution would not be perceptible' (p. 64):

> This is surely absurd. If each contribution is literally 'imperceptible' how can all the contributions together add up to anything? Conversely, if a hundred thousand members count for something, then each one contributes on the average a hundred-thousandth. If it is rational for workers in an industry to wish for a closed shop, thus coercing everyone to join the union, this must mean that the total benefits brought by the union are greater than its total costs. (Otherwise it would be better not to have the union.) But if this is so, it must mean that anyone who wished to maximise the gains of workers in the industry would join the union voluntarily.[2]

Others, who have spotted the underlying logic of Olson's argument, have simply thrown their hands up. Donald Regan, for instance, discussed the grass example in the context of an analysis of Lyons, but concluded that 'the problem of how imperceptible differences add up to perceptible differences is a certified stumper'.[3] This is true, but how can the central theory of twentieth-century economics and late twentieth-century political science be allowed to rest on 'a certified stumper'? We will inevitably need to come to terms with the general problem of negligibility, and how we do so is equally inevitably going to determine the kind of answer we give to Olson's question.

The paradoxical character of the argument is intensified when we realise that it is not simply a puzzle about social co-operation: negligibility or imperceptibility produces unacceptable conclusions in any form of cumulative behaviour, including (as we shall see) certain cumulative descriptions of the world. Suppose that we have a shepherd living by himself in the mountains. He needs to guide himself in the mist by cairns raised in suitable places; a cairn serves as a guide to him by being observable in the appropriate conditions, and its value consists solely in its observational properties. But the cairn is composed of many separate stones, each one of which is moderately

2. Brian Barry, *Sociologists, Economists and Democracy* (London: Collier-Macmillan, 1970), p. 32.

3. He suggested tentatively that we should model these cases using a probability calculus, a notion discussed and dismissed below. Donald Regan, *Utilitarianism and Co-operation* (Oxford: Oxford University Press, 1980), p. 61.

heavy and time-consuming to lift and put into place; any particular stone makes no difference to the observational character of the cairn, as only the accumulation of stones is properly visible. (So an individual stone is equivalent to an individual crossing of the grass.) How should the shepherd reason about the best use of his time and effort? It is immediately clear that he is faced with at least a first-order problem, comparable to the first-order problem of the free rider; in calling it first-order, I mean to reserve judgement about whether there may be some higher-order solution based on reflection about the existence of the lower-order puzzle. Let us imagine (to avoid certain possible objections, and to bring the situation more closely into line with a free-rider case) that the shepherd somehow successfully constructed a cairn last week, and that he counted each stone as he put it in place. (It might be that he did not even realise what he had done until he had finished piling stones as a form of exercise.) This week he needs to duplicate the cairn beside another precipice; but it would clearly be irrational for him to drag up to the chosen site exactly the same number of stones that he used last week, since one stone *ex hypothesi* makes no difference to the outcome, and he will save himself an appreciable amount of work if he can manage with one less. So he lugs one less stone and gets a bit more rest. Next week he needs another cairn, and he makes the same calculation . . . And so on (you get the picture). Each week the plainly rational use of his time and effort is to drag one less, but the iteration of these rational calculations leads to an absurd result. The question then is, where did the shepherd go wrong in his thinking? And if he made a mistake, is it a mistake which is also made by a free rider involved in a collective enterprise?

I have, of course, constructed this example deliberately because of its connection to the most famous example of such a puzzle, which has been the focus of philosophical discussion about the issue for more than two thousand years, the 'sorites paradox', or paradox of the heap.[4] Despite the paradox's name, the commonest example of it in antiquity was in fact not the construction of (or failure to construct) a heap, but the description of a number as 'small' or a quantity as 'few'.

---

4. *Sorites* is the Latin transliteration of the Greek σωρίτης, meaning originally 'a heaper' (one who heaps), from σωρός, 'heap'. See Jonathan Barnes, 'Medicine, Experience and Logic', in *Science and Speculation: Studies in Hellenistic Theory and Practice,* ed. Jonathan Barnes, Jacques Brunschwig, Myles Burnyeat and Malcolm Schofield (Cambridge: Cambridge University Press, 1982), p. 32 n. 18.

It is not the case that two are few and three are not also; it is not the case that these are and four are not also (and so on up to ten thousand). But two are few; therefore ten thousand are also.[5]

But a heap does appear in the longest discussion which survives from the ancient world, in Galen's *On Medical Experience*.[6]

Wherefore I say: tell me, do you think that a single grain of wheat is a heap? Thereupon you say No. Then I say: What do you say about 2 grains? For it is my purpose to ask you questions in succession, and if you do not admit that 2 grains are a heap then I shall ask you about three grains. Then I shall proceed to interrogate you further with respect to 4 grains, then 5 and 6 and 7 and eight; and I think you will say that none of these make a heap. Also 9 and 10 and 11 grains are not a heap. For the conception of a heap which is formed in the soul and is conjured up in the imagination is that, besides being single particles in juxtaposition, it has quantity and mass of some considerable size [that is, a 'heap' is not simply a numerable set of grains]. . . . If you do not say with respect to any of the numbers, as in the case of the 100 grains of wheat for example, that it now constitutes a heap, but afterwards when a grain is added to it, you say that a heap has now been formed, consequently this quantity of corn becomes a heap by the addition of the single grain of wheat, and if the grain is taken away the heap is eliminated. And I know of nothing worse and more absurd than that the being and not-being of a heap is determined by a grain of corn. And to prevent this absurdity ad-

5. This is from Diogenes Laertius's summary of the puzzles discussed by Stoic philosophers; *Lives of the Philosophers* VII.82. The translation is by Barnes, 'Medicine, Experience and Logic', pp. 27–28. The prevalence of this version in the ancient texts, incidentally, makes it all the odder that in the 1970s it should have been thought that Hao Wang had produced a new version of the paradox when he argued that we cannot say definitely whether a number is 'small' (Michael Dummett, 'Wang's Paradox', *Synthese* 30 [1975]: 324).

6. Galen, *On Medical Experience*, ed. and trans. R. Walzer (London: Oxford University Press, 1944). 'Survive' is a generous description—the text was discovered in Istanbul in 1931, in the form of an Arabic translation of a Syriac translation of the Greek original. But it is a remarkably accurate translation, as was seen when it was compared with some existing fragments of the original. Because of this history, however, Galen's text was not known to philosophers before 1931; the most important ancient texts prior to that year were Diogenes Laertius, Sextus Empiricus (*Against the Philosophers* and *Against the Mathematicians*) and Cicero's *Academica*, though Barnes has counted in all thirty-three separate works in which the paradox is expressly discussed—a large number (Barnes, 'Medicine, Experience and Logic', pp. 65–66).

hering to you, you will not cease from denying, and will never admit at any time that the sum of this is a heap, even if the number of grains reaches infinity by the constant and gradual addition of more. And by reason of this denial the heap is proved to be non-existent, because of this pretty sophism.[7]

Ancient writers were well aware of the far-reaching character of the paradox. Galen was interested in the sorites in the first place because he took it potentially to call into question the whole idea of induction—how many instances are 'enough' to establish reasonable belief in (for example) the conjunction of symptoms and disease? He listed as things eliminated from the world by the sorites 'a heap of grain', 'a mass', 'satiety', 'a mountain', 'strong love,'[8] 'a row' (of objects), 'strong wind', 'a city', 'a wave', 'the open sea', 'a flock of sheep', 'a herd of cattle', 'a nation' and 'a crowd,'[9] 'youth', 'manhood' and 'baldness'.[10] Cicero instanced 'rich' and 'poor', 'famous' and 'obscure', 'many', 'few', 'great', 'small', 'long', 'short', 'broad' and 'narrow,'[11] and the great sceptical philosopher Carneades is reported to have used the sorites argument to deny the existence of God (not unreasonably, given the continuum of divine and semi-divine beings in a polytheistic religion).[12] All these cases are matters of description, and not (or at least not in the first instance) action; but Burnyeat has observed that behind most of the ancient discussions is the presumption that there will be an actual debate, as in a law court, in which an adversary is being forced to commit himself to paradoxical conclusions,[13] so the implications of the paradox for action of various kinds was well understood by the ancient writers. The Roman lawyers were familiar with it, and it is twice referred to in the *Digest*, presumably because

7. Galen, *On Medical Experience*, pp. 115–116, translation corrected by Barnes, 'Medicine, Experience and Logic', p. 33.

8. The Syriac translator observed that this was οἶστρος, overwhelming desire—when does tepid affection become overmastering passion?

9. All these are from Galen, *On Medical Experience*, p. 114. See Barnes, 'Medicine, Experience and Logic', p. 34.

10. These are from Galen, *On Medical Experience*, pp. 123–125. Baldness became the other proverbial example.

11. Cicero, *Academica*, II.xxix.92.

12. Discussed by Myles Burnyeat in 'Gods and Heaps', in *Language and Logos: Studies in Ancient Greek Philosophy Presented to G. E. L. Owen*, ed. Malcolm Schofield and Martha Nussbaum (Cambridge: Cambridge University Press, 1982), pp. 315–338.

13. Burnyeat, 'Gods and Heaps', p. 334.

the Romans, like modern lawyers, were well acquainted with slippery-slope arguments.[14] There are also hints in the ancient literature of a most fascinating Aristotelian use of the sorites in ethics: Aspasius, the early second-century commentator on the *Nichomachean Ethics,* and the first commentator whose work survives in more or less its entirety, remarked in his discussion of Aristotle on the mean that

> [w]hat he [Aristotle] said at the end, that it is not easy to determine to what extent and 'up to what point' (1109b20) a person deviating toward the more or toward the less is blameworthy, this follows on what is always being said by him, that it is impossible to determine exactly anything in matters of action, but rather in outline; nor indeed anything else among perceptible things, whence too the heap puzzles *[sorites]* derive. For up to what point is a person rich? If someone should posit that it is someone who has as much as ten talents, they ask: 'but if someone should take away a drachma, is he no longer rich? Or if two?' For it is not possible to determine exactly any such things, since they are perceptibles, in respect to the rich man and the poor. In the case of the bald man too they ask whether he becomes bald by [the loss of] one hair, and what about two, and what about three? From this the arguments are called 'bald' as well as 'heap'. For in the case of a heap they used to ask the same thing: if a heap is made smaller by one grain [is it no longer a heap?], and then if by two and so on. And it is not possible to say when first it is no longer a heap because no perceptible things are grasped exactly, but rather broadly and in outline. For it is not possible to say that a person who is angry to a certain extent is being angry at the mean or is excessive or deficient, because a deviation by a small amount to the greater or to the less escapes notice. This is why one needs practical wisdom, which recognises the mean in emotions and in actions.[15]

I will return later to the possible links between negligibility and Aristotelian ethical theory. The sorites was widely known outside philosophical cir-

14. Ulpian in *De verborum significatione, Dig* L.xvi.177; Julian in *De diversis regulis, Dig.* L.xvii.65.

15. Aspasius, *On Aristotle. Nicomachean Ethics 1–4, 7–8,* trans. David Konstan (London: Duckworth, 2006), pp. 56–57; for the original text, see *Aspasii in Ethica Nicomachea Quae Supersunt Commentaria,* ed. G. Heylbut (Berlin: Reiner, 1889), 56, 25–57, 5. See Barnes, 'Medicine, Experience and Logic', p. 61. See also the remarks of the anonymous commentator, ibid., p. 60. Barnes gives reasons for supposing that Aristotle himself was not thinking about the sorites when he constructed his ethical theory; ibid., pp. 38–41. For Aspasius, see *Aspasius: The Earliest Extant Commentary on Aristotle's Ethics,* ed. Antonia Alberti and Robert W. Sharples (Berlin: Walter De Gruyter, 1999).

cles and often treated as a game or joke;[16] but then, as now, its primary function was to expose the pretensions of those philosophers who claimed to be producing a 'scientific' account of the world, and of human conduct, disdaining common-sense accounts, but who, when faced with the sorites, invariably fell back on a common-sense dismissal of its force. The sceptics of antiquity, in particular, deployed it against their Stoic opponents; most of what we know about the various ancient views of the paradox comes from these debates. It is not entirely clear who invented it, though writers in antiquity often associated it with a contemporary of Aristotle's, Eubulides of Miletus; nor is it clear what was the original context in which it was developed (the idea that it was a deliberately anti-Aristotelian argument has largely been discarded). It is quite probable that the basic idea occurred more or less as soon as people began to think about the curious implications of enumeration—Genesis 18 records Abraham forcing God into an (albeit brief) stance of mercy towards Sodom by taking him through what amounts to a sorites.[17]

Aristotelian logic contains no discussion of sorites-like arguments, and in the heyday of Aristotelianism during the Middle Ages they were scarcely ever considered; indeed, the term 'sorites' had been applied in the Christian Aristotelian tradition since the work of Victorinus in the fourth century merely to a series of syllogisms linked (or piled) together, with no recognition that this might engender paradoxical conclusions. Christians of course disliked and despised all the old arguments of the sceptics. This lack of interest continued down to the fifteenth century; Bartolus, for example, skips over the passages from Ulpian and Julian in his commentary on Book L of the *Digest*. Characteristically, the first great Renaissance logician, Lorenzo Valla, devoted some pages to the ancient sorites arguments in his *Dialecticarum disputationes*, citing Horace, Cicero and Abraham and quoting Cicero's extensive list of possible problems; though he included in the sorites (or *coacervatio,* as he called it, in his good Latin) any non-transitive set of propositions, including those where the non-transitivity does not arise from indiscernible changes—as in the standard example, Themistocles rules Athens, his wife rules Themistocles, her son rules Themistocles' wife, but her son

16. Barnes, 'Medicine, Experience and Logic', p. 36. See, for example, Horace, *Epistles* II.i.36–49.

17. This was used as an example of a sorites by Lorenzo Valla in his *Dialecticarum disputationes*. Presumably the passage represents Mesopotamian reflections on the number system, if indeed it does not represent Greek speculation (depending on when one dates Genesis). If even God cannot handle a sorites, what hope is there for the rest of us?

does not rule Athens.[18] But most logic textbooks from the sixteenth century to the nineteenth century continued to define a sorites in the Victorinan manner.

Its absence from works on logic in the period does not, however, mean that the issue itself was not of great interest. With the revival of scepticism in the late sixteenth and early seventeenth centuries, and with the development of what I have elsewhere termed 'post-scepticism' among the great philosophers of the mid-seventeenth century, sorites-type arguments were fully understood as part of the repertory of the sceptic, to be met with the same resources which were brought to bear on the other sceptical arguments, such as the inherent fallibility of human perception and the radical character of human moral disagreement.[19] Thus Hobbes included the sorites in his list of contentious matters which could be decided only by the fiat of the sovereign.

> In the state of nature, where every man is his own judge, and differeth from other concerning the names and appellations of things, and from those differences arise quarrels, and breach of peace; it was necessary there should be a common measure of all things that might fall in controversy; as for example: of what is to be called right, what good, what virtue, what much, what little, what *meum* and *tuum,* what a pound, what a quart, &c. For in these things private judgements may differ, and beget controversy . . . Consequently the civil laws are to all subjects the measures of their actions, whereby to determine, whether they be right or wrong, profitable or unprofitable, virtuous or vicious; and by them the use and definition of all names not agreed upon, and tending to controversy, shall be established. As for example, upon the occasion of some strange and deformed birth, it shall not be decided by Aristotle, or the philosophers, whether the same be a man or no, but by the laws.[20]

18. Valla, *Dialecticarum disputationes* (Cologne, 1541), p. 275. On Valla and the Renaissance use of the sorites, see Lisa Jardine, 'Lorenzo Valla and the Intellectual Origins of Humanist Dialectic', *Journal of the History of Philosophy* 15 (1977): 161–162, and 'Humanism and the teaching of logic' in *The Cambridge History of Later Medieval Philosophy,* ed. Norman Kretzman, Anthony Kenny and Jan Pinborg (Cambridge: Cambridge University Press, 1982), pp. 798–799. The Renaissance civil lawyers treated the subject in the same way in their commentaries on *Digest* L; see, for example, Jacques Cujas, *Ad titulum De verborum significatione commentarius* (Frankfurt, 1595), pp. 346–351.

19. For my earlier discussion of this issue, see Richard Tuck, *Philosophy and Government* (Cambridge: Cambridge University Press, 1993), pp. 285–293.

20. Thomas Hobbes, *Elements of Law* II.10.8.

This list runs together both moral disagreement ('what is to be called right', and so on) and the sorites in its standard ancient form ('what much, what little'); it also includes an example of a borderline problem of great interest, the definition of a human being. Hobbes's solution recognises that there is to be no natural answer to the sorites—there simply has to be an abrupt commitment on our part to a particular number (or its equivalent), and we have to recognise that questioning that commitment opens up a slippery slope on which we will find no stopping place.[21]

The point to stress, however, is that Hobbes fully understood the force and importance of sorites arguments, as did John Locke. Whereas Hobbes's answer involved a *collective* decision simply to stipulate a particular cutting-off point, Locke's answer (in line with his general philosophical response to Hobbes) was that a decision indeed had to be made, but it must be made by everyone separately and individually—disagreement was an inherent and ineliminable feature of sorites cases, and in practice discussion of heaps, monsters and so forth had to find the areas in which people's individual stipulations overlapped.[22] Strikingly, Locke (like some later philosophers) took the view that *all* descriptions of species potentially suffer from sorites problems, and hence that our language of kinds and essences is comprehensively stipulative. G. W. Leibniz, in his response to the *Essay,* did not dissent from Locke's view that individual stipulation is required in borderline cases, but argued that such cases are actually—and fortunately—much rarer than Locke believed, and that our language of species could map onto natural kinds with relatively little difficulty.[23] But something like Locke's view seems to have been standard among broadly empiricist philosophers in the eighteenth century, and indeed to have been taken for granted: David Hume, for example, nowhere discusses borderline cases as such, but his general account of human understanding was clearly compatible with the post-sceptical view that there are no sharp boundaries in nature, that our classificatory schemes are both ungrounded and radically contentious, but that they are necessary for us to live effectively in the world. To suppose otherwise came to seem an obvious example of fallacious reasoning. For example,

---

21. See also Gassendi's remarks on the sorites as one of the *sophistici ratiocinandi modi* categorised by Eubulides, in Chapter 3 of his *De Logicae Origine, et Varietate,* Book I of *Syntagmatis Philosophici Pars Prima, quae est Logica* and in his *Opera Omnia* (Lyons, 1658), I, p. 41; see also p. 51 for the Stoics' use of the sorites.

22. See John Locke, *Essay Concerning Human Understanding* III.vi.26–28.

23. Leibniz, *Nouveaux essais* III.v.9 and III.vi.27. See Timothy Williamson, *Vagueness* (London: Routledge, 1994), pp. 33–34 for a good discussion of the Locke-Leibniz debate.

Richard Whately, in his early nineteenth-century *Elements of Logic,* writing of the so-called fallacy of composition,[24] observed that

> [t]his is a Fallacy with which men are extremely apt to deceive *themselves:* for when a multitude of particulars are presented to the mind, many are too weak or too indolent to take a comprehensive view of them; but confine their attention to each single point, by turns, and then decide, infer, and act, accordingly: *e.g.* the imprudent spendthrift, finding that he is able to afford this, *or that,* or the other expense, forgets that *all of them together* will ruin him.[25]

This tradition of thinking about the problem, from the late Renaissance to the early nineteenth century, had at its heart the idea that a *judgement* of some kind is going to take place on the part of anyone faced with a sorites: we will not simply respond mechanically to the fact that two things are indiscriminable by treating them in the same way, but will reflect on the implications of doing so and discriminate even where there is no observational (or appropriate non-observational) basis for the discrimination. The naive versions of stimulus-response theory which became prevalent in the human sciences from the late nineteenth century onwards, infecting ideas of language itself as well as sociology, psychology and economics, made this a harder view to adopt. One result was that by the early twentieth century it became possible for economists to take seriously the claim that a negligible contribution to a common enterprise should be disregarded, a development which I shall be tracing in detail in Chapter Five. At the same time most philosophers were relatively uninterested in the issue, since they believed (like Gottlob Frege, Bertrand Russell and the early Ludwig Wittgenstein) that an ideal language with uniquely and determinately referring terms was theoretically possible, and that an ordinary language which lacked this feature was merely a flawed version of the ideal.[26]

24. A term which goes back to the scholastics.

25. Whately, *Elements of Logic,* 2d ed. (London: J. Mawman, 1827), p. 175. Though this work was criticised by the Benthamites for its general approach (not its view about this 'fallacy')—see George Bentham's *Outline of a New System of Logic: with a Critical Examination of Dr. Whately's Elements of Logic* (London: Hunt and Clarke, 1827), based on his uncle's papers—J. S. Mill admired it and quoted freely from it, including this passage, in his own *System of Logic.*

26. For a late example of this, see Hempel's response to Max Black: Carl G. Hempel, 'Vagueness and Logic', *Philosophy of Science* 6 (1939): 163–180.

As Timothy Williamson has observed,[27] two things had to change in order to render the sorites once again of philosophical interest. The first was the awareness from the late 1950s onwards that an ideal language of that kind eliminated a wide range of features of our ordinary language which are crucial to our use of language as such, as well as to our functioning effectively in the world. But this awareness in itself did not prompt renewed interest in the sorites (as can be seen from its relative absence in the writings of the later Wittgenstein and the ordinary-language philosophers of the 1950s); after all, no one expected to be able to capture the vagueness of ordinary language in a systematic and logical structure, and it was therefore not at all startling or interesting that the sorites should apparently confirm this. The second change in philosophical assumptions, which came largely in the 1970s, was a new hope that a systematic account of ordinary language *might* be given, and that it was not impossible to model it in a formal system—just impossible to do so with the old Frege-Russell logic. The sorites then became a critical stumbling block, and a series of papers and books from the mid-1970s onwards wrestled with its implications.[28] They have now provided us with the resources to deal in a new way with the problem of negligible contributions to collective goods.

We should clarify what is involved in the problem. First, a number of philosophers (including Russell and Crispin Wright) have written about the sorites as if it is a problem created by the coarseness of our observational or perceptual categories, as in the case of the original 'heap', or (the example Wright particularly was interested in) the colours on a spectrum—there is no determinate point at which red becomes orange. Observational predicates are clearly very prone to sorites problems, and they provide many of the best examples, but the problem can also arise in the case of predicates which are not observational, or at least not as straightforwardly observational as a colour description. Observation is the *only* determinant of an ob-

---

27. Williamson, *Vagueness*, pp. 70–73.

28. In addition to Williamson's book, a useful survey of the literature is in *Vagueness: A Reader*, ed. Rosanna Keefe and Peter Smith (Cambridge, Mass.: MIT Press, 1996). See also *Vagueness*, ed. Terry Horgan, *Southern Journal of Philosophy* 33, Supplement (1994). It was not just philosophers of language who began to suspect in the 1970s that the sorites was important: see, for example, my 'Is there a free-rider problem, and if so, what is it'? in *Rational Action: Studies in Philosophy and Social Science*, ed. Ross Harrison (Cambridge: Cambridge University Press, 1979), pp. 147–156, and James Fishkin's *The Limits of Obligation* (New Haven, Conn.: Yale University Press, 1982), pp. 54–57.

ject's colour: there simply is no other way of establishing the fact of the matter (to be told that it is reflecting a certain part of the visible spectrum is, of course, not to be told what *colour* it is). But a sorites is generated, for example, by the predicate 'rich'—one penny is not sufficient to render someone rich who was not rich without it; but whether someone is rich or not is not an observational question, in the simple sense of 'observation' which is conclusive for the use of a colour predicate. People do not necessarily look rich. The essence of a sorites is rather that the predicate is 'tolerant' (in Wright's terminology) with regard to what we might call the 'elements' which (at some level) comprise the object to which the predicate is applied. The character of the elements can vary: at their most basic, they are simply separable and numerable material objects, like grains; but they might be conventional divisions of a material continuum, like a second—when I spend an hour lecturing, the 'hour' is tolerant with regard to the seconds marked on my watch.

They might be rather more complex. An interesting example is provided by another way of thinking about the application of colour predicates. Though it is natural to suppose that colour predicates are tolerant with regard to wavelengths of light, if we did not know anything about the underlying physics, we could still construct a sorites using colour patches distinguished according to the criteria suggested by Nelson Goodman. Though patch B might be observationally indistinguishable from both patch A and patch C, patch C might be observationally different from A, and could therefore be distinguished *purely by observation* from B. The patches could thus be arranged in an ordering which would as a matter of fact standardly correspond to the ordering generated by our knowledge of the physics of light but would not depend on such knowledge. However, though we could in this way distinguish the patches using observational criteria, as Michael Dummett has emphasised, the 'Goodman property' of a particular patch is not itself what we normally think of as a perceptual or phenomenal property: it remains true that any two adjacent 'Goodman patches' are perceptually indistinguishable, and although we can use further consideration and inspection of the patches in the Goodman manner to distinguish between them, this does not eliminate the sorites. After all, the essence of a sorites is that *in some fashion* the elements can be distinguished, if only by numeration; the problem is not that we cannot distinguish between them, but that the relevant predicate is tolerant at the level of the elements, and that is true of colour predicates at the level of Goodman patches.

For a predicate to be tolerant in this fashion, furthermore, it is not sufficient that there be borderline or undetermined cases for its application. There has instead to be what some writers have termed 'higher-order' vagueness about the boundaries between clear and not-so-clear instances of the relevant property. For example, it is quite possible to have a no-man's-land between states, where the boundaries of the no-man's-land are entirely precise. We may be uncertain about whether territory in the no-man's-land is in State A or State B, and it may even be the case that the closer a piece of land is to one state, the more likely it is to be agreed on as belonging to that state, so that we have something like an ordered continuum running from A to B; but we know precisely where our uncertainty ends and where no one will dispute the nationality of a millimetre of land. The peculiar difficulty of a sorites is that (on the face of it) no such minimal change[29] in the description of the object in terms of the specified elements can motivate a change in the application of the tolerant predicate. If it is the case that 100,000 grains of wheat are definitely a heap, there can *ex hypothesi* be no point at which the subtraction of one grain changes a definite heap into something which is not definitely a heap.[30] Insofar as there might be boundaries to the area in which something is 'definitely' x, those boundaries must themselves be 'fuzzy', that is, there must be vagueness in the application to any object of the description 'beyond the boundary'. This higher-order vagueness is iterable, in the sense that there are (1) boundary cases between x and not-x; (2) boundary cases between x and 'the boundary cases between x and not-x'; (3) boundary cases between x and 'the boundary cases between x and the boundary cases between x and not-x'; and so on. Mark Sainsbury has argued persuasively that the prospect of such iteration means that vague concepts are better described as 'boundaryless' rather than as having borderline cases—there is no border *at all*.[31]

The second general point of clarification to make at this stage is that responses to the sorites always face a double problem. Either we accept vagueness, in the form that common sense suggests to us, and so cannot make a decision about what is to count as, say, 'rich', even in obvious cases; or we deny it, and then appear to be committed to a rigid boundary, which is

29. That is, a move to an object differing by only one element from the first object to which the predicate was applied.

30. See Keefe and Smith, eds., *Vagueness: A Reader*, p. 15.

31. Mark Sainsbury, 'Is There Higher-Order Vagueness?', *Philosophical Quarterly* 41 (1991): 179–180. Though J. A. Burgess has argued that the iteration terminates at a finite point; see 'The Sorites Paradox and Higher-Order Vagueness', *Synthese* 85 (1990): 417–474.

equally preposterous. This becomes particularly clear in cases like the shepherd building his cairn: he must be able to accomplish his task, but equally it cannot reasonably be the case that if he fails to reach a precise figure, he should reckon that he has failed. We would regard someone who clung to a specific number of elements in order to accomplish his task as obviously obsessive, particularly if he did so at some cost to himself—and by definition in a sorites, there must be some unnecessary cost involved in going right up to any proposed boundary. Is it possible to produce any analysis of the sorites which preserves our intuitions? As we shall see, there is at least one, though it has problems of its own; but at least it suggests the kind of shape a plausible analysis will take.

Philosophers currently distinguish between four different ways of responding to the sorites, though some of them can be combined. They have been termed 'nihilism', 'degree theories' (including variants of 'fuzzy logic'), 'supervaluationism' and 'the epistemic view'. I will deal with them in turn.

By 'nihilism' is meant the claim that the sorites shows that predicates which are vulnerable to it are strictly meaningless: there are no heaps, no one is rich (or poor), nothing is red. We initially have to differentiate this claim from the similar claim that there are no heaps and so on, since all there is in the world is a particular specification of fundamental particles, and the only meaningful language is one which describes that specification (this was essentially the Frege-Russell view). The modern nihilist is normally committed to a less far-reaching claim, that ordinary language can in general be meaningful even if it does not refer to the physical specification, but that predicates which are vulnerable to sorites arguments are in a special category of unacceptable terms. One powerful response is then to push the nihilist on the boundaries of this category: on inspection, almost every predicate which we might exclude from it begins to resemble those inside it. Even conventional physical objects, as has often been observed, become vulnerable to the sorites: it cannot be the case that removing *one* atom from Nelson's Column transforms it into a different object, unless one is employing an extreme version of the Frege-Russell theory. The essence of this response is that we cannot accept the meaningfulness of ordinary language and exclude this aspect of it; instead, we have to go all the way back to the radical claim that meaning consists in the accurate designation of the particles which exist, and as a consequence lose the whole of our natural languages—and, it should be remarked, lose the only explanatory categories we have in the actual practice of the human sciences.

A possible reply from the nihilist (discussed by Williamson) is that there are nevertheless some predicates where nihilism is appropriate and others where it is not. If we stipulate a particular bounded set of instances for, say, 'rich', the nihilist might argue, we have not *ipso facto* changed the meaning of the term: there is nothing about the predicate which necessarily requires that we use it in a way which opens up the sorites. So with those predicates, we could have a kind of reformed and sharpened language which still has some (albeit loose) relationship to our original language. But there are other predicates where that is not possible—in particular observational predicates, where (as we have seen) the only criterion for the correct application of the term is how it looks to an observer. If using a term on the basis exclusively of how something looks inevitably gives rise to a sorites, then these predicates (argues the nihilist) have to be eliminated. But the idea that we can sharpen *any* non-observational sorites-inducing predicate and preserve its meaning cannot be taken for granted. It has to be shown to be possible, presumably through one of the methods which we are presently going to consider, and if those methods work, then they do not (on the face of it) distinguish between observational and non-observational predicates. So while a 'global' (Williamson's description) nihilism seems to eliminate far too much of our ordinary conceptual apparatus, a 'local' or partial nihilism does not seem to offer anything which the other approaches do not.

For these reasons, nihilism has not in general been a very popular response to the sorites. Much more popular has been the second response, the idea that we can avoid the worst consequences of the sorites by employing a degree-theoretic approach; if my students are anything to go by, this is nowadays most people's first suggestion. The idea goes broadly as follows. The kinds of terms which give rise to a sorites do not bear ordinary truth values—that is, it is not the case in any instance that something must be either *x* or not-*x*. Instead, they have the equivalent of probabilities: in any particular application, the proposition 'This is an *x*' has a degree of truth, ranging (for example) from 0 for wholly untrue to 1 for wholly true. The analogy with probabilities can go a long way—Dorothy Edgington, for example, has argued that on the degree-theoretic view there can be the equivalent of conditional probabilities in conjunctions of propositions.[32] As usually presented,

---

32. That is, the truth of the conjunction *p & q* is not determined simply by the truth of *p* and *q* separately. With degrees of 'truth', the 'truth' of *q* might be conditional upon the 'truth' of *p*—for example, if *b* is redder than *a*, deciding that *a* counts as red obliges us to describe *b* as red also. See Edgington, 'Vagueness by degrees', in Keefe and Smith, eds., *Vagueness: A Reader*, pp. 294–316, an extension of her 'Validity, uncertainty and vagueness', *Analysis* 52 (1992): 193–204. See also the editors' remarks in *Vagueness: A Reader*, p. 45.

the degree of truth of the proposition in many sorites situations corresponds with the number of elements under consideration—it is 'more true' that a pile of 50 grains is a heap than that a pile of 49 is (though, plainly, not by much). An obvious implication of this is that in most instances we will not be able to say *simpliciter* of any pile that 'it is true that it is a heap', since the addition of one grain makes it 'more true' that the object is a heap, and it is always possible to add another grain. So in effect, a degree-theoretic approach changes a sorites predicate into a comparative—things are not heaps, they are heaper than their alternatives. (Again, the analogy with probability holds.) This was also the approach of the so-called fuzzy set theorists and fuzzy logicians, whose ideas enjoyed a certain vogue in the 1970s and 1980s (at one time one could buy 'fuzzy logic' washing machines): their idea was that things belonged to sets to measurable degrees (standardly between 0 and 1), such that one could say of something (for example) that it belonged to the set of heaps to the degree a, and to the set's complement (not-heaps) to the degree $1 - a$.

There are a number of technical objections to the degree-theoretic approach,[33] but there is also one overwhelming and non-technical problem. The implication of the approach is that it is truer that the richest man in the world is rich than it is that the second-richest man in the world is rich, and that seems preposterous. It is clearly true that the richest man in the world is *richer* than his nearest rival, but both are rich, or else the term 'rich' has lost its conventional meaning. You do not have to be equally rich to be, equally, rich. This is a general truth which applies beyond the domain of sorites-generating predicates: Williamson has given the example of 'acute angle', where an angle of 20° is more acute than one of 30°, but they are both acute. What this illustrates is the general difficulty of accommodating the sorites: its force is precisely that we want to accept *both* that there is some determinate property which we want to ascribe in a straightforward way to something—this is unquestionably a heap—*and* that there is no particular point at which we are authorised to ascribe the property. It is easy to 'solve' the sorites by abandoning one of these aspects, and a purely degree-theoretic approach in general abandons the first in order to formalise the second. There may, however, be room for some element of a degree theory within the next approach.

The third attempt to deal with the sorites has been termed 'super-

33. See, for example, Williamson, *Vagueness*, pp. 127–141.

valuationism'. On this view (associated particularly with Kit Fine), there is an indefinite set of possible 'precisifications' of any vague predicate—some people may draw the line for 'rich' at $200,000 a year, some at $300,000, some at $1 million, some at $3 million, and so on. For any precisification, it is true that there is a point at which there is a determinate border to the predicate's applicability. The free-standing proposition 'A man with x is rich' is then true if it would be true under any precisification, or for what Fine called 'all admissible and complete specifications'; truth in this case is conveniently labelled *supertruth*. If the proposition would not be true under all precisifications, it would be neither supertrue nor superfalse (superfalsity, of course, being when no precisification would admit the proposition's correctness). Consequently, it is possible for it to be supertrue that 'A man with x is rich', but neither supertrue nor superfalse that 'A man with $(x − 1)$ is rich'. This does not imply a sharp boundary to the concept of 'rich', however, as there will *ex hypothesi* be no sum such that on all precisifications its possessor counts as 'rich' and one dollar less makes him 'not rich' (this would be the defining characteristic of a sorites-inducing predicate). The appeal of supervaluationism is that it seems to capture exactly the features we wanted: we can say confidently of at least one object that it is a true instance of the relevant property, while not being committed thereby to the claim that there is a determinate boundary to its application. One might also rather naturally link supervaluationism to a degree theory, avoiding the problems of a pure degree theory as outlined above. Any supertrue proposition will count as true to, say, degree 1, a proposition which is true under all but one precisification will be true to some appropriate degree less than 1, and so on until we reach superfalsity at degree 0.[34]

A number of different doubts have been raised about supervaluationism, but two in particular are quite formidable. One is the meaning of an 'admissible' or 'possible' specification or precisification. One might propose that the possible specifications are those which one would actually find among native speakers of the language, so that one could settle on a supertrue proposition by finding the description of an object upon which everyone, with no exception, would agree (again, this view is often popular among my students). But if by 'would agree' we mean 'would agree even on reflection or higher-order consideration of the meaning of the term', then the statisti-

---

34. Something along these lines is suggested by David Lewis in his 'General semantics', *Synthese* 22 (1970): 18–67.

cal survey collapses back into the question of what ought to count as a precisification and has told us nothing. If we mean by it 'would agree as a matter of fact and without further reflection', then the problem is that by getting the native speaker to (for example) think through a sorites argument, we should be able to get him to change his usage and thereby undermine the utility of the survey (another example of the difficulties of the human sciences—see the discussion above). If we were to prescind completely from ordinary usage and suppose that admissible stipulations include all *possible* precisifications, however strange, we would have to accept that in the case of 'rich', they must in principle include any possible numeration of dollars and that there could therefore be no number which would be described as 'rich' on all specifications. And if we were to insist that 'admissible' means something like 'reasonable', we would have to build into our account of what is reasonable some grounds for ignoring the force of the sorites argument in the first place, since otherwise it would be 'reasonable' on reflection to conclude that no number of dollars makes someone rich. We might take 'reasonable' and 'strange' to be themselves vague notions, but then we confront higher-order or iterative vagueness.

Higher-order vagueness is also an aspect of the second doubt. It centres on the question of whether supervaluationism really eliminates sharp boundaries without itself being vulnerable to sorites arguments. It is supertrue that 'A man with x is rich', but neither supertrue nor superfalse that 'A man with $(x − 1)$ is rich'. x is therefore a sharp boundary for what we might call (following Fine) 'definite' richness; but the essence of the sorites seems to be that there cannot be sharp boundaries to concepts of *this* kind either. If I am definitely rich at x, surely I cannot cease to be definitely rich by the subtraction of one dollar? 'Definite richness' will have to be treated as a vague predicate, to be handled in the same way as 'rich'. But then the same problem arises at the level of what is to count as definitely 'definitely rich', and so on. These iterations in both the concept of admissibility and the concept of definiteness are, of course, parallel to the iteration which is a feature of the basic sorites: if we are not troubled by iteration in the case of supervaluationism, then by the same token we should not have been troubled by it in the case of the original sorites, and therefore would not have needed to develop a supervaluationist account in the first place. If this is correct, then supervaluationism cannot offer an escape from the fundamental difficulties of the sorites argument.

The last of the ways of dealing with the sorites which I listed above is the 'epistemic view', that is, that our failure to perceive a determinate point at which something becomes a heap is a form of *ignorance*, though of an exceedingly unusual kind. It is probable that all four of the responses were known in some fashion in antiquity, but the only ancient reply of which we have any clear sense seems to have been essentially the epistemic argument. It was associated with the greatest of the Stoic philosophers, Chrysippus, who was committed in general to the claim that every proposition is either true or false, and could therefore not accept any of the solutions we have just been considering. He seems to have argued that there must be a cut-off point for the application of any vague term, but no one can know where it is; faced with a soritical argument, one should 'fall silent' (ἡσυχάζειν) some steps *before* one ceases to be confident that one has a true instance of the property, in order to avoid committing oneself to a false proposition. Cicero depicted Carneades attacking the Chrysippan view and imagined Chrysippus's reply (Carneades was still a child when Chrysippus died, so presumably this was an imaginary dialogue):

'As far as I'm concerned,' says Carneades, 'he can snore as well as fall silent. But what good does it do? Someone will come along and wake you from your sleep and question you in the same way: "Take the number you fell silent at—if I add one to that number, will they be many?" Why say more? You confess that you can tell us neither which is last of the few nor which is first of the many. And that sort of error spreads so widely that I do not see where it may not get to.' 'That doesn't hurt me,' he says; 'for, like a clever charioteer, I shall pull up my horses before I get to the end, and all the more so if the place where the horses are coming to is steep. Thus,' he says, 'I pull myself up in time, and I don't go on answering your captious questions.'[35]

Chrysippus's idea thus presupposed that one can 'be silent' when one knows the truth of a proposition, and this infuriated Cicero's imagined Carneades.

If you've got hold of something clear but won't answer, you're acting arrogantly . . . if [you stop at cases that are clear] simply in order to be silent, you gain nothing; for what does it matter to the man who's after you whether he catches you silent or talking? But if up to nine, say, you answer without hesitation that they are few, and then stop at the tenth, you are withholding assent from what is certain and perfectly plain—and you don't let *me* do that in cases that are obscure.[36]

35. Cicero, *Academica* II.xxix.93–94.
36. Ibid.

The modern version of Chrysippus's argument is that presented in Williamson's *Vagueness*.[37] The advantage of the epistemic view is clear, as it preserves classical logic and prevents incoherence; but as in antiquity, the principal problem which the view has to overcome is the flat implausibility of its claim: how can there be a fact about the sharp border of a vague concept of which we are irremediably ignorant? And on the face of it, it plainly violates the second of the two conditions which (I said earlier) a solution to the sorites will ideally satisfy, that there is some leeway in our determination of when a task is completed. Surprisingly, however, as we shall see presently, the epistemic view (at least in Williamson's version) is the one approach which does provide a way of satisfying this condition.

As the first step in his argument, Williamson outlines a general paradox about vague knowledge.[38] It can be summarised as follows. Suppose that we are looking at a large crowd of people: we cannot count them, but we know by inspection that there are (for example) not exactly six people there, nor exactly six thousand—those are the kinds of crowds that we could distinguish from the one in front of us. But that leaves a wide range of possible numbers of people present—all the numbers where we would not know when a crowd of that size was in front of us. This set of the numbers which we cannot say correspond or do not correspond to the number of people in the crowd must have a lowest member; call it n. (To help with the later stage of the argument, I will put what is known or not known between markers.) So

(1) I do not know <the crowd is not n>

And accordingly

(2) I know <the crowd is not $n - 1$>

But knowledge of the numbers of people in a crowd, or any similar phenomenon, has in general a margin of error: it is intrinsically unreliable, such that any assertion I make about the size of the crowd may be mistaken by a magnitude of at least one person either way. So

(3) I know <if the crowd is n, I do not know that the crowd is not $n - 1$>

37. See pp. 12–22 for his extensive discussion of what we know about Chrysippus's view.

38. Which, on his account, encompasses another famous paradox, the surprise examination—not to mention backward induction in a finite set of iterated prisoners' dilemmas.

But this appears to lead to a contradiction:

> (4) I know <(a) if the crowd is n, I do not know that the crowd is not $n - 1$ *and* (b) I know <the crowd is not $n - 1$>, *therefore* (c) the crowd is not n>

Point 4c, 'I know <the crowd is not n>', contradicts 1. Williamson argues that a contradiction of this kind is at the heart of the sorites, as well as the other paradoxes mentioned above, and that the fallacious step in the argument is 4b, the claim that 'I know <. . . I know <the crowd is not $n - 1$> . . .>'. Substitute for it simply the claim 'I know <. . . . <the crowd is not $n - 1$> . . .>' and no contradiction arises. If I know <if the crowd is n, I do not know that the crowd is not $n - 1$, *and* the crowd is not $n - 1$>, there is no paradox: it does not follow from the fact that the crowd is not $n - 1$ that the crowd *is* n, and therefore it does not follow that I do not know that the crowd is not $n - 1$. So the paradoxical consequences are given by the assumption that I know that I know something, which (as Williamson observes) is a principle which is clearly false in a variety of familiar contexts, though it had not previously been recognised as false (or possibly false) in this context.

This is an important and interesting new observation. But it should be asked, is Williamson's 'paradox of inexact knowledge' (as we may call it) the sorites paradox? Clearly, the fact that our knowledge is subject to a margin of error does not in itself give rise to a sorites problem. The example we have just been considering does not involve a vague predicate such as 'heap' (or, arguably, 'crowd'); the question is not, 'Is there a heap in front of us?' but, say, 'Are there 2,000 people in front of us?', and 2,000 is a perfectly precise predicate. So at best Williamson's paradox is a generic one, of which the sorites is a special case. He has brought it to apply specifically to the sorites by arguing that the object of knowledge subject to a margin of error in a sorites is *the meaning of the predicate itself.* The idea here is first that (as many philosophers would currently accept) meaning supervenes on use: that is, there cannot be identical patterns of use for a term but different meanings for it. The question of *how* meaning supervenes on use is left open. Equally, it is quite possible that different patterns of use might underpin the same meaning (this is a familiar feature of supervenient relationships—for example, different computer hardware can run the same program, but the program supervenes on the hardware). Williamson uses this feature to distinguish between vague predicates and other terms:

For any difference in meaning, there is a difference in use. The converse does not always hold. The meaning of a word may be stabilized by natural divisions, so that a small difference in use would make no difference in meaning. A slightly increased propensity to mistake fool's gold for gold would not change the meaning or extension of the word 'gold'. But the meaning of a vague word is not stabilized by natural divisions in this way. A slight shift along one axis of measurement in all our dispositions to use 'thin' would slightly shift the meaning and extension of 'thin'. On the epistemic view, the boundary of 'thin' is sharp but unstable.[39]

So one is constantly liable, with these predicates, to make slight changes in the current use of the term, and with them to change the meaning; there is no way of fixing the usage and assessing its accuracy in the light of a stable meaning. Even the usage of a single individual, his 'idiolect', will (according to Williamson) vary in a rather unstable way, depending on such things as mood and circumstance, so that one cannot even determine by inspection what one means by the term. Consequently, when I seek to determine from the pattern of use what the meaning of a vague predicate is, I am in exactly the same position as someone surveying the crowd: there is a fact of the matter about where the limits of the application of the predicate lie, just as there is a fact of the matter about how many people are in the crowd, but my knowledge of where the limits are is subject to a margin of error. The sorites paradox is then the consequence of this fact about my knowledge, together with the mistaken assumption that I know that I know something where a margin of error is concerned. The correct practical response to a sorites is then (on Williamson's account) broadly that of Chrysippus: to pull one's horses up short of the cliff is precisely to acknowledge the existence of a margin of error in one's capacity to judge where the cliff is, even though one knows that the edge of the cliff is not where one is pulling up.

Williamson's argument is powerful and elegant. But does it dispose of the problem of the sorites? There are two questions which it needs to answer. One is whether the correct conclusion to draw from it is that we should abandon the principle that we know that we know x in these cases. Williamson argues simply that there is a choice between doing so and abandoning classical logic (*modus ponens* in particular), and that since the 'know that we know' principle has already been abandoned in other areas, it clearly causes less conceptual damage to do likewise in these cases. But he has not given us

39. Williamson, *Vagueness*, p. 231.

any independent reasons for supposing that the principle is fallacious;[40] in other areas it has been abandoned because the people concerned have not reflected on their knowledge and therefore can reasonably be said not to know that they know something, but knowledge of my inexact knowledge is not like that, or at least not once reflection has been allowed to start on the subject. There is something odd about the claim that I do not know that I know that the number of people in the crowd is not one I can make out exactly—if I know something like that, *why* do I not know that I know it? If all the usual tests for knowledge have been satisfied, why should we reject it as knowledge on the grounds that to do so requires us to abandon classical logic? Did we ever suppose that knowledge as normally understood requires that classical logic be true? Almost as many problems may be raised by abandoning the principle as by all the other solutions to the sorites. Williamson acknowledges that any way of making sense of the sorites is going to violate common sense—'the truth about vagueness must be strange'[41]—and in the end his argument may come down to a choice between strangenesses.

The second and possibly more important question is whether his account of inexact knowledge applies to the meanings of vague predicates. Why should we suppose that vague predicates have 'sharp but unstable' boundaries? In particular, as various people have observed,[42] it might be possible for us to stipulate vague boundaries for a new term which we have coined and whose meaning wholly follows its stipulation. Jamie Tappenden exploited a well-known example: the U.S. Supreme Court in *Brown v. Board of Education* in 1954 famously ordered that desegregation was to advance 'with all deliberate speed'. Suppose that the Supreme Court had instead used a new word—Tappenden suggested 'brownrate'!—and had announced that integration would be recognised as having proceeded at a brownrate if it had been completed within a year, and not at a brownrate if it took more than five years. The question of whether it had proceeded at a brownrate if it was

40. And the example in which he works out the implications of its abandonment in cases of inexact knowledge ('Inexact Knowledge', *Mind* 101 [1992]: 221–222, and *Vagueness*, pp. 223–224) seems to presuppose that knowledge of our inexact knowledge would itself be inexact—but why should that be?

41. Williamson, *Vagueness*, p. 166.

42. See, for example, Jamie Tappenden, 'Some Remarks on Vagueness and a Dynamic Conception of Language', in Horgan, ed., *Vagueness*, pp. 197–201; R. M. Sainsbury, 'Vagueness, Ignorance, and Margin for Error', *British Journal for the Philosophy of Science* 46 (1995): 599–600; Rosanna Keefe and Peter Smith, 'Introduction', in *Vagueness: A Reader*, p. 21.

accomplished in between one and five years would have been deliberately left open, with no precise dividing line stipulated. On Williamson's view, this ought on the face of it to be impossible.

However, it should be said that one of the great merits of the idea that vague predicates have sharp but unstable boundaries is that—unlike all other treatments of the sorites—it does in fact come close to capturing the phenomenology of judgement in the presence of vagueness. The idea that from moment to moment our own definitions of the sharp boundary waver in an unstable fashion is what it *feels* like to make judgements in the face of vagueness: we make a decision to stop piling the stones *now*, but we do not believe that we are thereby committed to stopping in precisely the same place next time. We have done 'enough', but we are also aware that in principle we must have overshot the boundary (this being the equivalent in this instance of Chrysippus pulling up his horses short of the precipice). In this respect Williamson's approach does what no other approach has done, in that it both preserves classical logic *and* gives us grounds for respecting our intuition that sticking to a particular number in a repetitive or cumulative sequence may be obsessional or misguided. I think this feature of decision-making in these circumstances is one of the things that struck the Aristotelians who assimilated Aristotle's concept of *phronesis,* or practical wisdom, to the kind of judgement we make in front of a sorites. Aristotle famously said that the objects of phronetic judgement are 'things whose first principles are variable (for all such things might actually be otherwise)' (NE 1140ᵃ30), and at NE 1109ᵃ30 he gave an account of how we hit a mean in our choices which sounds very like Chrysippus later:

> [H]e who aims at the intermediate must first depart from what is more contrary to it, as Calypso advises—
>
> Hold the ship out beyond that surf and spray [*Od.* xii.219]
>
> For of the extremes one is more erroneous, one less so; therefore, since to hit the mean is hard in the extreme, we must as a second best, as people say, take the least of the evils.

That is, err on the safe side. The man of practical wisdom is not committed to repeating exactly the same judgement in what are apparently the same circumstances: whether they *are* the same circumstances is itself a matter of judgement. So no algorithm can be given which will straightforwardly pick out what he would choose. (This may be the most profound of all Aristotle's departures from Platonic teaching.) Though we might not like Williamson's analysis, something along the lines implied in the remarks of both Chrysippus and Aristotle seems to be the right way to think about the sorites.

What of the kinds of objection brought against this view by Tappenden and others? A reasonable response would be that the Supreme Court intended school boards to make these kinds of judgements rather than prescribing to them what judgement to make. It was giving them parameters (their own judgement would be relevant only in the space between one and five years), but it was not necessarily supposing that from the point of view of the school boards there was any vagueness in their decision that could not be handled by Williamson's or some other comparable account of the matter. What about from the point of view of the Court? Was it stipulating vagueness as part of the definition of 'brownrate'? This does not seem to follow. Suppose it had agreed as part of some decision that people could legally invest a minimum of $1,000 in some bond issue but could invest more, up to a limit of $5,000; would the Court be stipulating a vague concept of 'amount invested in bond scheme X'? As far as the Court would be concerned, the amount to be invested would be left up to the judgement of the individual investor, provided it fell between $1,000 and $5,000, and therefore it would in some sense be vague about the amount, but of course the individual investor's judgement about what would count as an appropriate amount would not be vague.

As I said, the merit of Williamson's approach is that it preserves the phenomenology of vague judgement better than its rivals; but it is not necessary for my purposes for us to accept his analysis. What is necessary, however, is for us to accept the phenomenology, that is, to agree that we should not be forced to revise our vague judgements in such a way that we lose their essential feature—namely, that at some point we will decide we have 'enough', but in an identical situation we could make a different decision. The decision is, so to speak, 'criterionless', but it is nevertheless a decision. To see the importance of this, let us return to my original problem about the shepherd piling up a cairn and assess possible answers to it in the light of what we been considering about the sorites. The first point to make is that, as I have just indicated, if we take the epistemic view, there is no problem: there is a real cutoff point for the cairn at some point, and so each stone genuinely makes a difference to the outcome, by virtue of contributing to the accumulation which eventually turns into a heap. The fact that the shepherd does not know *when* it turns does not affect the issue; a loose analogy would be with, say, lobbing stones into a pond with a target at the bottom of it. Throw in enough stones and we will eventually hit the target, though we might not know we have succeeded until we are able to drain the pool and inspect the bottom. But it would be crazy to keep throwing until the pond was full of stones, in order to make *absolutely* certain; at some point we decide that we have thrown enough, though the judgement of 'enough' is itself one of the most important soritical judgements. Similarly, there is a margin of error in the shepherd's assessment of the number of stones needed, but that does not undermine the causal efficacy of any particular stone. Contrast this with the situation if there is genuine vagueness: then the creation of the heap could have taken place without any particular stone's being put in position, so no single stone put in place during the construction of the cairn can be said to have had causal efficacy with regard to the outcome. With vagueness, there can be neither counter-factual nor pre-emptive causation in the case of a single stone: not counter-factual, because the stone was not necessary for the heap to be created, and not pre-emptive, because the stone did not as a matter of fact bring about any change in the character of the pile.

However, suppose the epistemic view is not correct: do the other views allow us to make sense of our intuitions about what the shepherd should do? Supervaluationism is undermined by the following considerations: we can assume either that the shepherd has his own precisification, or that he adopts a supertrue definition of 'cairn' as his objective, a 'definite cairn', in order perhaps to avoid uncertainty about the status of his own precisification. In each case he faces the basic dilemma which a resolution of the practical sorites ought to be able to solve: either he is committed to the precisification or he is not. If he is not, then the precisification is vulnerable to soritic reflection and is liable to be completely undermined, so that the shepherd is incapable rationally of putting any stone in place. But if he is committed to his precisification, the result is almost as absurd: any precise determination *known to the shepherd* creates the problem that he should feel obliged to reach that precise number of stones or fail in his project—and that cannot be a realistic model of behaviour in situations of vagueness, since once again it seems to mean that the only alternative to what we might call soritic drift is an obsessive anxiety about hitting a precise target. As I said, the great advantage of the epistemic view is that it avoids this dilemma, while supervaluationism does not.

This is not true of a degree theory: it should permit a certain flexibility in our choice of target, since its whole point is to avoid a sharp boundary, and that is, of course, one of the sources of its appeal. But it runs into major difficulties of its own. If we pursue the parallel with probabilities which is usually an integral part of a degree theory, the obvious conclusion to draw, as far as action in the face of vagueness is concerned, is that there should be the equivalent of maximising expected utility. But then we face problems caused by the central awkwardness of degree theories, that the scale has to be stretched to accommodate all possible instances of the predicate. To take a simple example, suppose that we impose an upper limit of 100 stones that could possibly count as a heap, but we know that something around 50 will do. Let us also suppose that the labour of lugging stones is such that the shepherd will get no overall benefit if he has to move more than 50 (and would obviously prefer fewer—hence the relevance of the paradox). If we set the degree of truth of the proposition 'This is a cairn' at 1 for 100 stones and 0 for 0 stones and do something like calculating expected utility on the basis of these degrees, we get the absurd result that no number of stones is worth the shepherd's effort, and that the disutility to him gets progressively greater the more stones he adds.[43] So the general arguments against degree theories, like those against supervaluationism, apply just as strongly to their use in the context of practical judgement.

One might suppose that the third alternative to the epistemic view, nihilism, has little to offer, but in fact there is a kind of nihilist theory of how to handle a practical sorites which has some intuitive appeal. According to this theory, there is no possible answer to the sorites: the reasoning is valid and the conclusion follows. But to *act* on the reasoning would be fatal, and so in the interests of an effective life we have to prevent ourselves in some way from thinking in a soritic fashion. We can construct a particularly clear example of this by slightly changing the shepherd example. As I set it up earlier, the shepherd was engaged in an iterative task of constructing many cairns, and reasoned each time that he should put one less stone in place. This example can be dealt with on the view we are about to consider, but the

---

43. We calculate the expected benefit to the shepherd as the relevant degree for that number of stones multiplied by the utility of having the cairn, which we might reckon to be 50 utiles, and deduct from this product the disutility of the appropriate number of stones, counting the disutility of lifting each stone as -1 utile. So, for example, for 100 stones, the calculation is $(1 \times 50) - (100) = (-50)$. It will quickly be seen that the disutility runs from (-50) for 100 stones down to (-0.5) for one stone. This is obviously a very stylised example, but it makes the general point.

psychological issues are brought out more clearly if we imagine that the shepherd is using soritic reasoning to plan a single task.[44] Suppose that he takes a stone up the mountain every day in pursuance of a long-term project of cairn-building, and he is considering whether to take one up today. He can reason that if the cairn will be good with n stones, that is, n days' work, it will be just a good with $n - 1$ stones. Immediate gratification is preferable, all other things being equal, to the same amount of gratification in the future—that is, he has some normal discount rate for future utility; the argument works even if it is very low. So he has a good reason for resting today and starting work tomorrow. But tomorrow he reasons in the same way . . . and so on. His desire to put the labour off until the following day is very understandable, and his reasoning will be familiar to all of us who procrastinate; on the view we are about to consider, there is nothing wrong with the reasoning *as such*, but it is wrong to let oneself be swayed by it.

Jon Elster, for example, has endorsed in this context what he calls 'the following, well-known chain of reasoning':

'(1) If I take a drink just this one time, I can abstain on the next occasion and no harm will be done. (2) But do I really have any reason to think that I shall behave differently on future occasions, which will be essentially similar to the present one? (3) On reflection, therefore, I had better abstain now since otherwise I shall almost certainly yield to temptation the next time.' Is this irrational? Observe first that we are not here talking about a genuine causal impact of the present choice on later choices, as in cases of habituation or addiction . . . Yet the first choice will typically be known to the person at the moment the later choices are made, unless he engages in a piece of genuine or self-deceptive forgetting. When he is about to make the later choice, the situation will differ from the earlier one in that he now has information about an earlier choice (or about more earlier choices). This information constrains his self-image in a way that may ease or obstruct the prudential decision. If this is self-deception it is of a benign kind, since it turns out to be self-fulfilling.[45]

---

44. If we wanted to use the original example, we could suppose that the shepherd needed some form of psychological self-control to force himself at some point to stop reducing the number of stones in each cairn. The merit of the revised version is that it is a much more familiar setting for us to find ourselves in; indeed, for some of us it is a basic feature of our lives.

45. Jon Elster, 'Introduction', in *The Multiple Self*, ed. Jon Elster (Cambridge: Cambridge University Press, 1986), pp. 8–9.

Elster's belief that we are not thinking about 'a genuine causal impact' on later choices is slightly hard to follow. If the first choice 'constrains his self-image' in a way that alters a subsequent decision, then on the face of it it has a 'causal impact' on the later choice. He seems to mean by 'genuine causal impact' an effect unmediated by subsequent reflection about the implications of the first choice, as in addiction, where (we might suppose) the first consumption of the substance alters in some significant fashion our physical response to the substance on its second consumption. But there is no reason that our actions cannot have causal effects in other ways, and Elster's argument surely presupposes that they do. The particular story that he tells about the connection between my early and my late actions is also difficult to understand. It seems to be that if I take the drink now, on the next occasion I will think of myself as the sort of person who takes a drink when tempted, and I will therefore act in accordance with my self-image and yield to temptation again. But that is to presuppose an oddly limited set of self-images. Why can I not think of myself (as, actually, I do) as the sort of person who occasionally yields to temptation but is not crippled by it? And even if there were to be a very restricted set of self-images, why should we suppose that the construction of one is so sensitive to a single instance? The natural view to take, assuming that the individual act 'makes no difference', is that it makes no difference to *anything*, including the formation of my image of myself.

A more plausible suggestion was made by Philip Pettit in a response to my 1979 statement of the shepherd's problem. He argued that 'the reason it is not sensible of me to put off adding today's stone may be that such an omission is likely to set up a disposition in me to postpone every addition and that would be fatal for the cairn'.[46] According to Pettit, though what is created is not a physical habit or addiction, like smoking (like Elster, he wants to exclude that), it is not a 'self-image' either. Rather, it is a *disposition*, an inclination to behave unreflectively in a certain way, and like many such dispositions it might be harmful unless checked. Pettit recognises that on his view the individual stone does have a causal role to play, though not a direct role in the formation of the cairn: not putting it in place (he thinks) causes the shepherd to have more of a disposition to procrastinate, and that in turn prevents the cairn from coming into existence. It is this fact, that the first choice by the shepherd has a causal effect on his subsequent choices, that

46. Pettit, 'The Prisoner's Dilemma and Social Theory: An Overview of Some Issues', *Politics* (*The Journal of the Australasian Political Studies Association*) 20 (1985): 8.

Pettit uses to distinguish this case from collective free riding, where one individual's action has no causal effect on the other individuals' actions. (We agree on that; we disagree about whether it has any effect on the production of the goal in question, *given* the other people's actions.) Pettit, as one might expect, assumes that soritic reasoning is correct—'grains of sand make a heap but no grain marks the divide between a heap and a non-heap'.[47]

Procrastination is an interesting example of conduct based on a kind of soritic reasoning: although at first glance it simply involves putting something off, where what is being put off may not be vaguely specified (for instance, there may be a real deadline for the task to be completed), in fact there is usually a vague element. The amount of time at my disposal to complete a non-vague task is often vague, and characteristically when I procrastinate, I say to myself that another hour (or day, or week) will make no difference to my effectiveness at completing the task on time.

However, though much more intuitively satisfying than Elster's idea, Pettit's suggestion is still not convincing. First, the link between the shepherd's individual action and the formation of his disposition is itself a loose or vague one: one action or omission could not be enough to determine whether or not one had a disposition or inclination towards a certain kind of action, any more than it could create a particular self-image. The gradual creation of a character through many separate choices is an excellent example of a sorites (and may indeed have been recognised as such by the ancient Aristotelians). Pettit assumes that the shepherd will be able to see the point of an individual act when it contributes to the formation of his disposition, but not when it contributes to the formation of his cairn. Second, and related to this, Pettit's answer, like Elster's, is vulnerable to the objection that in order to prevent each action from having no significance, it makes a single act *too* critical and important. If their approach were correct, any single omission would have serious consequences; but as I have frequently said, any adequate theory has to take into account the fact that our project has not failed if we omit one (or even a number) of actions, or procrastinate a bit, and to believe that it has failed is to be weirdly obsessive. What, after all, should we say to the shepherd who believes Pettit's argument but has failed to move the first stone? We could hardly tell him to abandon the whole project; and since he

47. Ibid., p. 5. It should be said that he has somewhat changed his position on the general question. See, for example, his 'Free Riding and Foul Dealing', *Journal of Philosophy* 83 (1986): 369–370.

knows in advance that this is so, he must recognise that the first stone is not critical to accomplishing his goal even via the means of a disposition.

It is, of course, not at all unreasonable that we should need help to keep us engaged in a repetitive and burdensome task, or to prevent us from procrastinating. But it is more reasonable to suppose that we need help because we are prone not to think clearly about these kinds of projects, and (notoriously) to be poor at comparing present gratifications to future ones. As Hume said, '[T]here is no quality in human nature, which causes more fatal errors in our conduct, than that which leads us to prefer whatever is present to the distant and remote, and makes us desire objects more according to their situation than their intrinsic value';[48] strikingly, it was precisely this quality which he adduced as an explanation of our incapacity to collaborate in large groups (see Chapter Four for a fuller discussion of this passage). Similarly, the author who has written most interestingly in our time about this trait and how to overcome it—Thomas Schelling—does not suppose that it is *irrational* not to procrastinate: just very hard.[49]

It would appear from this that of all the proposed solutions to the problem of the sorites, the epistemic view is most satisfactory both as an account of vague predicates generally and as an account of what I have termed the 'practical sorites'. But it is most satisfactory, as I have emphasised, because it is best at preserving the phenomenology of vague judgement; even if it is not true as it stands, it suggests that it might be possible to preserve the phenomenology, and therefore for us to believe that—as far as rational conduct is concerned—situations involving negligible contributions or increments are in fact threshold situations. At some point there will be 'enough' contributions, even though we cannot say in principle where a correct judgement will be made in any particular instance. While we have essentially inexact knowledge (in some fashion) of where the threshold is to be found in sorites cases, and we have exact knowledge in cases such as voting, the basic char-

---

48. David Hume, *Treatise* III.II.8.8.

49. See Schelling, 'The Intimate Contest for Self-Command', in Schelling, *Choice and Consequence* (Cambridge, Mass.: Harvard University Press, 1984), pp. 57–82, and 'Ethics, Law and the Exercise of Self-Command', ibid., pp. 83–102. In the case of repetitive jobs, Schelling pointed to the role which setting oneself a goal specified in round numbers can play in getting one to continue working. This was in effect an application to self-management of Schelling's famous notion of 'salience' in interpersonal affairs—another example of the parallelism between the management of one's own life and the management of a communal life.

acter of our reasoning in the two kinds of case will be the same. My contribution, even if it is negligible, has causal efficacy in bringing it about that the threshold is crossed, as long as enough other contributions have been made or will be made (the same condition that I discussed at the end of Chapter Two). Whatever reason I have for contributing in the examples considered in the previous chapter, I have the same reason for doing so in the examples considered in this chapter.

One interesting example of this, with implications for a wide range of human actions, is indeed the predicate 'enough'. In his *On Medical Experience*, Galen included 'satiety'[50] among the terms which were vulnerable to soritic reasoning, for obvious reasons—for something to be 'red enough' or 'good enough' is precisely to be at the kind of threshold which (on the epistemic view) is to be presumed in examples of the sorites. This is particularly interesting in that in the 1950s and 1960s there was a major attempt to produce a formal account of decision-making which centered on the idea of something's being 'enough', in the form of the economist Herbert Simon's well-known theory of 'satisficing'. Simon's idea has sometimes been treated as if it were solely a theory about the cost of information, but Simon himself certainly intended it to be much wider than that, and to be applicable to cases not unlike the shepherd's problem.

Simon's starting point was a dissatisfaction with the conventional economists' model of rational choice, in his case because of the stringent character of the demands which it made upon the agent. In particular, the maximising model (he argued) implies that a rational agent

> must be able to attach definite pay-offs (or at least a definite range of pay-offs) to each possible outcome. This, of course, involves also the ability to specify the exact nature of the outcome—there is no room in the scheme for 'unanticipated consequences'. The pay-offs must be completely ordered—it must always be possible to specify, in a consistent way, that one outcome is better than, as good as, or worse than any others. And, if the certainty or probabilistic rules are employed, either the outcomes of particular alternatives must be known with certainty, or at least it must be possible to attach definite probabilities to outcomes.[51]

50. Presumably the original Greek term lurking behind the Arabic and Syriac was ὁ κόρος.

51. H. A. Simon, *Models of Man* (New York: Wiley, 1957), pp. 245–246.

Given that these conditions seem to be so stringent as to rule out of the arena of rational action most actual human behaviour, Simon proposed to substitute for the idea of maximising the idea of 'satisficing'—that is, that agents do not seek to achieve the actual optimum but instead seek to achieve a result which is satisfactory for them, despite possibly falling short of the optimum. Essentially, this process as Simon depicted it involves setting a minimum (in economic terms, an 'aspiration level'), and then selecting any outcome which presents itself above the relevant minimum.

The example Simon used repeatedly was that of the chess game. A rational chess player does not seek to optimise, in the sense of finding the best move available to him at a particular stage in the game—the calculation involved in such a procedure would not merely be absurdly costly in terms of time, it would actually be impossible. Instead, he might rely on his very rough knowledge of the way in which the game could develop, select a move which on the basis of such knowledge looks promising, and simply work through what his opponent's possible responses to it would be. If it proves unsatisfactory—that is, if it clearly enables his opponent to beat him—then the proposed move will be abandoned; otherwise, it is reasonable to adopt it rather than to search for a better alternative. The 'aspiration level' of the chess player is set at generating moves which will keep him in the game with a good chance of winning, rather than at generating the optimal move at each stage in the game. (It should be said that the coming of chess-playing computer programs has so far vindicated Simon's analysis of the rationality of chess strategies.)

Simon took satisficing to be necessary as an account of rational conduct in any situations where we cannot have the kind of information which is regarded as essential to rational decision-making of the conventional kind. As the passage quoted above implies, there are several different reasons that we might not have the information; one (but only one) is the high cost of obtaining it—a cost which might outweigh any benefits which the information could give us—and it was on this reason that both Simon and many of his early critics initially concentrated. But Simon also believed that the inability to order alternatives coherently could be grounds for switching to a satisficing policy, and such an inability might not be the result of costly information; it might, he suggested, also be the result of (for example) the incomparability of payoffs. Simon was in fact always at pains to deny that satisficing should be interpreted as a kind of covert maximising, with the costs of information added into the calculations.[52]

However, there are obvious difficulties in Simon's theory, which come out clearly when we apply it to the shepherd's problem. There is a good reason that information costs have bulked so large in discussions of his work: whether it is the high cost of obtaining information or the impossibility of doing so at all which leads us to be ignorant of the better options than the one we take, Simon's arguments presuppose that we act on the basis of *ignorance*. There is no place in his theory, at least as he presented it, for someone who knows there is a better option but chooses not to take it. Simon's arguments are in fact concerned with the justification for our continuing in ignorance of certain possible outcomes, and to this extent the concentration on information costs has been true to the spirit, if not to the letter, of his thesis. Despite his disclaimers, Simon actually always remained quite close to the traditional maximising view. But we can see the difficulty of this view when we ask what Simon's answer to the shepherd's problem would be: the theory of satisficing would lead us to say that rational conduct for the shepherd would consist in selecting a particular number of stones as appropriate for a cairn, constituting that as his 'aspiration level', and then seeking to achieve that outcome, eschewing any attempt to improve on it by a process of incremental optimisation. But it would be quite wrong to say that the shepherd's problem arises because he is ignorant of a better option, or because his options cannot be ordered: the puzzle is precisely that on the face of it he knows that one stone less will always be better for him. We merely have to ask, once again, whether it could possibly be rational for such a shepherd, assuming his aspiration level is 50 stones, doggedly to insist on dragging up the fiftieth stone when it is absolutely obvious that it makes no difference. There is, as I have said, an obsessional character to such behaviour which we would rightly condemn; and in fact Simon's proposal (applied in this context) leads to something very like Elster's, and is vulnerable to the same objections. But equally, Simon's intuition might be salvageable with an inexact notion of 'enough'; the way we cope with sorites situations *feels* more like satisficing than optimising, in that we characteristically decide that we have done *enough* to reach our target, though we are well aware (as I have stressed) that on another occasion we might make a different judgement.

52. H. A. Simon, 'Theories of bounded rationality', in *Decision and Organization: A Volume in Honor of Jacob Marschak*, eds. C. B. McGuire and Roy Radner (Amsterdam: North-Holland, 1972), pp. 170–171; see also Jon Elster, *Ulysses and the Sirens* (Cambridge: Cambridge University Press, 1979), pp. 57–59.

Conclusion to Part I

In this part of the book, I have put forward two arguments against the sceptical account of social co-operation exemplified by, but by no means restricted to, Mancur Olson's *The Logic of Collective Action*. Olson and his successors have claimed that where my contribution to a co-operative activity is relatively insignificant—that is, it apparently makes no difference to the outcome whether I contribute or not—then I have no instrumental reason to play a part in the activity, though I may of course have any number of non-instrumental reasons to do so, such as a desire to express myself, to be fair to my fellow-participants, and so on. Though Olson argued that this difficulty could be alleviated by institutional solutions such as mechanisms of coercion, he failed to realise that if his general argument is correct, those solutions are not in fact available, for they require the agents concerned to believe that there is some point to eliminating actions which cause negligible harm to others, and if they believe this, then (on Olson's account) they are being irrational. For this reason, I distinguish more sharply than many writers between what I term 'true' prisoners' dilemmas and the Olsonian free-rider problem, as a true prisoners' dilemma is defined as one where the agents' actions have determinate effects on one another and strategic considerations of all kinds can therefore come into play, including institutional fixes of various sorts.

Against Olson, I argued first that if I am faced with a situation where an accumulation of relatively small contributions eventually leads to the crossing of some threshold which I would welcome, then in general I have a good instrumental reason to make one of the contributions, assuming that enough other ones will be made (either by me, as in the shepherd case discussedin Chapter Three, or by other people, or by nature). This is straightforwardly and uncontroversially the case where I know that the threshold is at a determinate number of contributions and I know that one less than that

99

number, and no more, has been or will be provided by the other agents (or, again, by myself at other times). In this situation, my contribution is necessary to achieve the outcome, and on any account of instrumental rationality I have a reason to add my bit, however small it may be. But—and this is, of course, much more controversial—I have argued that the same is true, though with a somewhat modified account of instrumentality, as we move away from this simple case. First, we might be in a position where only one more contribution is needed and there are at least two people able to make it. Here I might think of myself as playing a game of chicken with the other prospective contributors, and therefore fear that unless I contribute, no one else will (that being the essential element of a chicken game—that my opponents may have stronger nerves than I have and will go all the way even to destruction). If that is the case, then I am once again in a situation where I believe my contribution is necessary, and again I have a straightforward reason to contribute. But if I do not think of myself as playing chicken—that is, if I am reasonably confident that if I do not contribute, someone else will—I might still have a good instrumental reason to take part, and this is the first of my controversial claims.

It turns on a general argument about how to think about causation in these cases: that we should recognise that I will have brought about the outcome even if my action was not *necessary,* in the sense that without it the outcome would not have happened. It is enough for me to be able to claim causal responsibility for the outcome that my action was *sufficient,* given the other circumstances, for the outcome to occur. Only a view of this kind, I argued, makes sense of our familiar intuitions about causal agency: no one has successfully asserted that in cases of causal redundancy, or over-determination, the agent whose action was actually responsible for the outcome did not cause it, though whether this intuition can ultimately be fitted into the dominant view of causality as counter-factual necessity is still a matter of debate (I would say no, but the conclusion of this debate does not affect the general case I am putting forward). So the issue, I argued, is not whether or not I will be causally responsible for the outcome even if my action was not necessary; it is why I might *wish* to be causally responsible. This is a question which most accounts of rational choice have neglected, since they have vaguely supposed that the only causal relations are those of necessity, and that therefore the questions of why I might wish to be causally responsible for the event or outcome in question and why I might wish it to occur are the same question.

I suggested two possible answers to the question of why I might wish to be causally responsible for an outcome under these circumstances. One retains the idea that from the point of view of choosing rationally, I should choose only actions which are necessary to bring about an event, but includes as part of the event my feeling of having been responsible for the outcome. A desire to be responsible, on this account, is a separable and independent desire from the wish for there to be the thing for which one is responsible. That is the view taken by a number of economists. It is, however, a counter-intuitive view, despite the fact that it is intended in some fashion to preserve our intuitions about choice, since we do not usually make this kind of distinction either in our reflection about what we should do or in our evaluation of someone else's action. My second, albeit tentative, answer was intended to correspond more closely to what we actually think; it proposed (broadly following Mill) that there may indeed be only one general concept of causality, but it is one of sufficiency rather than necessity. On this account, our thinking about how to choose an action is what the conventional rational-choice theorists hold it to be, in the sense that we simply consider what we wish to bring about, compared with the other things we could bring about by acting in a different way (so we rank the alternatives); but 'bringing about' here can mean merely that our action is sufficient. To put it another way, the domain within which we choose is the set of actions which are sufficient to bring about desired outcomes; it may then be relevant to our deliberation within that domain that in some cases we are in a unique position with regard to the outcome, and that our action would be both sufficient and necessary, but that would be only one among many considerations which go into the deliberative process, and would be itself neither necessary nor sufficient as a basis for our final decision.

The second of the two general arguments which I put forward in this part of the book, and the other controversial claim, was that even in cases where an individual contribution appears to make no appreciable difference to the outcome, we have to deliberate *as if* there is a determinate threshold, so that all that I already said about the rationality of contributing would then be applicable to these cases also. I took the issue here to be essentially the same as the issue in the famous puzzle of the sorites, since our contribution is only 'negligible' or 'inappreciable' if it is the case that one contribution of this kind makes no difference to whether or not we achieve our goal; and for that to be true, it has to be the case that the goal is tolerant or vague with regard to an individual increment, since otherwise the contribution could be viewed as causally contributing to the outcome, as in the cases discussed above. So any solution to the sorites must be applicable to this question also, and the existence of the sorites should alert us to the fact that a claim of negligibility should always be made circumspectly, since it may have far-reaching and paradoxical implications. It is also the case that, as Williamson wisely observed, 'the truth about vagueness must be strange',[1] and that our unexamined intuitions are not going to get us very far in thinking about these issues.

There may be no wholly convincing solution to the sorites, but any pro-posed solution should preserve the sense we have both that it is possible to decide the point at which, say, an accumulation of stones becomes a heap, after which all additional accumulations are equally heaps, *and* that no such point is critical—no solution to what I have termed a 'practical sorites' would be acceptable if it implied that one was compelled to put in place a specific number of contributions, on pain of failing to achieve the desired result. Many solutions, such as straightforward stipulation or precisification, or a higher-order version of precisification such as supervaluationism, fail to meet this latter condition; others, including a degree-theoretic approach, fail to meet the former condition—for example, as we saw, the degree-theoretic view implies that a gigantic heap is more truly a heap than a smaller but equally indubitable one. The one approach which comes closest to meeting both conditions is Williamson's, according to which there is a determinate point, but its location is inherently unstable and unknowable. This view has its own problems, and my argument does not depend on Williamson's being correct in all (or any) respects, but it does depend on its being the case that at some point we reckon that we have reached our goal, though where that point lies cannot be determined either in prospect or in retrospect—that is, we cannot predict the appropriate number in advance of reaching it, and we cannot use as inductive evidence for the special appropriateness of the num-ber the fact that in the past we stopped there, for it is always open to us to stop somewhere else. But the fact that we can make this decision means that the general theory of contribution outlined in the course of making my first argument is equally applicable to sorites-like cases: each stone (to continue with that example) which I put in place before I make the decision has caus-ally contributed to the achievement of my goal.

The practical implication of this is that the correct way to think about con-

1. Timothy Williamson, *Vagueness* (London: Routledge, 1994), p. 166.

tributions in these vague situations is that if I believe that all of us who have an interest in the outcome have in some way co-ordinated our actions so that in my judgement 'enough' of us are contributing (say through a mixed strategy), and I am one of the group on whom the burden of contribution falls, I have a good reason to play my part. This is the equivalent in a sorites of co-ordination in a clear-cut threshold case, where the group has organised itself to deliver precisely the threshold amount; where the threshold is vague, the determination also has to be vague in the sense discussed in Chapter Three, that is, unstable, but in any particular instance it is possible to make the judgement that a certain amount is enough, and it then follows that I have a reason to contribute.

It might, of course, be the case that different people's judgement will differ over the appropriate amount, and then I have a good reason to contribute (in this respect) only insofar as the group converges on the figure I would have chosen myself. And it is certainly true that in such a situation, I might well be tempted to think that a figure less than the one proposed would still be 'enough' if my own contribution were to be omitted. But if the argument in Chapter Three is correct, this is a mistake—though a familiar kind of mistake. If we can make judgements at all about how to characterise a vague goal—and as I have stressed, the possibility of doing this is in fact inherent in the sorites paradox—then those judgements should determine whether or not we contribute, in just the same way as the recognition of an uncontroversial threshold determines our action. The natural test in practice would be to ask ourselves whether a certain amount would be appropriate, or 'enough', to achieve the goal if we were not ourselves contributing, and then to treat that amount as the threshold towards which we should direct our own actions. This is not to require ourselves to be altruistic, but simply to require ourselves to be rational in the way in which we think about vague goals.

An important implication of this is that collaborative conventions intended to provide vague benefits will be somewhat unstable but will not collapse: at some point, as people defect on the grounds that (in their neutral judgement) enough has already been provided and their contribution is not needed, the group will reach a point where an additional defection seems to at least one member to take the amount below the appropriate level, and that member will therefore contribute. All that I said in Chapter Two about chicken games also applies. As with straightforward thresholds, there may well be an incentive for the contributors to play chicken with one another, but there will also be the general and familiar reason to avoid such games; or, if they cannot be avoided, for enough players to chicken out and contribute. The unstable judgement of an individual faced with a sorites corresponds, we might say, to a kind of unstable communal judgement: the group's contributions will waver in an unpredictable fashion, but there is no more reason to suppose that they will completely fail to put together any contributions than there is reason to suppose that an individual will be completely inert in the face of a vague goal.

This unstable convention is the equivalent of a strict Schelling/Lewis convention, in which the group co-ordinates its activities in such a way that it hits the threshold and therefore provides its members with a straightforward reason to contribute. But as with non-soritic judgements, many cases will not be like this. Often they will be more like ordinary elections, where there has been no prior convention even of this unstable kind, and where the issue of redundant causation is therefore relevant; here too, however (if my argument has been correct), we might still have a reason to contribute. Even though I might know that other people will put a stone on the heap if I do not, there may be an instrumental reason for me to make my contribution, if I wish to think of myself as being responsible for the outcome, and if I believe that enough other people are going to do so. Exactly the same considerations about agency in the face of causal redundancy apply in sorites situations as in situations with precisely defined thresholds.

So does Tuck's arg have force if you don't care about being responsible? (e.g. profit maximizer)

It is important at this stage for me to be clear about what my arguments against Olson and the others do *not* imply, as people are often confused about what would follow were it the case that we have good instrumental reasons to contribute in these kinds of situations. The first point to stress is (as I said in Chapter Three) that on my account, I have a good reason to contribute *only if enough other people are going to do so*, or at least if I believe that that is the case. I take this in fact to be the key difference between an instrumental theory of collaboration and a Kantian one: on Kant's account (or on one plausible and familiar reading of Kant), we should deliberate in a particular instance on the assumption that all other rational beings would choose what we choose, and then compare that hypothetical outcome with our wants. Thus it is right for me (for example) to perform a just act even if no one else will, and wrong to break a promise even if all other men are in actuality promise-keepers and my act can have no real effect on the practice of promise-keeping. A desire to extract a principle of this kind from some non-Kantian, vaguely instrumental premises was also what motivated some of the founders of rule utilitarianism, as we shall see in more detail in Chapter Four: the idea that we should ask of a prospective action, 'What if everyone did that?', and then make the decision in accordance with our answer to that question, implies that even if no other people are actually going to contribute, we should nevertheless do so. But on my account the essence of an instrumental theory has to be that one believes that one is actually going to have some causal effect on the outcome, and if no one else is going to contribute to the enterprise, it is clear that one's action can have no effect. The mistake has been to suppose that if one's action has no effect in isolation, it still has no effect when in conjunction with other actions; this was the mistake made by Olson in the passage I have quoted a couple of times already.

> Selfless behavior that has no perceptible effect is sometimes not even considered praiseworthy. A man who tried to hold back a flood with a pail would probably be considered more of a crank than a saint, even by those he was trying to help. It is no doubt possible infinitesimally to lower the level of a river in flood with a pail, just as it is possible for a single farmer infinitesimally to raise prices by limiting his production, but in both cases the effect is imperceptible, and those who sacrifice themselves in the interest of imperceptible improvements may not even receive the praise normally due selfless behavior.[2]

This is true, but it does not follow (as Olson supposed that it did) that there is no point in using a pail to lower the flood if enough other people are doing likewise.

A related point is that my account provides a reason for continuing to participate in a working convention, once it is up and running, and therefore provides a reason for creating such a convention in the first place. On an Olsonian view, since there is no reason to abide by a convention, there is equally no reason to enter into one; the theory of convention worked out by Schelling and Lewis would then make no sense once the numbers were large enough. However, if one knows that one will have a reason to contribute if enough other people do likewise, and one knows that they know that, and so forth, then there is exactly the basis for constructing conventions which Schelling and Lewis presumed; the reason for participation, more-

2. Olson, *The Logic of Collective Action* (Cambridge, Mass.: Harvard University Press, 1971), p. 64.

over, applies whatever the numbers involved. As in their theory of convention, of course, there has to be a common interest, in the sense that we would all rather have whatever the convention creates than its absence. Where interests genuinely conflict, and where we want different general outcomes, a whole host of different considerations come to bear on the situation, and we will find ourselves in the world of fundamental political or ethical theory. My theory does not straightforwardly address those considerations, as my target has been the more limited (though practically very powerful) claim that even where we have a common interest as traditionally understood, we still cannot secure mutual co-operation. Whether we can do so in situations where we lack a common interest is another question; it may be that a desire to collaborate at some very deep level (that is, to enjoy social relations with other men at almost any cost) can lead us to convert a clash of more superficial interests into a common interest, but much of the classical political theory of our culture is devoted to various answers to this question, and my limited claim cannot provide a new answer. What it can do, however, is to suggest that ideas like those of Hobbes, Rousseau, Hume and Bentham (and maybe even Marx), in which we subordinate our partial interests to our more fundamental interest in living an orderly social life, though they may not actually be true, are at least not as logically flawed at their base as Olsonians would have us suppose.

I should also distinguish my argument from what is in many respects the closest analogy to it, the theory put forward by Derek Parfit in his *Reasons and Persons*.[3] In his third chapter, 'Five Mistakes in Moral Mathematics', Parfit characterises as among these 'mistakes' exactly what I too have criticised, namely, the assumptions that imperceptible effects should be disregarded and that what he calls 'overdetermined' actions do not have effects which we should take into account in our calculations about what we should do. He even at one point mentions the sorites paradox.[4] But (for reasons largely to do with his general project of calling into question the identity of the person or persons who should be the object of both our prudential and our moral thinking) Parfit was oddly unwilling to conclude from this that individual actions in these collective contexts have the kinds of effect which I have attributed to them. As he said at the end of Chapter 3, discuss-

---

3. Parfit, *Reasons and Persons* (Oxford: Oxford University Press, 1984).
4. Ibid., p. 78.

ing cases where someone makes a negligible contribution to an activity which collectively injures other people,[5]

> It is not enough to ask, 'Will my act harm other people?' Even if the answer is No, my act may still be wrong, *because* of its effects on other people. I should ask, 'Will my act be one of a set of acts that will *together* harm other people?' The answer may be Yes. And the harm to others may be great. If this is so, I may be acting *very* wrongly . . . We must accept this view if our concern for others is to yield solutions to most of the many Prisoner's Dilemmas that we face: most of the many cases where, if each of us rather than none of us does what will be better for himself—or better for his family or for those he loves—this will be worse, and often *much* worse, for everyone.[6]

Parfit used the same kind of argument in a slightly different context in Chapter 4, when he argued that in cases such as the classic prisoners' dilemma, a strictly self-interested reasoner would continue to conclude that he ought not to co-operate despite the fact that the end result is worse for him than collaboration would have been. This is so, he wrote, because

> [*we*] do better, but *each* does worse. If we both do A [that is, collaborate, or keep silent] rather than E [that is, defect, or confess], *we* make the outcome better for each, but *each* makes the outcome worse for himself. Whatever the other does, it would be better for each if he did E. In Prisoner's Dilemmas, the problem is this. Should *each* do the best he can for himself? Or should *we* do the best we can for each? If *each* does what is best for himself, *we* do worse than we could for each. But *we* do better for each only if *each* does worse than he could for himself.[7]

From Parfit's point of view, the distinction which I initially stressed between prisoners' dilemmas and free-rider problems does not matter; in a dilemma, 'each' of our actions (to use his terminology) has an adverse effect on the other player, while in a free-rider case, 'each' of our actions has little or no

---

5. For example, withholding a small amount of water from a large collective enterprise designed to rescue many men dying from thirst, or adding a tiny amount of extra power to some torturing machine. These are variants on a case devised by Jonathan Glover ('It Makes No Difference Whether or Not I Do It', *Proceedings of the Aristotelian Society* 49, supp. [1975]: 171–190), in which bandits deprive tribesmen of baked beans one by one.

6. Parfit, *Reasons and Persons,* p. 86.

7. Ibid., p. 91.

effect on the others, but in both cases 'we' do better by collaborating than 'each' would do by not collaborating. And the point of Parfit's general argument, set out with great subtlety in the rest of the book, is that we have good reasons for adopting the perspective of 'we', both in inter- *and* intra-personal deliberation.

However, as I argued in Chapter Two, we do not need to change our perspective in this way. There are many conditions which together allow my action in these sorts of cases to be sufficient to bring about the outcome; they include basic facts about my physical existence as well as a complex range of social facts to do with other people's actions. Given these conditions, as I stressed when discussing Lyons, *my individual action* has causal efficacy; it is not true, on my account, that 'each' does no harm in free-rider cases, any more than 'each' would do no harm in cases where there was an absolutely clear-cut and non-controversial threshold. A proper understanding of the causal character of the individual action, as Lyons realised, is enough to enable us to dispense with the need to change our perspective from the individual action to a set of actions, or from the individual person to a set of persons. It is particularly curious that Parfit did not take this position, as he himself had earlier said when discussing the question of how we share causal responsibility, and correctly denying that it is shared *pro rata* among the participants (the mistake I discussedin Chapter Two), that 'each counts as producing the *whole* of this total benefit . . . This is what each does, not by himself, but with the help of others'.[8] But each does it not just with the help of others, but with the help of nature and a whole host of other conditions; that does not oblige us to talk as if 'we', including in 'we' every relevant anterior circumstance, human and non-human, had produced the action.

But Parfit's account also provides a different and in some ways more difficult challenge to what I have been arguing. As has often been observed (and this is indeed a key aspect of Parfit's work), a theory of Parfit's kind seems to impose an immense moral burden upon us. Our participation in collective enterprises of an enormous size does not in any way reduce our responsibility for the outcomes; if our state kills people wrongly, then (assuming the existence of appropriate democratic structures) we are ourselves as responsible as if we had killed the people individually. For many readers of Parfit this has been a major stumbling block, as few have possessed the courage he possesses simply to accept this implication. Despite the differ-

8. Ibid., p. 69.

ences between our theories, on my account too we are each fully causally responsible for a collective outcome. Does this imply that we should carry the same moral burden to which Parfit condemns us?

My answer would be to separate causal responsibility from its moral implications, in ways with which we are familiar in other contexts. Our intuitions about moral responsibility are very complex, and influenced by many considerations other than how we ascribe causal responsibility; in particular, they are often very influenced by our assumptions about what would be an appropriate penal response to the act in question. This is familiar in cases where an action carries moral or legal responsibility even though it demonstrably has no causal effect, as in the example I have used before, of an illegal firing squad which follows the practice of assigning to the squad only one round of live ammunition. Each member of the squad would be treated equally by the law, and no one would (for instance) be treated as merely *intending* to kill the victim. It would be no defence for all but one of the squad to demonstrate that it was not their bullets which killed the victim; but a demonstration of this kind would certainly establish the fact that they did not cause his death. But the same is true in reverse; thus, in many instances where we would have expected that the ascription of moral responsibility would bring with it penal action of some kind, we often pull back from ascribing full moral responsibility to people who are involved in collective actions, even though we have no doubt about their causal responsibility. To take an extreme example, suppose that a large mob seizes someone and beats him to death. It is not at all unreasonable to say that all of them, or a substantial number, are causally responsible, given that an accumulation of blows will eventually kill someone. But suppose also that we believe in the need to punish murderers by capital punishment; we might then reasonably hold that it would not be appropriate to put every member of the mob to death as a punishment for the murder of one man. So, compared with a straightforward case in which one man kills another, our intuitive response to the mob's action might *appear* to involve the ascription of a different kind of responsibility to the members of the mob, but in fact the distinction between the two cases would be generated by our distaste at the consequences, where large numbers are concerned, of treating causal responsibility as the exclusive basis for punishment.

We can see how this could be so if we contrast it with a situation where people deserve praise or reward rather than blame or punishment. For example, we might well hold that soldiers who have collaborated in some brave action each deserve the same kind of praise which one brave soldier would receive for a comparable action he performed by himself. The difference between this case and the mob is most naturally understood as a response to the fact that excessive suffering is caused by capital punishment of all the members of the mob, whereas only pleasure is caused by our recognition that each brave soldier was responsible for the group's successful operation. Given the tremendous complexity of the relationship between the ascription of moral responsibility and the ascription of causal responsibility, it does not seem to me to be an argument against my account of collaboration (nor, it should be said, is it necessarily an argument against Parfit's account) that we do not suppose that members of large groups are to be treated as morally responsible for the action of the group in the same way or to the same degree as an isolated individual might be. One advantage of accepting that the causal structure will not (so to speak) uniquely determine the moral structure is that doing so allows a very wide range of possible responses to collective action, in which even whole nations might be punished, though in ways which would fall far short of what would be demanded for a single offender; one would not be required to treat the participants either as all innocent or as all guilty, at least in the sense that their guilt would carry the same implications as the imputation of guilt to a single person. This seems to me to correspond reasonably well to our intuitions about how to judge collective action.

I might also here make a more general point about calculation, both of a general welfarist kind[9] and of a more specifically utilitarian variety. As we shall see in Chapter Four, the classic utilitarians, from Bentham down to J. S. Mill, were not particularly committed to precise calculations of consequences, even as a theoretical possibility; rather, rough generalisations about the likely outcome seemed to them sufficient. Not until F. Y. Edgeworth's *New and Old Methods of Ethics* in 1872, I think, were utilitarians urged (at least by a friend of the movement) to recognise that their calculations should in principle be mathematically precise. One of the interesting implications of my discussion of the practical sorites is that the early utilitarians' instinct in this area may have been well grounded. The essence of soritic reasoning is that we know there is a determinate outcome but we cannot specify it; only a very rough or vague judgement could *as a matter of principle* be

---

9. To use the distinction pioneered by Sen; see, for example, Amartya Sen, 'Utilitarianism and Welfarism', *Journal of Philosophy* 76 (1979): 463–489.

enough to pick out the consequence of our action. This is true even where we are not engaged in an interpersonally collective action, as in my case of the shepherd in the hills: if he is to be an ideal utilitarian, with his own actions as the domain over which utilitarian calculations are to be made, he simply *cannot* be precise. Does this mean, however, that he cannot be a utilitarian? I do not see why this should be the case: he is still deliberating about the likely consequences of his actions, and choosing among the consequences so that something like his own utility is as great as it can be. The fact that the consequences include outcomes which cannot be precisely specified does not preclude utilitarian calculation; it merely precludes *precise* utilitarian calculation.

The last point which I wish to make at this stage about the general implications of my argument and how it is to be properly understood is that it must be understood as a *normative* claim, and not at all (or at least not much) as a predictive claim about how human beings will as a matter of fact behave. Notoriously, these two things have been extensively confused in the rational-choice literature, and even in the literature of neo-classical economics (as we shall see in Part II). The notion of rational conduct with which I have been concerned is an essentially instrumental one: conduct is rational if it is successful at securing a given goal or goals, and the character of the goals is (in this context) left unexamined—there is no such thing as a rational goal, unless the goal itself is taken to be an instrumental means to some further end. As I said in the Introduction, I am not committed to the idea that this is indeed the only meaning of rational action; but I am interested in seeing how far our common intuitions about collaborative behaviour can be sustained within a narrowly instrumental view of rationality. The appeal of this view, for economists in the first instance and then for rational-choice theorists in political science, was that it seemed to produce elegant and plausible explanations of observable activity; this was why its apparent failure in the case of such a central political phenomenon as voting caused political scientists such distress. But one of the constant problems about using the notion of 'rationality' as an explanatory category is that it must always be at the same time a normative category—all other things being equal, it is always better to be rational than irrational. (All other things may not be equal, and rationality cannot be an overriding value; but in this respect it does not differ from most—maybe all—of our other values.)

Confusion in this way between a predictive or explanatory category and a normative one is not at all uncommon (and has been at the basis of Charles

Taylor's remarks about the impossibility of a value-free social science, at least where the science resembles those practised today).[10] For another example, suppose that we possessed (as the Greeks believed they did) a 'science of virtue'—a systematic account of the dispositions which we regard as virtuous, and a corresponding awareness of the connection between possessing a particular virtue and acting in a certain way. Such a science would be eminently predictive; its subject-matter, after all, would precisely be good predictions about how people of a certain character behave (this is what it *means* to have a certain character or disposition). But all its propositions would at the same time be intended to possess normative force, and given the language employed in the science, one could not easily disentangle the predictive and the normative aspects. 'Rationality' is in this respect similar to 'virtue': one cannot wish away the normative character of describing an action or a person as 'rational'. This was recognised by one of the few economists to consider the real relationship between the normative and descriptive features of rationality, John Harsanyi. He was fully aware that (as he put it) 'already at a common-sense level, rationality is a *normative* concept: it points to what we *should* do in order to attain a given end or objective', and he remarked that

> [p]hilosophers, and social scientists outside the economics profession, have
> often expressed puzzlement about the successful use of the normative con-
> cept of rational behavior in positive economics—and, more recently, also in
> other social sciences—for explanation and prediction, and even for mere
> description, of human behavior. But there is nothing really surprising about
> this. All it means is that human behavior is mostly goal-directed, often in a
> fairly consistent manner, in many important classes of social situations.[11]

In other words, it is a contingent fact that people are actually rational, just as we might believe (if we had a social science based on the virtues) that people are actually brave, temperate or just, and we could use our account of those

10. See in particular his famous essay of 1971, 'Interpretation and the Sciences of Man', reprinted in Charles Taylor, *Philosophy and the Human Sciences: Philosophical Papers 2* (Cambridge: Cambridge University Press, 1985), pp. 15–57.

11. John Harsanyi, 'Advances in understanding rational behavior', in *Foundational Problems in the Special Sciences*, eds. R. E. Butts and J. Hintikka (Dordrecht: D. Reidel, 1977), pp. 315–343, reprinted in Paul K. Moser, ed., *Rationality in Action: Contemporary Approaches* (Cambridge: Cambridge University Press, 1990), pp. 271–293. My quotations are from the reprinted version, pp. 272 and 273.

virtues to predict and explain their behaviour—as of course we can and do even in the absence of such a science, when we are confident that a particular individual's character is virtuous in some respect.

Thus to deny that it is in the last analysis rational to defect from a large-scale collaborative activity is not to deny that as a matter of fact people may fairly consistently do so. As I remarked in the Introduction, Hume took the common-sense view that although it might be rational to collaborate, many people act irrationally in this area, and we should organise our institutions accordingly; such a view would preserve most of the practical implications of the idea that it is rational not to collaborate. In particular, it would preserve the obvious need for institutions of punishment to ensure that people do not defect. It is sometimes implied by discussions of this question (for example, by Michael Taylor in his *Community, Anarchy and Liberty*)[12] that traditional anarchist political theory would be to some extent vindicated were it possible to show that collaboration is rational, but of course that is not so. The likelihood of failure in reasoning, especially in areas where our immediate interest is very vivid, is sufficiently great that we will always need mechanisms to force collaboration; but at least on my account such mechanisms will not be adding insult to injury by asserting to their victims that they are being forced to act in ways which would in the absence of coercion be *irrational,* in order to bring about the common good.

The analogy for Hume (as we shall also see in detail in Chapter Four) was with people's characteristic failure of prudence with regard to their future good, and that is indeed the most plausible analogy. To say that it is not rational to defect from a large-scale enterprise is to say that the people who do so act in an extraordinary or demented manner, any more than all of us do when we are somewhat careless about the future. Some economists or political scientists, I think, are rather unwilling to say this, because lurking at the back of their approach is the idea (most notoriously associated with Ludwig von Mises)[13] that *all* intentional human action is rational, since it must correspond to the wishes which the agent possessed at the moment at which he performed the action. But that idea has been widely discredited, for obvious reasons: it reduces rationality to an empty and uninformative

12. Taylor, *Community, Anarchy and Liberty* (Cambridge: Cambridge University Press, 1982). See also his *Anarchy and Cooperation* (London: Wiley, 1976) and *The Possibility of Cooperation* (Cambridge: Cambridge University Press, 1987).

13. 'Human action is necessarily always rational'; Von Mises, *Human Action: A Treatise on Economics* (New Haven, Conn.: Yale University Press, 1949), p. 18.

category, which cannot even do the work which the positivist social scientist wants it to do, since it cannot explain in terms of a more general and consistent set of preferences why an individual behaves as he does on a particular occasion. It must be theoretically possible for an agent to act irrationally, in the sense that what he chooses to do does not correspond to a desire or set of desires which he possesses in a reasonably steady fashion and which he would, say, acknowledge in other circumstances as governing his conduct. It is in this sense that it is possible to say that we often do not act prudently or rationally with regard to the future, and that we often do not see the instrumental point of collaborating with many other people. But our irrationality in these kinds of situations is so familiar and pervasive that the positivist is still in a perfectly secure position to make predictions on the basis of observable conduct. My argument does not in any way necessarily imply that (for example) grain farmers in America will actually form effective cartels, though it does imply that if they do so, it is not some mistake of rationality on their part.

There are, however, a couple of qualifications to what I have just said. The first is that in some instances, my argument allows behaviour to be viewed as rational, within a broadly rational-choice view of politics, which was formerly seen as irrational. The most notable instance of this is the phenomenon of the bandwagon, which (if I am right) is a perfectly reasonable aspect of an electoral system, but which has proved remarkably intractable for conventional rational-choice theory. The second qualification is more important, and is connected to another part of Charles Taylor's case against the value-free social sciences. The essence of the social sciences as we currently possess them is that the categories they use are—by and large—the kinds of categories which people use, and have always used, in making sense of their lives. ('Rationality' is, after all, a prime example of this.) The consequence, as Taylor has repeatedly stressed, is that these 'scientific' theories quickly become just another element in the array of theories and beliefs which constitute the means of interpreting our lives to ourselves, and cannot maintain the separation from the objects of their analysis which is inherent in the natural sciences—the planets are not going to take up the law of gravity as part of their own self-understanding! This being so, we can often point to changes in people's behaviour as influenced by the pervasiveness of a particular social scientific theory; a vivid example of this process is the slide in psychoanalysis from the science envisaged by Freud to the philosophy of life which it largely is today.

Equally, I think it is not unreasonable to say that the prevalence in modern economics and political science of the idea that it is not instrumentally rational to collaborate in large groups may well have led people to adjust their conduct accordingly, and to treat actions as legitimate which in the late nineteenth century they would have taken to be illegitimate or imprudent. A particularly good illustration of this is provided by the observation of J. M. Clark in 1923 (which I discuss in more detail in Chapter Five) that 'one of the commonest ways of expressing the forces which restrain competitors from carrying price-cutting to the limit is to say that they are held back by a sentiment against "spoiling the market"'.[14] In other words, competitors in 1923 believed that it was imprudent to cut costs too far, whereas such a sentiment seems ridiculous in 2008. The history of voting almost certainly constitutes another such example: it is unlikely that low participation rates in modern Western democracies have no connection with fifty years of academic theorising about the irrationality of voting. While a failure to collaborate may well be in part a familiar failure of reasoning, and while no one would rely on people's capacity to think clearly about collaboration, it may also be the case that people are less likely to collaborate than they would have been had the academic study of social action not taken this particular turn. So in Part II I take up the theme of the history of ideas about collaboration, and show that the notion of what constitutes common-sense rational behaviour in this area is indeed highly historically variable.

14. Clark, *The Economics of Overhead Costs* (Chicago: University of Chicago Press, 1923), p. 439.

History

CHAPTER FOUR

Rule and Act Utilitarianism

What I have outlined in the first part of this book is a set of arguments designed to suggest that the modern view of the reasoning underlying what I have called 'Olson's problem' is mistaken. The arguments have involved quite abstract considerations, and in at least one case (my endorsement of the epistemic view of vagueness) have required the acceptance of a very counter-intuitive theory. So it might be supposed that the power of common sense is all on Olson's side, and that however odd their views might seem on laborious inspection, ordinary political and economic agents, and ordinary economists, are simply acting on the basis of what has always been obvious. But as I have stressed, both the technical arguments which I have been putting forward—on pre-emptive causation and the epistemic view of vagueness—have the merit that they correspond more closely than their rivals to our familiar intuitions about human action and judgement. And as I observed in the introduction to Part I, a notable feature of Olson's idea is that it would have been accepted by scarcely any theorist, let alone ordinary political actor, before the twentieth century. Collaboration in pursuit of common goals seemed on the whole to be pre-eminently rational, and the mechanisms to enforce it were designed to guard against the irrationality and imprudence to which human beings are all too prone. One of the principal reasons for supposing that Olson was wrong is indeed that what he took to be self-evident was a very recent and—in its day—controversial view about the rationality of collaboration, and that in areas away from the academic discipline of economics it continues to possess an air of casuistry. In this part, I shall trace the history lying behind Olson's use of the idea, and show how it had come to be taken for granted among economists themselves a relatively short time before Olson wrote. Much of the discussion will concentrate on the history of economics, since it was economists who put

forward the argument in its most precise and explicit form, but I shall begin
by looking at the history of ideas about co-operation among (broadly defined) utilitarians, from whose ideas the economists at first borrowed much
of their discourse, but who were (as we shall see) late in coming to their
own version of Olson's problem; indeed, it is arguable that it is only with
Jonathan Harrison's article of 1953, discussed in Chapter Two, that utilitarian philosophers clearly stated the puzzle.

A number of writers have supposed that the modern problems about
collaboration, and even the prisoners' dilemma itself, can be traced back
to Thomas Hobbes; but I have given elsewhere reasons for being sceptical
about a reading of Hobbes that would locate him in a setting of either prisoners' dilemmas or Olson's problem.[1] These puzzles can arise only when an
agent would be better off in some way by defecting from the co-operative
enterprise; they thus require, as a minimum, some form of comparability
between the good secured by the action of the co-operative enterprise and
the good secured by the individual defection. The point about Hobbes is that
(at least on one plausible reading of the texts) there is no such comparability,
and furthermore, that it is on the absence of such comparability that Hobbes
relies to make his argument work.

His primary concern was to find a category of actions which would be universally describable by all men in all societies in the same moral terms, as a
'duty' or a 'right', and he believed that he had found such a category in actions intended for one's self-protection: men must always be allowed the
'right' to protect themselves. He was, however, quite clear that there is no
such 'right' to do anything other than protect oneself; there are things one
might want to do but cannot be said to have the right to do, because they
cannot be interpreted as a means to self-defence. The examples he gave
were drunkenness and cruelty (that is, vengeance 'without regard to future
good'), 'for I can not see what drunkenness or cruelty . . . contribute to any
man's peace or preservation'.[2] But there would be genuine dispute about
most of the circumstances in which such a right could be exercised—for example, in a 'state of nature' with no civil society, was a particular individual
apparently harmlessly wending his way a threat to other men or not? He
might be, and it might be a reasonable judgement that he was a danger and
should therefore be attacked. This epistemic uncertainty about the circum-

---

1. See Richard Tuck, *Hobbes* (London: Oxford University Press, 1989), pp. 106–109.
2. Thomas Hobbes, *De Cive* III.27 note.

stances in which it would be correct to exercise one's undeniable right of self-preservation is what leads (in Hobbes's theory) to a state of war in nature.

The solution to the problem of endemic conflict was for all men to transfer to a single authority their judgement about what, in uncertain situations, was in fact a danger to them. This authority would not know the truth about these situations, any more than the natural men did—there is (Hobbes believed in general) no truth to be known about anything in the external world. But if the authority's judgement was canonical for its subjects, there would be intersubjectivity, without objectivity. This authority was, of course, the state, and it could reasonably require (for example) its subjects to fight in its armies, since it was the only source of information about whether, say, the Dutch were actually a threat or not. If the sovereign pronounced the Dutch a threat, then it was as rational for his subjects to fight the Dutch as it would have been for each one of them in the state of nature to fight whomever they believed to be threatening them.

Hobbes persistently argued that there would be no rational grounds for anyone to defect from civil society as long as the sovereign's judgement was generally accepted by his subjects (if that was not the case, of course, then private judgement had re-appeared and all men were potentially back in the state of nature). This is the antithesis of the free-rider argument, in which the best point to defect from the common enterprise may be when one can be assured that others will not do likewise. But Hobbes was clearly correct to argue this, in the terms of his own argument: for one had no right to do anything which one did not sincerely believe conduced to one's preservation, and all judgement in situations of uncertainty had been transferred to the sovereign on condition only that all other men did likewise. In situations of certainty, it is true, one could act on one's own initiative—thus the condemned man on the way to the gallows was entitled to struggle, for it was clear that he was directly under attack. But he should have been condemned only because of some earlier failure of rationality on his part, in posing his own view about what he had the right to do against that of his sovereign.

This whole argument is obviously very far removed from a theory of perfect competition and its Olsonian derivatives. Hobbes's men cannot rightfully or rationally snatch a competitive advantage over their fellows by defecting from a common social enterprise, and it is not the prospect of this collapse which prompts the emergence of the leviathan state. What Hobbes was concerned with above all was the conflict not of interests but of ideologies—of dogmatic beliefs which forced their bemused followers into actions deeply against their own interests, culminating in the civil wars which had wasted Europe since the Reformation. It was mistaken or contentious beliefs, not rational self-interest, that led to defections from the social enterprise.

It is among eighteenth-century writers that we encounter in a developed form a more familiar account of rational collaboration in the pursuit of a variety of different goods. Francis Hutcheson, in particular, seems to have put into circulation the idea that moral value was in general attached to actions which conduced to 'the public interest', and that the relationship between the action and the general interest could be somewhat remote. To express this, he used extensively a terminology which became central to this tradition, that of the 'tendency' of an action. Thus 'an action is called *materially good* when in fact it tends to the interest of the system, as far as we can judge of its tendency', where by 'the system' Hutcheson meant 'the general good, or a particular good consistent with it.'[3] Similarly, he explained rights in this fashion—'every proper right is some way conducive to the publick interest, and is founded upon some such tendency'. And for 'remote reasons . . . the interest of society' might require that we accept arrangements which look at first glance to be undesirable, such as leaving a miser in possession of money which could have been spent charitably by someone else.[4] This particular example was picked up by David Hume,[5] and the puzzle represented by such cases, where the maintenance of property rules seemed to work against people's interests in a particular instance, became the central puzzle for this whole tradition.

Hutcheson did not develop a stringent philosophical justification for these ideas, nor properly discuss the relationship between benevolence and altruism. But Hume provided the fullest and most persuasive theory of the complex relationship between individual short-term interest, individual long-term interest and altruism. As is well known, Hume was interested in distinguishing between 'natural' and 'artificial' virtues, the former including (for example) benevolence, the latter including particularly justice. In both

3. Hutcheson, *A System of Moral Philosophy* (London, 1755), I, p. 252. See also p. 232 and many other places in Hutcheson's works.

4. Ibid., pp. 257, 259.

5. Hume, *Treatise*, III.II.2.22. See also his well-known use of the example of Cyrus deciding which boy to give a coat to, in Appendix III to his *Enquiry Concerning the Principles of Morals* (*Enquiries* 256).

cases, both our own self-interest and our disinterested care for other people would lead us to praise certain kinds of actions and to blame others. The key distinction between the two types of virtue was that the former involved actions which were directly beneficial to another man or men, whereas the latter were only indirectly beneficial, through their congruence in a general practice.

> The social virtues of humanity and benevolence exert their influence immediately by a direct tendency or instinct, which chiefly keeps in view the simple object, moving the affections, and comprehends not any scheme or system, nor the consequences resulting from the concurrence, imitation, or example of others . . .
>
> The case is not the same with the social virtues of justice and fidelity. They are highly useful, or indeed absolutely necessary to the well-being of mankind: but the benefit resulting from them is not the consequence of every individual single act; but arises from the whole scheme or system concurred in by the whole, or the greater part of the society. General peace and order are the attendants of justice or a general abstinence from the possessions of others; but a particular regard to the particular right of one individual citizen may frequently, considered in itself, be productive of pernicious consequences . . .
>
> The happiness and prosperity of mankind, arising from the social virtue of benevolence and its subdivisions, may be compared to a wall, built by many hands, which still rises by each stone that is heaped upon it, and receives increase proportional to the diligence and care of each workman. The same happiness, raised by the social virtue of justice and its subdivisions, may be compared to the building of a vault, where each individual stone would, of itself, fall to the ground; nor is the whole fabric supported but by the mutual assistance and combination of its corresponding parts.[6]

It is clear from this passage, and comparable passages in the *Treatise*, that Hume, like Hutcheson, was well aware that a particular act may be a disbenefit taken by itself, and yet the practice or co-operative enterprise of which it is a part may be greatly beneficial. But as far as he was concerned, this was not a problem: if we recognise that the long-term effect of collaboration is beneficial, we will reasonably conclude (if we are not allowing ourselves to be swayed by our immediate feelings) that we should co-operate in

6. Hume, *Enquiries*, 255–256.

the collaborative enterprise. The long-term utility of the practice was in itself a sufficient reason for action; in particular, the parties to the enterprise certainly did not need to have *promised* one another that they would collaborate. After all, Hume's principal target in much of this discussion was precisely the social contract theory, which (he claimed) supposed that such things as allegiance to government and the recognition of property rights derived from a promise by the members of the society to obey the law. Hume repeatedly made the point that no prior agreement, at least in this sense, was required for the principles of justice to have a purchase on us: all we need is to recognise the ultimate advantage to us, and to other people, of the collaborative enterprise we are engaged in. He said in the *Treatise* that our 'common sense of interest . . . produces a suitable resolution and behaviour' when it 'is mutually expressed, and is known to' the parties,[7] but as David Lewis pointed out, the mutual expression could be of an extremely general kind, and might be very far removed from what we customarily think of as an agreement.[8] 'Thus two men pull the oars of a boat by common convention for common interest, without any promise or contract: thus gold and silver are made the measures of exchange; thus speech and words and language are fixed by human convention and agreement'.[9] Like Hutcheson, Hume freely used the terminology of *tendency*—thus he observed of the 'artificial' virtues that 'the tendency of qualities to the good of society, is the *sole* cause of our approbation, without any suspicion of the concurrence of another principle', and of the rules of justice that they have 'all of them a direct and evident tendency to public good, and the support of society'.[10]

Two essential features of the Olsonian theory are missing from Hume's account. The first feature is the sense that a defection may be rational because it will in fact make no difference to the outcome, and the second (related) feature is an awareness of the effect that large numbers may have on a situation. Hume was as happy to use the analogy of two men rowing a boat as he was to use that of a vault, and yet one rower cannot defect without the most dramatic and catastrophic effect on the overall enterprise. Ironically, a vault can in fact stand perfectly well if an individual stone drops from it (as is often obvious after war damage), and yet Hume used the image of a vault in order to persuade his readers that an individually beneficial act should not be per-

---

7. Hume, *Treatise*, III.II.2.

8. See his *Convention: A Philosophical Study* (Cambridge, Mass.: Harvard University Press, 1969), pp. 33–36.

9. Hume, *Enquiries*, 257.

10. Hume, *Treatise*, III.III.1.8 and III.II.6.6.

formed if it meant dropping out of a socially beneficial enterprise. A clear sense that certain actions may make no difference, and that because of this there is a special problem about co-operative enterprises which rely on many such actions, is absent from Hume's work.

There is one passage in the *Treatise* which has been used (for example, by Russell Hardin and Michael Taylor) as a statement of Olson's problem. It is the passage I have already cited (see p. 95) about our lack of foresight. In it, Hume is discussing the advantages of government:

> [N]ot contented to protect men in those conventions they make for their mutual interest, it [that is, government] often obliges them to make such conventions, and forces them to seek their own advantage, by a concurrence in some end or purpose. *There is no quality in human nature, which causes more fatal errors in our conduct, than that which leads us to prefer whatever is present to the distant and remote, and makes us desire objects more according to their situation than their intrinsic value* [my emphasis]. Two neighbours may agree to drain a meadow, which they possess in common; because 'tis easy for them to know each others mind; and each must perceive, that the immediate consequence of his failing in his part, is, the abandoning the whole project. But 'tis very difficult, and indeed impossible, that a thousand persons should agree in any such action; it being difficult for them to concert so complicated a design, and still more difficult for them to execute it; while each seeks a pretext to free himself of the trouble and expence, and wou'd lay the whole burden on others. Political society easily remedies both these inconveniences.[11]

One of the striking features of this passage, however, is that Hume does not commit himself to the proposition that the individual act makes little or no difference to the outcome. In fact, he is clear that the prospective partners are straightforwardly (though understandably) mistaken in what they conclude is in their interests—this is the point of the sentence which I have put in italics. According to Hume, it is a mistake of prudence which leads to non-co-operation where there are large numbers, a mistake comparable to one person's preferring an immediate gratification to a more distant but much greater one; the passage occurs in a section which is principally concerned with the 'natural infirmity' by which one tends to prefer a 'present good' to a more remote one. Indeed, the passage continues,

11. Ibid., III.II.7.8.

> Magistrates find an immediate interest in the interest of any considerable part of their subjects . . . And as the failure of any one piece in the execution is connected, tho' not immediately, with the failure of the whole, they prevent that failure, because they find no interest in it, either immediate or remote.

So Hume assumed that there was some causal relationship, albeit of a remote kind, between an individual act and the collective outcome. Government is necessary because rational action becomes psychologically more difficult where there are lots of people involved, not because rational action changes its character in such situations. Hume's general view, expressed in all these passages, was that it is reasonable to talk about collaborative enterprises (such as, famously, promise-keeping or political allegiance)[12] as being in the interests of the people who constitute the enterprise, and that this is in itself a good reason for the individuals to contribute their support to it. Psychological features, such as the propensity to think about short-term outcomes, or a general ignorance of the instrumental point of collaboration, might induce people not to co-operate, but this (though understandable, and predictable on Hume's account of human character) was an error of reasoning. The numbers of people did not affect the nature of the reasoning involved, though it might well make the practical problems more intense.

The same thought is, more or less, expressed in the well-known passage at the end of the *Enquiries* in which Hume says that

> according to the imperfect way in which human affairs are conducted, a sensible knave, in particular incidents, may think that an act of iniquity or infidelity will make a considerable addition to his fortune, without causing any considerable breach in the social union and confederacy. That *honesty is the best policy,* may be a good general rule, but is liable to many exceptions; and he, it may perhaps be thought, conducts himself with most wisdom, who observes the general rule, and takes advantage of all the exceptions.[13]

Hume confessed that it was hard to answer this 'knave'; but the difficult issue, to which indeed Hume had no answer, was the question of why there should be *universal* compliance to a general rule. In this tradition, as we saw

---

12. See particularly his remarks in his essay 'Of the Original Contract', in *Essays Moral, Political, and Literary,* ed. Eugene F. Miller (Indianapolis: Liberty Fund, 1985), pp. 479–482.
13. Hume, *Enquiries,* 232.

in Part I, it makes sense for there to be a certain number of breaches of a general convention, and if we are interested (as Hume was in this passage) in moral psychology, it is indeed somewhat hard to explain how the preparedness to break rules can be experienced as a matter of morality, familiarly understood. Hume accepted that any social practice will be breached, but he did not suppose that the breaches would lead to the collapse of the practice.

Accordingly, writers in the broadly Humean tradition, who included in this respect the utilitarians, often drew their readers' attention to the problems involved in securing collaborative behaviour, but they almost invariably assumed that if the collaboration secured beneficial outcomes for the individuals concerned, that was in principle a good reason for the individuals to contribute voluntarily to the enterprise. Jeremy Bentham in particular thought hard about these issues, and produced what was clearly a very influential statement of the theory when he discussed taxation in *An Introduction to the Principles of Morals and Legislation* (1780); in it for the first time he addressed an Olsonian kind of argument head on. The benefit to the community of an individual's paying his taxes might fail, he said, because the tax was mis-spent, but

> the act of payment, when referable to any particular sum, especially if it be a small one, might also have failed of proving beneficial on another ground: and consequently, the act of non-payment, of proving mischievous. It is possible that the same services, precisely, might have been rendered without the money as with it. [That is, the contribution makes a negligible difference.] If, then, speaking of any small limited sum, such as the greatest which any one person is called upon to pay at any time, a man were to say, that the non-payment of it would be attended with mischievous consequences; this would be far from certain; but what comes to the same thing as if it were, it is perfectly certain when applied to the whole. It is certain, that if all of a sudden the payment of all taxes was to cease, there would no longer be any thing effectual done, either for the maintenance of justice, or for the defence of the community against its foreign adversaries . . . Upon the whole, therefore, it is manifest, that in this case, though the mischief is remote and contingent, though in its first appearance it consists of nothing more than the interception of a *benefit*, and though the individuals, in whose favour that benefit would have been reduced into the explicit form of pleasure or security, are altogether unassignable, yet the

mischievous tendency of the act is not on all these accounts the less indis-
putable.[14]

The terminology of *tendency* to capture the causal character of an insignificant contribution continued to be extremely popular among the utilitarians.[15] A particularly good example is provided by John Austin in *The Province of Jurisprudence Determined* (1832), dealing with the same question of
taxation.

> If I evade the payment of a tax imposed by a good government, the *spe-
> cific* effects of the mischievous forbearance are indisputably useful. For the
> money which I unduly withhold is convenient to myself; and, compared
> with the bulk of the public revenue, is a quantity too small to be missed. But
> the regular payment of taxes is necessary to the existence of the govern-
> ment. And I, and the rest of the community, enjoy the security which it
> gives, because the payment of taxes is rarely evaded.
>
> [In this case] the act or omission is good, considered as single or insulated;
> but, considered with the rest of its class, is evil. In other cases, an act or
> omission is evil, considered as single or insulated; but, considered with the
> rest of its class, is good . . .
>
> It, therefore, is true generally (for the proposition admits of exceptions),
> that, to determine the true tendency of an act, forbearance, or omission, we
> must resolve the following question:— What would be the probable effect
> on the general happiness or good, if *similar* acts, forbearances, or omissions
> were general or frequent?
>
> Such is the *test* to which we must usually resort, if we would try the true
> *tendency* of an act, forbearance, or omission: Meaning, by the true *tendency* of
> an act, forbearance, or omission, the sum of its probable effects on the gen-
> eral happiness or good, or its agreement or disagreement with the principle
> of general utility.[16]

14. Bentham, *A Fragment on Government with an Introduction to the Principles of Morals and
Legislation*, ed. Wilfrid Harrison (Oxford: Basil Blackwell, 1948), p. 274.

15. Indeed, in the eyes of William Whewell, a critic, utilitarianism could be *defined*
as 'deducing the Rules of action from considering the tendencies of actions to produce
human pleasure or pain'; *The Elements of Morality, Including Polity*, 4th ed. (Cambridge:
Deighton, Bell, 1864), p. v.

16. Austin, *The Province of Jurisprudence Determined*, ed. H. L. A. Hart (London: Wei-
denfeld and Nicolson, 1955), pp. 39–40.

The language allowed the utilitarians to talk about an individual action as possessing a kind of causal relationship to the collaborative outcome even when individually it appeared to be insignificant; they did not spell out precisely what they meant by it, but it is clear that their intuition was that in some loose and rather remote way, any individual contribution to a collective good, assuming the existence of a system of some kind (that is, the provision of enough comparable contributions), did have a causal efficacy over the outcome. Though Austin proposed that the 'test' for determining the tendency of the action was 'What would be the probable effect on the general happiness or good, if *similar* acts, forbearances, or omissions were general or frequent?', I think it would be mistaken to conclude that he intended by this the kind of sub-Kantian theory which later became popular among rule utilitarians. The 'test' is a means to determine rather vaguely and approximately the 'effects' of the act, not to replace the question of its effects with another question; it picks out the existence or potential existence of a set of actions which together produce a benefit, and within which each action will (or would) possess a causal relationship with the outcome. As we saw in Part I, my individual action has an effect on the outcome *if there are enough comparable actions,* and to ask 'What would happen if there were frequent examples of such an action?' is in this context to ask 'Suppose there were enough such actions for my action to contribute to bringing about a particular outcome; would I want to do so?' Would I want to go down to the beach with the other villagers and launch the lifeboat?

I have stressed the vagueness or inexactitude of the test—we are comparing large-scale social practices, not making minute calculations about individual utilities and the consequences of our actions. Our particular action, as in voting, may not actually be part of the causally efficacious set, but if the probability that it will be is high enough (and 'enough', as we have seen, is inherently a rather vague notion), I have a good reason to take part. This may seem the antithesis of at least Benthamite utilitarianism, but in fact (as Ross Harrison in particular has stressed) Bentham was not committed to the kind of interpersonal comparison of utility and summing utilities with which he is often associated. He persisted in describing the Utility Principle as 'the greatest happiness of the greatest number', and the *numbers of people* rather than precisely the quantity of their utility was often what mattered. In his *Constitutional Code,* the legislator is required to recognise as the sole end of government the greatest happiness of all without exception, in so far as possible: of the greatest number on every occasion on which the nature of the case renders it impossible, by rendering it matter of necessity to make sacrifice of a portion of the happiness of a few, to the greater happiness of the rest.[17]

Something rather like Rousseau's radical democratic politics was what Bentham envisaged—indeed, he remarked once that he had been 'fascinated by Rousseau . . . to the highest pitch of fascination'.[18]

Bentham returned to the question of large-scale collaboration in a different context forty years after the publication of *An Introduction,* in an essay of 1821, 'Observations on the Restrictive and Prohibitory Commercial System', in which he attacked a recent Spanish ban on the importation of various manufactured articles.

> In proportion as an individual, engaged in any one branch of industry, sees or fears to see his performances outdone by any competitor, whether foreign or domestic, he is interested in putting a stop to such rival labour, if possible; or to lessen its produce as far as he is able. The individual feeling is necessarily communicated to any body of individuals in the same situation; their common bond of union against those who are prejudiced by the employment of these productions, is much stronger than the motives to rivalry against one another. Hence, to obtain benefit for themselves and each other, individually and collectively considered, at the expense of all but themselves, is of course at all times the wish, and, as far as any prospect of success presents itself, at all times the endeavour, of all persons so connected and so situated. . .
>
> There are . . . two distinct interests; interests opposed to each other: the interest of producers, the particular interest; the interest of consumers, the universal interest. The individuals who compose the particular interest always are, or at least may be,—and have to thank themselves and one another if they are not,—a compact, harmonizing body; a chain of iron: the individuals making the universal interest are on every such occasion an unorganized, uncombined body; a rope of sand. Of the partakers in the uni-

17. Ross Harrison, *Bentham* (London: Routledge, 1983), pp. 233–234. See also Harrison's remarks about the rule-utilitarian element in Bentham, pp. 237–244.

18. Bentham to Étienne Dumont, 14 May 1802, in *The Correspondence of Jeremy Bentham, Vol. 7: January 1802 to December 1808,* ed. John R. Dinwiddy (Oxford: Oxford University Press, 1988), pp. 25–26. At the same time he expressed scepticism about the notion of a social contract. See also Harrison, *Bentham,* Chapter 8.

versal interest, the proportion of interest centred in one individual is too small to afford sufficient inducement to apply his exertions to the support of his trifling share in the common interest. Add to which the difficulty, the impossibility, of confederacy to any such extent as should enable the exertions of the confederates fairly to represent the amount of the general interest,—that general interest embracing, with few exceptions, the whole mass of society . . .

Even of the manufacturing interests, it is not every class that has the power to associate and combine in support of the common interest of the class: that power only exists where similar manufactures are concentrated in small districts; where means of intercourse are frequent and easy: or where large numbers are employed by large capital in the hand of a single individual, or of a single partnership. What facilities of general association or combination are possessed by individuals employed as general shop-keepers, bakers, butchers, tailors, shoemakers, farmers, carpenters, brick-layers, masons, &c.? None whatsoever.

Had every one individual in every one of these classes his vote in the business, all would indeed be as it should be: the sum of all the several distinguishable interests being thus framed and ascertained, would constitute the universal interest; in a word, the principle of universal suffrage would be applied.[19]

Again, these passages show Bentham aware of what was to be Olson's argument but not fully countenancing it, and not moving away in essentials from the position he had taken up in *An Introduction*. The distinction between what he here called the 'particular' interest and the 'general' interest was primarily a distinction between a focused common enterprise, in which the producers thought of themselves exclusively as the producers of a particular commodity, and the much more diffuse common enterprise of being consumers—something in which we all share, whatever our other concerns, but which it is hard to specify very precisely. This is not exclusively a question of numbers, as the producers of a single commodity might be very numerous; though in those circumstances Bentham recognised the practical difficulties of communication to which Hume had drawn attention. And Bentham's solution to the problem of the disparate interests of consumers,

19. Bentham, 'Observations on the Restrictive and Prohibitory Commercial System,' in *Jeremy Bentham's Economic Writings*, ed. W. Stark (London: Allen & Unwin, 1952–1954), III, pp. 404, 406, 408.

like Rousseau's, was a voting system, which of course on Olson's argument was no solution, as there would be (if the premises are correct) no reason to vote.

Something like Bentham's view remained a staple of utilitarianism, at least until the time of Henry Sidgwick. For example, John Stuart Mill, though often (as is well known) critical of Bentham, was extremely interested in the idea of a *tendency* in both natural and social science, and advocated its use as an essential category in causal explanation. In his essay 'On the Definition of Political Economy' (originally published in 1836), he warned against the 'truism' that 'there are *exceptions* to all rules. Such is the current language of those who distrust comprehensive thinking, without having any clear notion why or where it ought to be distrusted'. Instead, we should think of each element in a causal explanation of some event as a 'tendency', or 'power acting with a certain intensity in that direction' which could always be modified by another 'tendency' operating in a different direction.

> Thus if it were to be stated to be a law of nature, that all heavy bodies fall to the ground, it would probably be said that the resistance of the atmosphere, which prevents a balloon from falling, constitutes the balloon an exception to that pretended law of nature. But the real law is, that all heavy bodies *tend* to fall; and to this there is no exception.[20]

He repeated this at greater length in *A System of Logic*, remarking that it was not strictly true to say that a body moves in a certain manner 'unless prevented . . . by some counteracting cause':

> it *tends* to move in that manner even when counteracted; it still exerts in the original direction the same energy of movement as if its first impulse had been undisturbed, and produces, by that energy, an exactly equivalent quantity of effect. This is true even when the force leaves the body as it found it, in a state of absolute rest; as when we attempt to raise a body of three tons weight with a force equal to one ton . . . These facts are correctly indicated by the expression *tendency*. All laws of causation, in consequence of their liability to be counteracted, require to be stated in words affirmative of tendencies only, and not of actual results.[21]

20. Mill, *Essays on Economics and Society*, ed. J. M. Robson (London: Routledge, 1967), I, pp. 337–338.

21. Mill, *A System of Logic*, III.10.5.

These examples were from the physical sciences, but he said the same about the moral sciences:

> It is enough that we know that certain means have a *tendency* to produce a given effect, and that others have a tendency to frustrate it. When the circumstances of an individual or of a nation are in any considerable degree under our control, we may, by our knowledge of tendencies, be enabled to shape those circumstances in a manner much more favourable to the ends we desire than the shapes which they would of themselves assume. This is the limit of our power, but within this limit the power is a most important one.[22]

And when he composed his *Principles of Political Economy* in 1847, he consistently talked about such things as the 'tendency' of profits to equality.[23]

Mill also gave one of the most carefully considered accounts of the problem of co-operation to come out of this tradition, in Book V of the *Principles*, in which he discussed the 'limits of the province of government'. He drew attention to an exception to the general principle of non-intervention by government in economic affairs, an exception 'to which, as it appears to me, the attention of political economists has not yet been sufficiently drawn.

> These are matters in which the interference of law is required, not to overrule the judgement of individuals respecting their own interest, but to give effect to that judgement; they being unable to give effect to it except by concert, which concert again cannot be effectual unless it receives validity and sanction from the law.[24]

Essentially, this was Hume's argument about the need for government to co-ordinate a large-scale operation; Mill's example was already what became the standard modern example for these puzzles, a trades union. He observed that an agreement among workers to work, say, nine hours a day instead of their former ten, but for the same pay each day which they had formerly received, might be in each of the workers' interest, but 'however beneficial the observance of the regulation might be to the class collectively, the immediate interest of every individual would lie in violating it; and the more numerous those were who adhered to the rule, the more would individuals

22. Ibid., VI.5.4.
23. Mill, *Principles of Political Economy*, II.15.4.
24. Ibid., V.11.12.

gain by departing from it', since each individual would be able to earn more for his extra time.

> If nearly all restricted themselves to nine hours, those who chose to work for ten would gain all the advantages of the restriction, together with the profit of infringing it; they would get ten hours wages for nine hours work, and an hour's wages besides. I grant that if a large majority adhered to the nine hours, there would be no harm done: the benefit would be, in the main, secured to the class, while those individuals who preferred to work harder and earn more, would have an opportunity of doing so. This certainly would be the state of things to be wished for . . . Probably, however, so many would prefer the ten hours work on the improved terms, that the limitation could not be maintained as a general practice: what some did from choice, others would soon be obliged to do from necessity, and those who had chosen long hours for the sake of increased wages, would be forced in the end to work long hours for no greater wages than before.

Mill concluded that 'there might be no means of their attaining this object but by converting their supposed mutual agreement into an engagement under penalty, by consenting to have it enforced by law', and that this

> serves to exemplify the manner in which classes of persons may need the assistance of law, to give effect to their deliberate collective opinion of their own interest, by affording to every individual a guarantee that his competitors will pursue the same course, without which he cannot safely adopt it himself

—though he added with characteristic caution, 'I am not expressing any opinion in favour of such an enactment, which has never been demanded, and which I certainly should not, in present circumstances, recommend'.[25]

This was essentially a judicious version of Hume's argument, applied in a new context. Negligibility as such plays no part; when Mill said that 'the more numerous those were who adhered to the rule, the more would individuals gain by departing from it', he had in mind the conditions for the success of the trades union in securing a new wages agreement, rather than the fact that an individual worker might be making a negligible contribution to the outcome. If there were only a few highly skilled workers, they might be able to secure a better deal from their employers if most agreed to work

25. Ibid.

short time, but not if only one or two did so, and yet each worker would be making a significant contribution to output. Mill described the defection of the workers as driven by 'immediate' interest, and this contrast between short-term and long-term interest is, of course, characteristic of the Humean or the Benthamite account of these problems. He was also to some extent open-minded on the question of whether workers would actually defect, as is shown by his interesting remarks about the desirability of a situation in which some people worked long hours and others did not. Elsewhere in the *Principles,* and in his later writings on trades unions, Mill wrote eloquently in defence of co-operation as a new industrial principle which would transform modern economies.[26] It is also no doubt the case that the views on preemptive causation which I attributed to Mill in Chapter Two disposed him to a more realistic sense of the rationality of co-operation.

The idea that we have a long-term interest in collaborating, or sticking with a convention which we believe to be beneficial, found expression in Mill's well-known remarks in Chapter II of *Utilitarianism* (1861) on the role of rules in utilitarianism: 'To consider the rules of morality as improvable is one thing; to pass over the intermediate generalization entirely and endeavour to test each individual action directly by the first principle is another'. These remarks became the centre of interest in the 1950s, when some philosophers thought that they marked the beginnings of rule utilitarianism and the repudiation of an act utilitarianism, which they took to have been the classic Benthamite position. But in fact Mill added little in this respect to what had been commonplace in his father's generation, though for personal reasons he insinuated that he had done so. No one, I think, in the mid-nineteenth century supposed that Mill had said anything new in this passage, and they all recognised that Bentham too had believed in the importance of intermediate rules from which we had no good utilitarian reason to derogate in ordinary circumstances.

Indeed, one of the main criticisms of utilitarianism levelled by its midcentury opponents was that the utilitarians inconsistently endorsed intermediate rules, not that they disregarded them. William Whewell, for example, Knightbridge Professor of Moral Philosophy at Cambridge from 1839 to 1855 (as well as Master of Trinity from 1841 to 1866), published in 1845 *The*

---

26. See, for example, *Principles*, IV.7.6, and his remarks in 'Thornton on Labour and its Claims' (1869) and 'Chapters on Socialism' (1879), in *Essays on Economics and Society,* pp. 658–668 and 705–753.

Elements of Morality, including Polity, which (under the curious Cambridge system) became a textbook at first for the Mathematical and Classical Triposes and subsequently for the Moral Sciences Tripos. In it (sixteen years before Mill's *Utilitarianism*) he criticised the utilitarians for what he took to be their casualness in talking about calculating the 'sum of human happiness'.

> I wish to know whether I may seek sensual pleasure; whether I may tell a flattering lie. I ask, Will it increase or diminish the Sum of Human Happiness to do so? This mode of putting the question cannot help me. How can I know whether these acts will increase or diminish the Sum of Human Happiness? The immediate pleasure of gratified sense or of gratified vanity, I may, perhaps, in some degree, estimate; but how am I to estimate the indirect and remote effects of the acts, on myself and others; and how am I to measure the total effect thus produced, on Human Happiness? By a sensual act, or by a lie, I weaken, it may be said, the habit of temperance and of truth in my own mind; and by my example I produce a like effect on the minds of others. Suppose, then, that I regard this consequence, and see that the act thus leads to something of unhappiness; still, this effect is perhaps slight and precarious; how am I to balance this result, against those direct gratifications which are produced by the acts now spoken of?[27]

He understood that the utilitarians had not in fact wished to make these kinds of calculations about the detailed consequences of actions, but, he continued,

> the mode in which Moralists have been able to apply this Principle, of aiming at the greatest amount of Human Happiness, to the establishment of Moral Rules; has been, by assuming that man must act according to *Rules*. I say, *assuming;* for it does not appear, that we can *prove* that the Principle of increasing as much as possible the Happiness of man requires us to act by general Rules. The man who is tempted to sensual pleasure, or mendacious flattery, may say, I do not intend that what I do now should be a Rule for myself, or for others. At present I seek to promote Human Happiness, by making an exception to Rules: in general I shall conform to Rules. To this, the Moralist replies, that to speak and think thus, is to reject Rules altogether: that Rules are not recognized, except they be applied in all cases, and relied upon as the antagonists of the temptations which particular cases

27. Whewell, *The Elements of Morality, Including Polity* (London: 1845), I, pp. 362–363 (Chapter XXV, §548).

offer. In short, he says, that man, by his nature, must act by Rules; and that he, the Moralist, who has to decide respecting the character of human action, has to establish Rules of human action. Thus he assumes, in addition to his Principle of the Greatest Amount of Human Happiness, another Principle, of the Universality of Rule; and it is this latter Principle, which really gives a Moral character to his results.[28]

Already in these remarks, in the 1840s, we see one of the themes which was to preoccupy writers in the act-rule utilitarianism debate of the 1950s, that because utilitarians could not consistently suppose that a general rule should be followed in all cases, when in any particular case an increase in utility might be caused by breaching the rule, the requirement to follow a rule must be added on in some way to the principle of utility and could not be deduced from it. Whewell's own philosophy was an interesting attempt to revive a seventeenth-century natural rights theory, with an explicit reliance on Grotius, and he took morality to be essentially the recognition of a set of fundamental rights the existence of which laid corresponding obligations upon us; so he was not troubled by the problem of collaboration to the same degree that the utilitarians were. His ideas failed to attract many followers, but the criticisms he made stung utilitarians into a response, particularly (no doubt) because Whewell's commanding position in what was taught at Cambridge for thirty years affected a large part of Victorian intellectual culture. In the course of the 1870s, a modern utilitarianism was put together which conceded some of the points which Whewell and other critics had made, and which presented itself explicitly as (in F. Y. Edgeworth's words) a 'new method of ethics', to be contrasted with the 'old method' represented by Mill and his predecessors.[29]

The principal work in this movement was, of course, Henry Sidgwick's *The*

---

28. Ibid., p. 363 (Chapter XXV, §549). See also his remark in the *Supplement* added to the fourth edition (1864): 'That the existence and prevalence of Moral Rules promotes human happiness, we are quite ready and willing to assert. And even more than this;— that if there be any Rule which, by its prevalence, increases human happiness, rightly estimated, then this Rule is consistent with Morality, and is a part of Morality. But this is a very different thing from accepting a system which deduces *all* its Moral Rules from the Principle of increasing human happiness, because we do not think we *can* determine in all cases what does increase human happiness. The calculation is too vast, vague and complex'; *The Elements of Morality, Including Polity* (Cambridge, 1864, p. 582.

29. Francis Ysidro Edgeworth, *New and Old Methods of Ethics* (Oxford: James Parker, 1877).

Methods of Ethics (1874). A book of often infuriating judiciousness, its object was, as Sidgwick put it, 'to expound as clearly and as fully as my limits will allow, the different methods of Ethics that I find implicit in our common moral reasoning; to point out their mutual relations; and where they seem to conflict, to define the issue as much as possible'.[30] Sidgwick refused to declare any moral view correct; his plan was to clarify what was at stake in each major moral theory and to invite the adherents of each one to be clearer about what was implicit in their beliefs. Part of his unwillingness to declare himself was based on his keen sense that no moral theory had actually solved the problem of motivation, of giving us a reason to sacrifice our own interests to those of other people, something he wrote movingly about in the autobiographical fragment annexed posthumously to the sixth edition of the book.[31] So there could be on his part no thorough-going commitment to any existing theory, though among the competitors, he evinced a certain practical regard for utilitarianism, partly because (he believed) it actually corresponded rather well to our workaday moral ideas. There were, however, two issues which he recognised as providing substantial difficulties for utilitarianism as a sytematisation of common-sense morality. The first was an objection which had been raised in the previous decade by Whewell's successor in the Knightbridge chair, John Grote. In his posthumously published *An Examination of the Utilitarian Philosophy* (1870; Grote died in 1866, and the *Examination* had been written as a critique of Mill's *Utilitarianism*), Grote had singled out more or less for the first time, among other objections, the most profound criticism of utilitarianism.

> [T]he fact is, two pleasures cannot be tasted with a view to the comparison of them, as a chemist may taste two fluids: the utilitarian is led astray by his language, talking as he does about pleasures as if they were separate entities, independent of the mind of the enjoyer of them: the pleasures are always mixed with something from ourselves, which prevents us speaking, with any philosophically good result, of this sort of independent comparability among them. . .
> As a matter of fact we do not look upon pleasures as independent things

30. Henry Sidgwick, *The Methods of Ethics* (London: Macmillan, 1874), p. 13.

31. Indeed, he is reported to have remarked gloomily just after the appearance of the first edition (of which it is true) that 'the first word of my book is "*Ethics*", the last word is "failure"'; F. H. Hayward, *The Ethical Philosophy of Sidgwick* (London: Swan Sonnenschein, 1901), p. xix.

to be thus compared with each other, but as interwoven with the rest of life, as having their history and their reasons, as involving different kinds of enjoyment in such a manner that our being able to enter into one kind is accompanied with a horror of another kind, which would entirely prevent the comparison of the one with the other as pleasures. Besides this, it must be remembered that, in the interval between the one pleasure and the other, the mind is changed: you have no permanent touchstone, no currency to be the medium of comparison. Supposing a man whose youth has been grossly vicious, whose mature age is most deeply devout: according to disposition, the view as to past life in this case will probably much differ: but most commonly I think the man will wonder that he was ever able to find pleasure at all in what he once found pleasure in. Earnestness in the later frame of mind, whatever it is, would only preclude the possibility of a cool comparison of it, as to pleasure, with the earlier one. . .

We have, most of us, our own pleasures, and other people's pleasure often seem to us none at all. I cannot understand a happiness for everybody, after we have gone beyond our universal wants of meat, drink, and shelter, and till we arrive at a sphere where pleasure may be of a temper and nature which at present we cannot enter into.[32]

Sidgwick recognised the force of this point, agreeing that 'the represented pleasantness of different feelings fluctuates and varies indefinitely with changes in the actual condition of the representing mind (or minds in so far as we elect to be guided by others)', and concluding apropos of utilitarianism that

the assumption is involved that all pleasures are capable of being compared quantitatively with one another and with all pains . . . This assumption is involved in the very notion of Maximum Happiness: as the attempt to make 'as great as possible' a sum of elements not quantitatively commensurable would be a mathematical absurdity. Therefore whatever weight is to be attached to the objections brought against this assumption which was discussed in c.3 of Book II [from which the earlier sentence was taken] must of course tell against the present method.[33]

He left the point there—the object was to clarify the extent to which utilitarianism in this respect rested on an ungrounded assumption, rather than to

32. John Grote, *An Examination of the Utilitarian Philosophy,* ed. Joseph Bickersteth Mayor (Cambridge: Deighton, Bell, 1870), pp. 53–55.
33. Sidgwick, *The Methods of Ethics* (1874), pp. 129, 384.

call the assumption into question (something his successors, as we shall see, were much less cautious about).

The second difficulty which, he accepted, could not easily be solved by the utilitarians was the problem of rules and collaboration. The key passage is in *The Methods of Ethics*, Book IV, Chapter 5. Discussing exceptions to moral rules, Sidgwick remarked that among them there is one kind

> which Utilitarianism seems to admit: where the agent does not think it expedient that the rule on which he himself acts should be universally adopted, and yet maintains that his individual act is right, as producing a greater balance of pleasure over pain than any other conduct open to him would produce.
>
> And certainly we cannot argue that because a large aggregation of acts would cause more harm than good, therefore any single act of this kind will produce this effect. It may even be a straining of language to say that it has a tendency to produce it: no one (e.g.) would say that because an army walking over a bridge would break it down, therefore the crossing of a single traveller has a tendency to destroy it. And just as a prudent physician in giving rules of diet recommends an occasional deviation from them, as more conducive to the health of the body than absolute regularity: so there may be rules of social behaviour of which the general observance is necessary to the well-being of the community, while yet a certain amount of non-observance is rather advantageous than otherwise.

He had earlier acknowledged the force of a generalisation principle of a Kantian kind, 'that a right action must be one which the agent could desire to be done under all similar circumstances', though only as a corollary of any realist view of ethics, rather than as a principle which could determine the actual content of a moral theory. But he observed that there was no reason not to 'include among relevant "circumstances" the belief (supposing it to exist) that the action will not be widely imitated'; for example, celibacy might be endorsed precisely on the assumption that it was unlikely to be widespread. So breaking a rule in this fashion could be accommodated within the generalisation principle. It followed that

> there would be a discrepancy between Utilitarianism and Common-sense morality of a very curious kind: as it is the very firmness with which the latter is established which becomes the rational ground for relieving the individual of its obligations. A and B are supposed to see that the happiness of a community will be enhanced (just as the excellence of a metrical composi-

tion is) by a slight admixture of irregularity along with a general observance of rules: that is, by a little of what is commonly blamed as vice, along with a great deal of what is commonly recommended as virtue: and convinced that others will supply the virtue, A and B think themselves justified, on Utilitarian grounds, in supplying the vice.

It does not seem to me that this reasoning can be shewn to be necessarily unsound, and therefore it is important to call attention to this point, as constituting a real peculiarity of the Utilitarian method.[34]

Elsewhere he described this as one of the 'swarm of puzzles and paradoxes' which beset utilitarianism.[35]

The Methods of Ethics undoubtedly moved the interpretation of utilitarianism substantially in an act-utilitarian direction. For Whewell, the inability of utilitarianism properly to handle universal rules (that is, rules which ought to be universally followed) was an argument against adopting the philosophy; for Sidgwick, it was simply a feature of any consistent version of utilitarianism. It prised it away (he believed) from common sense, but that was not in itself a decisive objection, as Sidgwick rather admired the revisionary spirit of people like Bentham. It is easy to mistake the novelty of Sidgwick's analysis of utilitarianism, concealed as it was beneath his punctilious and reasonable manner, but F. Y. Edgeworth, reading the book in the mid-1870s while training for the law in London, immediately saw the significance of what Sidgwick had done. In 1877 he published *New and Old Methods of Ethics*, in which Sidgwick was hailed as the inventor of a new kind of utilitarianism, alongside Gustav Fechner, the German psychologist who had proclaimed the possibility of precise measurement of sensation in his *Elemente der Psychophysik* of 1860. Edgeworth labelled this new kind of utilitarianism 'exact': 'the doctrine of Fechner and Sidgwick may be termed exact utilitarianism, as distinguished from Hume's non-quantitative principle of utility, and the not very explicit greatest-happiness principle of Bentham and his followers, including J. S. Mill'.[36] Edgeworth had seen precisely what was at stake, applauding remarks such as the following in *The Methods of Ethics*—

---

34. Ibid., pp. 450–451. See also his discussion of lying, in Book III, Chapter 7, pp. 293–294.

35. Ibid., p. 453.

36. Edgeworth, *New and Old Methods of Ethics*, p. 35. For Edgeworth's ideas, see the introduction by Peter Newman to his edition of Edgeworth's works, *F. Y. Edgeworth's Mathematical Psychics and Further Papers on Political Economy* (Oxford: Oxford University Press, 2003).

that our practical Utilitarian reasonings must necessarily be rough, is no reason for not making them as accurate as the case admits: and we shall be more likely to succeed in this if we keep before our mind as distinctly as possible the strict type of the calculation that we should have to make, if all the relevant considerations could be estimated with mathematical precision.[37]

—and praising (though with one reservation)[38] Sidgwick's clear recognition (in the passage quoted earlier) that utilitarianism must involve a commitment to sum 'quantitatively commensurable' elements and that this commitment should not be dodged. From now on, writers on utilitarianism almost all supposed that according to the utilitarians, as T. H. Green put it, 'ultimate value lies in pleasures as such, not in the persons enjoying them. A pleasure of a certain intensity, enjoyed by three persons, is of no more value than a pleasure of threefold intensity enjoyed by one'.[39] Edgeworth spotted something else which was of great importance in Sidgwick: though Sidgwick did not himself propose a mathematical analysis of human conduct, either in his ethical writings or in his extensive and important writings on political economy (see Chapter Five), his philosophy was consistently treated by both Edgeworth and W. S. Jevons as friendly towards such an analysis.[40] Again, a contrast with Whewell is instructive: though Whewell was an excellent mathematician, he viewed the idea of mathematical precision in human affairs as unachievable, and indeed (as we have seen) used the impossibility of calculating utility as one of his prime arguments against the utilitarians. Writing on political economy in 1831, he observed prophetically that 'any attempt to make this subject at present a branch of Mathematics, could only lead to a neglect or perversion of facts, and to a course of trifling speculations, barren distinctions, and useless logomachies', and criticised

37. Sidgwick, *The Methods of Ethics*, p. 386.

38. This was on the issue of equality. Sidgwick supposed that Bentham's principle of equality was a reasonable part of utilitarianism (p. 387), whereas Edgeworth in both *New and Old Methods of Ethics* and *Mathematical Psychics* argued that exact utilitarianism would not necessarily issue in equal treatment (for the familiar modern anti-utilitarian reasons). See particularly *Mathematical Psychics* (London: C. K. Paul, 1881), pp. 124–125.

39. Green, *Prolegomena to Ethics* (Oxford: Oxford University Press, 1883), p. 378. This was written between 1877 and his death in 1882.

40. See Sidgwick's plea for greater clear-headedness among economists about the importance of quantitative reasoning, 'Economic Method', *Fortnightly Review,* February 1879, pp. 310–311.

the idea that one could approximate the complexities of economic life.[41] There is nothing of comparable hostility in Sidgwick.

However, it does not follow from Sidgwick's act utilitarianism that he believed that collaboration in large numbers was impossible for the utilitarian. Though the remark '[W]e cannot argue that because a large aggregation of acts would cause more harm than good, therefore any single act of this kind will produce this effect' sounds rather like Olson's or Harrison's point, and though it is striking that Sidgwick began to call into question the language of 'tendency', the way he developed his argument illustrates that what he had in mind was a situation where we can be very confident that there will be no (or very few) similar actions. In other words, he was considering a case like my lifeboat example, where I know that the other villagers will not turn up and I therefore have no (instrumental) reason for doing so myself. As we have repeatedly seen, the essence of Olson's problem is that *irrespective* of what other people do, I have no reason to take part in collaborative activity, and Sidgwick in this passage was not yet saying that. The substance of his idea was in fact closer to Lyons's than to that of a straightforward act utilitarian, something of which Lyons himself was well aware.[42] Like Lyons's rules, the rules which Sidgwick envisaged were potentially quite different from those which earlier utilitarians had conventionally supported, such as the familiar laws of private property. General adherence to the rules *up to a certain point* was what Sidgwick (like Lyons) had in mind; the utilitarians of the late nineteenth and early twentieth centuries accepted that utilitarianism could not justify the kind of universal rule-following which their predecessors had assumed, but they did not conclude that no collaborative practices were possible for utilitarians. Implicitly, Sidgwick accepted that there must be some sort of threshold at which taking part in the practice might become justifiable (or might cease to be justifiable, depending on the circumstances), and this was made explicit by some of his successors.

For example, C. D. Broad, a great admirer of Sidgwick, writing in 1916, made clear that this strand of utilitarianism would not entail the *exceptionless* following of rules. Attacking the 'false hypothesis' that we should ask our-

---

41. Whewell, 'Mathematical Exposition of some of the Leading Doctrines in Mr. Ricard's "Principles of Political Economy and Taxation"', *Transactions of the Cambridge Philosophical Society* 4 (1833): 197; see pp. 167–168 for remarks on approximation (the paper was read in 1831).

42. David Lyons, *Forms and Limits of Utilitarianism* (Oxford: Oxford University Press, 1965), p. 112.

selves in moral matters 'Suppose everybody did what you propose to do?', he argued that it was misplaced as an explanation of why we ought to co-operate in enterprises 'when the part contributed to the whole good by each member of the group is very small'.[43] Broad pointed out that 'it is quite true that A's abstention *would* have bad consequences if it took place together with the abstention of a great many other people. But it does not in the least follow that it *will* have any bad consequences if it takes place together with but few other abstentions'. It may easily be the case that defection from the co-operative enterprise could be justified in utilitarian terms:

> Let us suppose that a group G is cooperating to produce a certain result. Let us suppose that n people have joined the group and let us further suppose that, however great n may be, the joining of the group by an $n+1$th individ-ual entails certain sacrifices on him. It is probably reasonable to suppose (a) that the sacrifices made by each individual are lessened as the number of members increases but that the rate of decrease diminishes as n grows greater; (b) that the amount of good produced by the group (apart from the sacrifices) increases as n increases, but that after a certain point the rate of increase diminishes as n grows greater. If now we call $s(n)$ the total sacrifices made where there are n members and $g(n)$ the total good produced by their efforts (apart from the sacrifices) it is quite likely that a point will be reached where
>
> $$g(n + 1) - s(n + 1) < g(n) - s(n)$$
>
> When this point is reached it would seem to be the duty of people to re-fuse to join the group, and if they let themselves be guided by the mere fact that $g(0) = 0$ and decide to join, they will presumably decide wrongly.[44]

He used another example to make the same kind of point, in which he asked whether a utilitarian should worry about picking an ear of corn in a field on the grounds that if a million people picked ears of corn the crop would be devastated (an unknowing—I think—reprise of the original sorites). His an-swer was that

> it seems perfectly possible that no one's state of mind is in the least better or worse for the plucking of one ear and yet that it may be very much the

43. Broad, 'On the Function of False Hypotheses in Ethics', *International Journal of Ethics* (now *Ethics*) 26 (1916): 385.
    44. Ibid., pp 386–387.

worse for the plucking of a million. There is absolutely no logical reason against this and it seems to me to be true. The most probable account of the matter is that the plucking of a certain finite number n (varying of course with the circumstances) is absolutely indifferent, while the plucking of any greater number leads to consequences which get worse as the number gets greater. It is no objection to this view that we cannot state exactly what the number n is; for it is no objection to any theory that it does not presuppose omniscience in its supporters.[45]

And he later remarked that 'probably in most cases upper and lower limits could be given for it.'[46]

Broad was as clear as anyone before Lyons that utilitarianism can perfectly well justify co-operative behaviour on the assumption that there is a determinate threshold which the accumulation of collaborative acts will cross; he was also quite clear that this form of collaboration would fall short (potentially, well short) of universal compliance, and that that should perhaps not trouble anybody. The only justification for universal compliance he could suggest was a general and non-utilitarian principle of fairness (though even then he was cautious about whether the principle required *universal* compliance—why *ruat coelum*?).[47] (It should be stressed that Broad was analysing the logic of utilitarianism rather than endorsing it, though as with Sidgwick, an effective analysis might slide into an element of endorsement.) Disagreement with what we might term the Sidgwickian view centered not on the claim that some compliance was possible—nobody until the 1950s seems seriously to have doubted that—but on the claim that universal compliance was undesirable. G. E. Moore, for example, writing thirteen years before Broad, and attempting in general to refute Sidgwick, based his argument for universal respect for a rule on the idea that we should take into account our inability to calculate utilities correctly:

> [W]ith regard to any rule which is generally useful, we may assert that it ought always to be observed, not on the ground that in every particular case it will be useful, but on the ground that in any particular case the probability of its being so is greater than that of our being likely to decide rightly that we have before us an instance of its disutility.[48]

45. Ibid., pp 383–384.
46. Ibid. p. 387.
47. Ibid., p. 389.
48. Moore, *Principia Ethica* (Cambridge: Cambridge University Press, 1903), p. 162.

But this was a rather feeble argument and has not as it stands been especially persuasive, for there is no reason to suppose that the probabilities will work out in this way; in Austin's example of tax evasion, for example, there is every reason to suppose that the defaulter has made a correct calculation about the direct disutility of his action.

Another attempt at defending universality was made in 1936 by an Oxford economist, Roy Harrod, in the course of an article trying to uphold utilitarianism against its modern critics such as Moore. Harrod, interestingly, was a leading theorist of the doctrine of 'increasing returns'—the idea that costs diminished in large-scale organisations—and in this article tried to generalise the theory to social and political life.[49] Accordingly, he argued that

> [t]here are certain acts which when performed on n similar occasions have consequences more than n times as great as those resulting from one performance. And it is in this class of cases that obligations arise. It is in this class of cases that generalising the act yields a different balance of advantage from the sum of balances of advantage issuing from each individual act. For example, it may well happen that the loss of confidence due to a million lies uttered within certain limits of time and space is much more than a million times as great as the loss due to any one in particular. Consequently, even if on each and every occasion taken separately it can be shown that there is a gain of advantage (the avoidance of direct pain, let us say, exceeding the disadvantages due to the consequential lack of confidence), yet in the sum of all cases the disadvantage due to the aggregate loss of confidence might be far greater than the sum of pain caused by truth-telling.

He concluded from this that 'an act which is expedient in the circumstances but would be inexpedient when done by all in precisely relevant circumstances must be judged to be wrong by a more refined utilitarian system. Thus the Kantian principle is embodied in utilitarian philosophy'.[50] The prevalence of truth-telling was an instance of increasing returns—the more

49. See his remark that '[i]t is interesting to notice that the system of free competition does not allow for the application of the Kantian principle in the purely economic or katallactic field. And it is precisely the phenomena of "Increasing Returns"—analogous to those requiring the application of the Kantian principle in everyday conduct—which have given one of the strongest arguments in justification of the demand for "economic planning"'; R. F. Harrod, 'Utilitarianism Revised', *Mind* 45 (1936): 150.

50. Ibid., pp. 148, 149.

people who joined together to tell the truth, the better the consequences for all of them. Harrod made clear that he had in mind conscious and potentially innovative collaborative activity, rather than merely the following of existing social norms; even if many people in a society did not tell the truth, it was conceivable that a subgroup who practised truth-telling among themselves could reap collective benefits, and that this could offset the disbenefits created by widespread neglect of truth-telling (the parallel with the benefit of increasing returns for an individual sector is obvious). Adherence to the rule of the practice would still be universal, but it would be universal only among people who thought of themselves as having a common purpose. This should still be contrasted with Sidgwick's view, where the utilitarians who wanted an 'admixture of irregularity' saw themselves nevertheless as engaged in a common enterprise. But, of course, without further argument Harrod's general conclusion does not follow: if it is the case that individual producers remained small independent entities—in other words, if they did not form wholly integrated united economic agents—then (as opponents of a widespread use of the doctrine of increasing returns were to make clear)[51] each one's contribution might be regarded as having a negligible effect on the overall reduction of cost for the industry. So a single agent could free-ride on the cost-cutting forced by big cartels on, say, the suppliers to the industry. Similarly, one could argue that the difference between the loss of confidence if one million lies are spoken and the loss if one million minus one are spoken is likely to be infinitesimal, and that therefore the deleterious consequences of one lie must be infinitesimal. The question is not whether there is an n (all threshold theorists would suppose that there is), but whether any additional contribution above n makes a difference to the outcome. If it does not, then the correct conclusion is that utilitarians should simply settle as n, as Sidgwick had supposed; and it is very hard—as Lyons discovered—to show that contributions above n are necessary in the same sense as those below it.

In the 1950s some moral philosophers suggested a new reason why men motivated either by self-interest or by any kind of altruism might think it rational to follow general rules even in particular adverse cases. This was an argument (clearly influenced by the post-war teachings of Wittgenstein) according to which the question 'Why should I keep this promise?' was to be

51. See, for example, Edward H. Chamberlin, *The Theory of Monopolistic Competition,* 5th ed. (Cambridge, Mass.: Harvard University Press, 1946), pp. 85–88.

answered simply by saying that the *point* of the practice of promise-keeping is that everyone keeps his promise, and that therefore only the general rules or practices could be scrutinised or challenged in this manner. The first person to argue this seems to have been Stephen Toulmin, in *An Examination of the Place of Reason in Ethics* (1950—and therefore before the publication of Wittgenstein's *Philosophical Investigations* in 1953; but see p. 206 n. 1 for an apposite reference to Wittgenstein's current views, and p. xiii for a reference to Wittgenstein's lectures in Cambridge). Toulmin argued about the question 'Why ought you really to keep your promise to return a book to someone?' that

> I can answer, in succession, 'Because I ought to do whatever I promise him to do' . . . , 'Because I ought to do whatever I promise anyone to do' . . . , and 'Because anyone ought to do whatever he promises anyone else that he will do' or 'Because it was a promise' . . . Beyond this point, however, the question cannot arise: there is no more general 'reason' to be given beyond one which relates the action in question to an accepted social practice.[52]

A number of matters were left unclarified by Toulmin's avowed sketch, and the next few years saw the appearance of a number of articles which took rule utilitarianism further, and more out of Wittgenstein's shadow. The most important was, of course, John Rawls's famous 'Two Concepts of Rules' (1955), which grew out of a review of Toulmin's book in 1951.[53] Rawls insisted that one could not intelligibly talk about justifying a particular action within a practice such as promising because

> the point of the practice is to abdicate one's title to act in accordance with utilitarian and prudential considerations in order that the future may be tied down and plans coordinated in advance. There are obvious utilitarian advantages in having a practice which denies to the promiser, as a defense, any general appeal to the utilitarian principle in accordance with which the practice itself may be justified. There is nothing contradictory, or surprising, in this.[54]

52. Stephen Toulmin, *An Examination of the Place of Reason in Ethics* (Cambridge: Cambridge University Press, 1950), p. 146.

53. John Rawls, 'An Examination of the Place of Reason in Ethics', *Philosophical Review* 60 (1951): 572–580.

54. Rawls, 'Two Concepts of Rules', *Philosophical Review* 64 (1955): 16.

Later in the article he expanded on this:

> Practices are set up for various reasons, but one of them is that in many areas of conduct each person's deciding what to do on utilitarian grounds case by case leads to confusion, and that the attempt to co-ordinate behavior by trying to foresee how others will act is bound to fail . . . From this one sees that a practice necessarily involves the abdication of full liberty to act on utilitarian and prudential grounds.[55]

Rawls was well aware that one might read his argument (as, indeed, some did) as implying that a rule, defined in some simple way, must *always* be kept. He responded as follows.

> Is this to say that in particular cases one cannot deliberate whether or not to keep one's promise? Of course not. But to do so is to deliberate whether the various excuses, exceptions and defenses, which are understood by, and which constitute an important part of, the practice, apply to one's own case. Various defenses for not keeping one's promise are allowed, but among them there isn't the one that, on general utilitarian grounds, the promisor (truly) thought his action best on the whole, even though there may be the defense that the consequences of keeping one's promise would have been *extremely* severe . . . It would be said of someone who used this excuse without further explanation that he didn't understand what defenses the practice, which defines a promise, allows to him. If a child were to use this excuse one would correct him; for it is part of the way one is taught the concept of a promise to be corrected if one uses this excuse. The point of having the practice would be lost if the practice did allow this excuse.[56]

So Rawls's point was that in at least *some* circumstances, the self-binding character of the practice required that we do something which we know to be utilitarianly suboptimal, and that was sufficient to refute what he called 'extreme' utilitarianism (his own brand he termed 'restricted').

Rawls's argument turned on his claim that utilitarians could not co-ordinate their activities without (at least to some extent) renouncing individual utilitarian calculation, and if people were allowed to think for themselves, they would undermine their collective endeavour. This is clearly broadly similar

55. Ibid., p. 24.
56. Ibid., p. 17.

to Olson's idea, and different from the view of a Sidgwick or a Broad that in principle utilitarians could manage to hit some target of participation in a collaborative enterprise, such that enough people would take part to secure the relevant good. Indeed, J. J. C. Smart's response (as representative of the older utilitarianism) to the debate in the 1950s over rule utilitarianism was (as we have seen) to insist on precisely this.[57] Rawls at this stage, however, never spelt out just what the impossibility of co-ordination consisted of. He said in the passage quoted above that attempts by utilitarians to think for themselves would 'lead to confusion', but that is compatible with several different interpretations. The least interesting is that Rawls believed that utilitarian calculation was often inaccurate, and that allowing people to make decisions about how to act based on fine distinctions of utility would often produce suboptimal results. Clearly that is true, and the original utilitarians almost certainly believed something like it; but Rawls seems to have wanted to make a more far-reaching point—that even if we *know* that breaking a rule will lead to a better outcome and there can be no question of our having made a mistake, restricted utilitarianism will still prescribe that the rule be kept. It should be noted that knowing that the breach of the rule is utilitarianly superior to keeping it is not the same as knowing that a *major* disutility will be caused if we stick to the rule; it is possible in principle to know without question that a relatively minor disutility will occur, and that is the kind of case Rawls seems to have had in mind. Like most people, he accepted that rules must be broken in the interests of preventing enormous disutilities.

It is hard to see what Rawls may have based this stronger version of his claim on, other than something like a utilitarian version of Olson's argument. Only if we think that there is a fundamental problem about individual increments to a cumulative utilitarian enterprise will we be inclined to believe that even accurately calculating utilitarians' thinking about their own contributions will necessarily lead to the failure of collaboration. As it happens, just that view was being put forward at about the time Rawls was writing, in Jonathan Harrison's famous article of 1953, which we have already discussed. Rawls had apparently not read the article when he wrote 'Two Concepts of Rules', but the problem which Harrison diagnosed is very simi-

---

57. See my discussion of Smart's ideas in Chapter Two. His praise for Sidgwick's analysis of utilitarian rule-following is noteworthy: 'I think that this is the best book ever written on ethics, and that these chapters are the best chapters of the book'; J. C. C. Smart, 'Extreme and Restricted Utilitarianism', *Philosophical Quarterly* 6 (1956): 347.

lar to Rawls's, and when David Lyons in the early 1960s took on the task of refuting Harrison, he was aware that in doing so he was to some degree refuting Rawls—the chairman of his committee—also.[58]

As we saw, Harrison used two examples which became very familiar in the literature of the 1950s and 1960s.

> There are some actions which we think we have a duty to refrain from doing, even though they themselves produce no harmful consequences, because such actions would produce harmful consequences if the performance of them became the general rule. I think I have a duty to vote for that person whose party I think would govern the nation best, although I do not think that the addition of my vote to the total number of votes which are cast for him is going to make any difference to the result of the election, simply because I realise that, if all his other supporters were to do as I do, and fail to go to the polls, the man would not be elected. I refrain from walking on the grass of a well-kept lawn, not because I think that my walking on the grass is going to damage the lawn to such an extent as to detract from anybody's pleasure in contemplating it, but because I realise that, if everybody else who walked in the park were to do likewise, the grass in the park would be spoilt.[59]

Harrison was well aware that it was hard to justify such actions in terms of their long-term damage to practices, observing (about Hume's account of justice) that 'it is simply false that the performance of every just action is necessary if the good produced by the practice of justice is to be secured. If this were true, the human race would have perished miserably many years ago'.[60] One of Harrison's great merits was that he was more conscious of this key fact—that practices are not vulnerable to a specifiable amount of defection—than almost anyone else at the time. Indeed, he spotted that if one accepted Harrod's argument about the collective leverage acquired by individ-

58. See his remarks about 'Two Concepts of Rules' in *Forms and Limits of Utilitarianism,* pp. 182–194. Of course, by the time of Lyons's book (1965), Rawls had moved on from his earlier position towards something resembling his later famous theory; see Lyons's acknowledgement of this, pp. 195–196.

59. Jonathan Harrison, 'Utilitarianism, Universalization, and Our Duty to Be Just', *Proceedings of the Aristotelian Society* 53 (1952–1953): 107. See also A. K. Stout, 'Suppose Everybody Did the Same?', *Australasian Journal of Philosophy* 32 (1954): 16, and Smart, 'Extreme and Restricted Utilitarianism', p. 346.

60. Harrison, 'Utilitarianism, Universalization, and Our Duty to Be Just', p. 111.

ual acts, 'not every member of the class of actions in question must be performed if the others are to continue to have any value. I may omit to perform any one (or any two, or any three) of those actions which themselves produce no consequences, without detracting from the value of those which do'.[61]

Having stated the problem in this fashion, in his 1953 paper Harrison answered it simply by asserting (rather like Rawls was to do) that 'hence we must perform certain actions, which produce no good consequences, or even harmful consequences themselves, because, if everybody took the liberty of infringing the rule demanding their performance in the same circumstances, its utility would be lost.'[62] It was the gap represented by this 'hence' that Lyons jumped into ten years later, having noticed that, on the face of it, the conclusion does not follow. As it happens, Harrison returned to the subject twenty-five years after his original article and tried to make his reasoning clearer, recognising that it had been widely misunderstood; and in this paper he introduced an explicit use of the sorites. He argued that he should be thought of not as a rule utilitarian but as what he now called a 'cumulative-effect' utilitarian:

> I call it cumulative-effect utilitarianism because it presupposes that the repetition of similar actions often has a cumulative effect. Doing something once may do no harm and may even do good, but repeating the same thing over and over again may eventually become very harmful. One straw does no harm to a camel, but enough straws break its back. I do no harm by not paying my income tax, but if no-one paid, modern government would be impossible.[63]

One might suppose from the analogy with a straw breaking the camel's back that Harrison was a threshold theorist all along, and that Lyons's critique missed its mark; but Harrison denied this, saying that the 'attempt to reduce cumulative-effect utilitarianism to act utilitarianism . . . is a manifestation of a fallacy which I shall call the "last straw fallacy".

> It is . . . quite untrue that anyone's putting one single straw on the camel's back ever does the camel any harm. Even if I put a straw on the camel's back

61. Ibid., p. 121.

62. Ibid.

63. Jonathan Harrison, 'Rule Utilitarianism and Cumulative-Effect Utilitariansm', *Canadian Journal of Philosophy* 5, Supp. (1978): 28.

the fraction of an instant before its back breaks it cannot be that it was my straw that broke it. The camel's back is never sensitive to individual straws, and is just as little sensitive to them when there is nothing on its back, as when it is carrying as much as it can, or as when its back is actually breaking. Those who suppose that there must be such straws simply do not grasp the fact that the effects of a number of repetitions of an action, which individually do no harm, can do harm. They instinctively, but illogically, feel that if the repetitions collectively do harm, this must be accounted for as the sum of the harm by the individual actions which are repeated. This, however, is simply not so; nor is there any breach to the laws of mathematics or of logic in saying that it is not so. There is a threshold such that stimuli of certain degrees of magnitude which fall below it produce no effect. Putting a straw on a camel's back is an instance. Nothing below this threshold has any appreciable effect, but this, of course, does not mean that *repetitions* of occurrences below this degree of magnitude should not have a very appreciable effect, if not a disastrous one, as in the case of the camel.[64]

Accordingly,

no individual action by itself ever does any harm [in these cases], whether it is the only one of its kind which is performed, or whether everybody or almost everybody performs actions of a similar kind. The effects of my action (and, of course, theirs) on the harm done all of them collectively is always nil, whether others do what I do or whether they do not.[65]

The example of a camel is not a happy one, as the whole point of the proverb is that in that instance there was a clear threshold, but Harrison was plainly trying to express the reasoning of the sorites. Having done so, he restated his original claim more clearly: because no distinction can be drawn in a practice (such as paying taxes) between actions which have an effect and those which do not (since no actions have an effect), there can be no describable subset of actions which are permitted while the rest are forbidden. In these cases one has to prescribe all actions or none, and one must therefore usually prescribe all. This is not so far removed from Lyons's argument that in situations like voting one has to treat what one might call 'pre-' and 'post-' threshold cases the same because one cannot distinguish between them; the difference is that the difficulty in genuine threshold cases is

64. Ibid., pp 32–33.
65. Ibid., pp 33–34.

the practical difficulty of distinguishing among similar actions, whereas in sorites-like cases it is a more fundamental difficulty—there may really *be* no difference between the actions, as it may be that *none* contributes to the crossing of a threshold. But this in fact makes an important theoretical difference from Lyons's position, as on Lyons's account there actually are a number of actions which have genuine causal power over the result, but we cannot practically determine which, whereas on Harrison's account no action has causal power. As a result, Harrison's view seems to break the link between consequences and what it is right for us to do: we *know* that what we are doing cannot have an effect, and yet we are still required to do it. In his 1978 article Harrison acknowledged this:

> It is true that it [cumulative-effect utilitarianism] cannot go on to say why one ought to perform an action which is such that the effects of everybody's performing it would be good. But then, ordinary act utilitarianism, if it were a fact, would be an ultimate fact beyond which act utilitarianism could not go.[66]

This also seems to have been his view in 1953, though he nowhere made it as explicit then as he did later. And it was, of course, this aspect of his theory which Lyons was most at pains to combat. It may, incidentally, be very significant that in his critique of Harrison, Lyons reintroduced and freely used the expression 'the tendency of an action', something Harrison had barely (if at all) used.[67] As we saw, the language of 'tendency' was always used by earlier utilitarians to signify that they were talking about the loose causal relationship between a negligible contribution and the overall outcome, and Lyons seems instinctively to have resurrected it to have the same meaning.[68]

66. Ibid., p. 30.
67. See Lyons, *Forms and Limits of Utilitarianism,* for example p. 53 ff.
68. A view rather similar to Harrison's 1978 position was also hinted at by Peter Singer in a 1972 article in the *Philosophical Review,* in which he remarked that

> [a]lthough some act-utilitarian writers may have assumed that only consequences for which the act is a necessary or sufficient condition should be taken into account, there is no good reason for an act-utilitarian to do so. An act may contribute to a result without being either a necessary or sufficient condition of it, and if it does contribute, the act-utilitarian should take this contribution into account. The contribution that my vote makes toward the result I judge to be best in an election is a relevant consideration in deciding whether to vote, although it is, almost certainly, neither a necessary nor a sufficient condition of that result; for if this were not so, the

Though Harrison did not make his use of a soritic argument at all clear in 1953, it is reasonable to accept his claim in 1978 that this was in effect what he had believed all along. It certainly explains his unusual use of the examples of voting and walking on the grass, and would align him very neatly with the move towards using this kind of reasoning in political science represented at almost the same moment by Downs's work. But as we have seen from looking at the whole story of the way in which utilitarians thought about collaborative action, Harrison's view was *original:* utilitarians had not in general supposed that there could be *no* threshold, and that individual actions could have literally *no* effect on an outcome. To them (brought up on the classics as they all were) this would have seemed unacceptably paradoxical, and no serious basis for a political theory. It also helps to explain why Olson thought that he was applying in a wider arena of politics an idea which had hitherto been largely the preserve of the economists: it was indeed the case that philosophers and political theorists had *not* thought in this way until very recently. In the next chapter I shall accordingly turn to the story of how the idea developed among economists; there too we shall see that it was a disconcertingly modern way of looking at social activity, and that economists themselves had thought in this way for only a few decades before Olson wrote.

---

act-utilitarian view would leave us with a result which was unconnected with the actions of any of the voters, since what is true of my vote is equally true of every individual vote. ('Is Act-Utilitarianism Self-Defeating?', *Philosophical Review* 81 (1972): 103)

It is hard to see how something can have consequences without being either a necessary or a sufficient condition for the outcome, but both Harrison and Singer seem to have wanted to solve the problem in this way.

CHAPTER FIVE

Perfect Competition,
Oligopoly and Monopoly

As we have seen, the essence of Olson's approach to politics was the transfer to a wider sphere of the ideas about competition which were taken for granted among economists in the middle of the twentieth century. In particular (to recapitulate), he relied on the distinction between monopoly, oligopoly and perfect competition. In a monopoly, one producer controls the whole supply of a commodity, and (if he is operating against a background of competitive *purchasing*, an assumption which will in general be made in what follows) can set production levels (or prices) in such a way as to maximise his profits. (If a monopolist is faced by a monopsonist, the result is dictated by the general theory of bilateral bargaining.) In an oligopoly, a few (paradigmatically two, 'duopolistic') producers lack total control, but are big enough to be able to affect the market price by their price and production decisions. (Again, competitive purchasing is assumed.) In perfect competition, the producers are so small relative to the overall size of the market in their product that they can make no difference to the price whatever they choose to do about their levels of production; in the modern terminology, they are 'price-takers'. Under oligipoly, strategic interaction is possible, and Olson was accordingly not interested in it as a model for his problem; free riding makes sense only on the assumption of perfectly competitive behaviour.

This structure played an enormous part in twentieth-century economics, but as the more historically informed economists themselves were aware, it is extremely hard to find it before the twentieth century.[1] *Competition*, of

1. See above all George Stigler, 'Perfect Competition, Historically Contemplated', *Journal of Political Economy* 65 (1957): 1: 'Only slowly did the elaborate and complex concept of perfect competition evolve, and it was not until after the first World War that it was finally received into general theoretical literature.'

course, played a crucial role in political economy from its beginning, but competition does not mean specifically *perfect* competition; as we shall see, for most pre-twentieth-century writers, there was no significant difference between what would later be termed oligopoly and perfect competition. The theoretical difficulty that had to be overcome was precisely what we have been studying in this book so far: is it reasonable to suppose that because one's contribution to a collaborative enterprise is very small relative to the whole, one should therefore discount its effect on the outcome? If one thought that it was not reasonable, then one would presume that rational producers would think of themselves as (in this context) maintaining a collaborative enterprise against the consumers, and perfect competition among rational agents would not be distinguishable from oligopoly and even from monopoly (with some qualifications, which we will touch on as we proceed).

Given the philosophical background of early utilitarianism as I have depicted it, in which the difficulties of voluntary collaboration were acknowledged, but in which the number of people concerned was not especially salient to the argument, it should first of all come as no surprise that the political economists who belonged to this tradition failed to make anything like the modern distinction between perfect competition and oligopoly or monopoly. As we saw in the previous chapter, Hume, Bentham and Mill all supposed that in principle collaboration makes sense, but they also acknowledged that human nature is such that people often do not recognise their real interests (though it would not follow that they should be made to do so—that was for all of them a quite separate question, as is shown by Mill's caution in the passages quoted in Chapter Four). As a result, political economists who started from these premises would not have a very systematic account of competition: they understood the appeal of cartels and combinations, but they also understood their difficulties, and were happy to exploit those difficulties if a wider social good was the result of doing so. Adam Smith, for example, Hume's most faithful follower, when he wrote about competition did not suppose that merchants who combined in order to push up prices were acting irrationally, at least in any straightforward sense of the term. One of his most famous passages, after all, assumes just this:

> People of the same trade seldom meet together, even for merriment and diversion, but the conversation ends in a conspiracy against the public, or in some contrivance to raise prices. It is impossible indeed to prevent such

meetings, by any law which either could be executed, or would be consistent with liberty and justice.

The best the law can do is not 'to facilitate such assemblies; much less to render them necessary'.[2]

But he also assumed that informal collaboration was potentially quite fragile in practice, even declaring at one point that 'in a free trade an effectual combination cannot be established but by the unanimous consent of every single member of it, and it cannot last longer than every single member of it continues of the same mind'.[3] He had in mind the trading practices of the artisans of a small town, where a decision by one tradesman to cut his prices in order to take a high proportion of the available sales might lead to a cascade of price-cutting and the end of the cartel. Such behaviour by one of the artisans need not be strictly rational, but given that irrational or imprudent conduct—in particular, as Hume would have said, preferring short-term to long-term gain—is not uncommon, the abolition of legal constraints on free trade would make it more likely. These are (it should be said) somewhat unusual circumstances—as later economists often pointed out, there were a number of reasons why one defection might not lead to comprehensive price-cutting, notably the fact that one producer might not be able to satisfy as much of the local demand as would be needed to force the other producers to lower their prices to his level. (In other words, he might sell out all his stock very quickly, and then purchasers would need to pay high prices to the loyal members of the cartel if they were to acquire the product.)

In general, however, the classical theorists pinned their hopes not on the breakdown of an existing combination but on free entry into any trade and the free movement of capital between different producers. As long as it was possible for anyone to join a particular industry or profession and market his product at a lower price than that of the existing tradesmen, they consistently asserted, cartels would not be able to maintain high prices; and as long as capital could move freely, capitalists would constantly and restlessly shift their resources into any industry that was currently offering high profits, make as much money as they could until the profits fell as a result of expan-

---

2. Smith, *An Inquiry into the Nature and Causes of the Wealth of Nations*, ed. R. H. Campbell, A. S, Skinner and W. B. Todd (Glasgow edition) (Indianapolis: Liberty Fund, 1981), I.x.ii.27.

3. Ibid., I.x.ii.30.

sion, and then move on. Capital movement (on their view) acted as the equilibrating force in the economy, in the long term bringing all rates of profit down to a single rate which constituted (with the costs of production) the 'natural' price for each commodity.[4] The advantage of this view was precisely that it did not require them to have any great confidence in the tendency of cartels to fall apart spontaneously through defections, though its disadvantage was, of course, that it led them to be less interested than later economists in the many informal means (including strategic price-cutting followed by price rises) which monopolists or oligopolists can use to keep new entrants out of their industry.

The number of producers, on their view, was relevant to competitive behaviour in a couple of ways, but neither of them led to the modern theory of perfect competition. Both, as we have seen, were familiar considerations in Hume and Bentham. First, the more producers there were, the more likely it was that one of them would act imprudently and defect from an informal cartel—and given that these theorists believed that one defection was often enough to weaken the cartel radically, the larger the industry, the less easy it would be to maintain a combination. Second, and much more importantly, they believed that some degree of communication was necessary between the members of a collusive cartel, and that communication of the requisite kind became more difficult as the number of the producers grew and as they become more geographically dispersed. This applied particularly to agriculture. As Smith said,

> Were it possible, indeed, for one great company of merchants to possess themselves of the whole crop of an extensive country, it might, perhaps, be their interest to deal with it, as the Dutch are said to do with the spiceries of the Moluccas, to destroy or throw away a considerable part of it in order to keep up the price of the rest. But it is scarce possible, even by the violence of law, to establish such an extensive monopoly with regard to corn; and, wherever the law leaves the trade free, it is of all commodities the least liable to be engrossed or monopolised by the force of a few large capitals, which buy up the greater part of it.[5]

4. This point is put extremely clearly by the Benthamites James Mill in his *Elements of Political Economy* (London: Routledge/Thoemmes, 1992), pp. 92–93, and J. R. McCulloch in his *Principles of Political Economy* (London: Routledge/Thoemmes, 1995), pp. 328, 334–335.
    5. Smith, *Wealth of Nations*, IV.v.b.4.

When corn first comes from the ground,

> it is necessarily divided among a greater number of owners than any other
> commodity; and these owners can never be collected into one place like a
> number of independent manufacturers, but are necessarily scattered through
> all the different corners of the country. These first owners either immedi-
> ately supply the consumers in their own neighbourhood, or they supply
> other inland dealers who supply those consumers. The inland dealers in
> corn, therefore, including both the farmer and the baker, are necessarily
> more numerous than the dealers in any other commodity, and their dis-
> persed situation renders it altogether impossible for them to enter into any
> general combination.[6]

It must be stressed once again that it was the farmers' inability to communicate readily with one another, rather than the simple fact that there were
large numbers of them, which was picked out by Smith as the principal reason for their failure to form combinations. If they could have co-ordinated
their production decisions effectively (his argument implies), their sheer
numbers would not *in themselves* have led to non-co-operation (though they
might have made an individual defection more likely). This should, among
other things, always give pause to anyone who thinks that an argument
based so avowedly on the way of life in the rural areas of *ancien régime* Europe is readily applicable to the conditions of a modern developed economy,
which has speedier communications around the entire world than a farmer
in eighteenth-century England had with his neighbour.[7]

These writers said the same about trades unions, when modern unions
appeared in England in the 1820s. Though common law may always have

6. Ibid.

7. One exception to this claim, that classical political economists had no theory about
the fundamental relevance of numbers to competition among producers, has been proposed by Reghinos Theocharis in his *Early Developments in Mathematical Economics,* 2d ed.
(London: Macmillan, 1983), pp. 153–155. It is the Milanese contemporary of Smith, Pietro
Verri, whose *Meditazioni sulla economica politica* (1771) and essay on the grain trade both
contain a claim that prices will fall as the number of producers increases. But this is simply
an aspect of Verri's rather fanciful theory that price is determined simply by the ratio of
sellers to buyers, a theory which was widely criticised for its obvious failings, for example
by Condorcet; see Verri, *1771 Reflections on Political Economy,* trans. Barbara McGilvray,
ed. Peter Groenewegen (Sydney: University of Sydney Department of Economics, 1986),
p. xxix). Otherwise Verri agreed with Smith and the physiocrats that open entry would
succeed in breaking up cartels.

made combinations of workers or manufacturers illegal, their illegality was enshrined most clearly in the Combination Acts of 1799 and 1800. Benthamite radicals consistently attacked the acts, Bentham himself observing that '[o]ppression [is] well exemplified by anti-combination and anti-emigration laws. Anti-combination acts prevent men from earning subsistence at home; anti-emigration acts from earning it abroad: both join in driving men into the poor-house and suborning suicide'.[8] The acts were repealed in 1825–1826, largely through the efforts of Bentham's protégé Francis Place, though some penalties on workers' combinations remained (the famous Tolpuddle Martyrs, for example, were prosecuted not for combining, but for administering an oath—that is, enforcing the combination upon its members). As we have seen, even Smith was unwilling to make associations of producers actually illegal, though he was very sure that they should not be facilitated by government action, and the Benthamite political economists consistently supported the principle of voluntary combinations for labourers. J. R. McCulloch was particularly interested in this issue, and in an *Encyclopaedia Britannica* article on *Combination* (written in his old age for the eighth edition, 1853) he argued that

> workmen are not allowed freely to dispose of their labour, if they be prevented from concerting with each other the terms on which they will sell it. Capacity to labour is to the poor what stock is to the capitalists. Now a hundred or a thousand capitalists may form themselves into a company, or combination, take all their measures in common, and dispose of their property as they may, in their collective capacity, judge most advantageous for their interests:— And why should not a hundred or a thousand labourers be allowed to do the same by their stock?[9]

But McCulloch was also confident that trades unions could not actually benefit their members by securing higher wages, as he believed that any rise in wages would reduce the competitiveness of the industry in the search for markets and capital, and end by relatively impoverishing the workers (a version of the so-called wages-fund argument which governed British discussion of trades unions in the mid-nineteenth century). He also believed

8. Jeremy Bentham, *Economic Writings*, ed. W. Stark (London: Allen & Unwin, 1954), III, p. 52.

9. J. R. McCulloch, *Syllabus of a Course of Lectures on Political Economy; Articles from the Encyclopaedia Britannica [etc]*, ed. D. P. O'Brien (London: Routledge/Thoemmes, 1995), p. 162.

that as a matter of fact free associations of labourers would not be particularly cohesive, though if they were, they might obstruct free entry to their trade, to the detriment of 'the manufacturing and commercial prosperity of the country' and (ultimately) of their own interests. In remarks which resembled those of Mill, he observed that

> the reason that combinations among numerous bodies are rarely injurious is, that the motives which individuals have to break off from the combination are so numerous and powerful, that it can seldom be maintained for any considerable period. But if those who adhere to combinations were to be allowed to maltreat and obstruct those who secede from them, this principle would be subverted, and combinations might become so very injurious as to require the interference of the legislature for their suppression.[10]

So McCulloch essentially restated the Smithian or Humean view in this new context: collaboration often made sense, but people frequently had 'powerful' motives for breaking away from the co-operative enterprise. In the case of trades unions, there was in actuality no long-term benefit to the members from keeping wages high, so the question of the rationality of the seceding workman did not arise (unlike in Mill's remarks five years earlier); but McCulloch, like Hume and Smith, and indeed Mill, preserved an open mind on the question of whether long-term benefits of collaboration provided in themselves a good reason for the members to co-operate.

As a new way of thinking about economics developed in the late nineteenth century, some of this attitude to competition changed; but the modern theory on which Olson and Buchanan drew was still not straightforwardly a product of this new 'neo-classical' or 'marginalist' economics. Indeed, some of the most interesting neo-classicists were very resistant to the idea which is at the heart of the modern theory, that defection from large-scale enterprises is rational. What the new style of economics did provide was a sharper distinction between behaviour in small and in large groups, and in the process nineteenth- and early twentieth-century economists explored most of the issues which were later to be discussed by game theorists under the heading of the prisoners' dilemma. But they still left undiscussed the question of whether defection from a large group is rational in a way that defection from a small group is not.

The new style of economics, with its greater emphasis on mathematical

10. Ibid., p. 166.

modelling, began in France, and was indeed viewed with some suspicion by contemporary English political economists (many of whom, as it happens, were excellent mathematicians). Although there were some forerunners (notably the revolutionary activist Nicholas-François Canard, whose political loyalties no doubt led to his work's falling into disfavour at the restoration), it is generally agreed that the first significant example of mathematical economics was Augustin Cournot's *Recherches sur les principes mathématiques de la théorie des richesses* (Paris, 1838).[11] Cournot's principal object in his little book was to show how many important issues in economics could best be handled using the apparatus of classical calculus. To do so, he needed to show first that the relationship between the quantity of an article produced and its price was a *continuous function,* comparable to the continuous function which in dynamics linked, say, the altitude of a projectile and its velocity. So familiar has this notion become subsequently, and so enshrined in such a commonplace apparatus as the graphical depiction of supply and demand curves, that its theoretical difficulty has been forgotten. And yet there was a perfectly good reason why earlier writers (many of them entirely familiar with the calculus, which, after all, was a basic part of higher education in eighteenth-century Europe) had not looked to continuous functions as a good representation of economic relationships. Projectiles do actually follow a continuous path—there is an infinity of distinguishable points in any line connecting two points. Expressing what happens during their flight in terms of a continuously varying function is therefore an obvious thing to do, once the technical difficulties in the way of such a mathematics had been solved by Newton and his successors. But human tastes are not like that; nor are the other entities with which economists usually deal, such as a currency.

Cournot was fully aware of this, and answered it as follows. Speaking of a function $F(p)$ which expresses the relationship between the demand for an article and its price, he remarked that we must assume it to be

a *continuous function, i.e.* a function which does not pass suddenly from one value to another, but which takes in passing all intermediate values. It might be otherwise if the number of consumers were very limited: thus in a certain household the same quantity of firewood will possibly be used whether wood costs 10 francs or 15 francs the stere [that is, the cubic

11. Available in English as *Researches into the Mathematical Principles of the Theory of Wealth,* trans. Nathaniel T. Bacon (New York: Macmillan, 1897), reprinted with notes by Irving Fisher (New York: Macmillan, 1927).

metre], and the consumption may suddenly be diminished if the price of the stere rises above the latter figure. But the wider the market extends, and the more the combinations of needs, of fortunes, or even of caprices, are varied among consumers, the closer the function $F(p)$ will come to varying with p in a continuous manner. However little may be the variation of p, there will be some consumers so placed that the slight rise or fall of the article will affect their consumptions, and will lead them to deprive themselves in some way or to reduce their manufacturing output, or to substitute something else for the article that has grown dearer.[12]

So Cournot (unlike many of his modern successors) believed that his continuous functions had to be seen as the representation of the behaviour of large groups, in which any one person's conduct made a (literally) infinitesimal difference to the overall outcome. Even if a single individual were ascribed a demand or supply function, for this ascription to make sense he had to be seen as a kind of idealised representative of the whole aggregate of possible consumers or producers.

But many of Cournot's contemporaries had substantial doubts about the appropriateness of this model, particularly (as I said) in England. A good example would be William Whewell, whose scepticism about mathematical economics I touched on in Chapter Four. Writing in 1831, he was highly sceptical about the possibility of talking about an equilibrium between supply and demand, even as a 'first approximation' to 'the true state of things'. He used as an analogy the difference between the physics of tides and that of waves (both problems he was independently interested in). It might be reasonable to do as Newton did, and treat the complex motions of the tides in a simplified form as a problem of equilibrium, but

> [i]n order however that solutions of this nature may have any value, it is requisite that the principles, of which we estimate the operation, should include *all* the *predominant* causes which really influence the result. We necessarily reject some of the circumstances and tendencies which really exist: but we can do this with propriety, only when the effects of these latter agents are, from their small amount or short duration, inconsiderable modifications only of the general results. The quantities which we neglect must be of an inferior *order* to those which we take into account; otherwise we obtain no approximation at all. We may with some utility make the theory

12. Ibid., pp. 49–50.

of *tides* a question of equilibrium, but our labour would be utterly misspent if we should attempt to consider on such principles the theory of *waves*.

It appears to be by no means clear that the irregular fluctuations and transitory currents by which the elements of wealth seek their natural level may be neglected in the investigation of the primary laws of their distribution. It is not difficult to conceive that the inequalities and transfers produced by the temporary and incomplete action of the equalizing causes, may be of equal magnitude and consequence with those ultimate and complete changes by which the general tendency of such causes is manifested. A panic may produce results as wide and as important as a general fall of profits.[13]

And he concluded this paper with the observation from which I quoted in Chapter Four, that

the pretensions of Political Economy to such a scientific character, are as yet entirely incapable of being supported. Any attempt to make this subject at present a branch of Mathematics, could only lead to a neglect or perversion of facts, and to a course of trifling speculations, barren distinctions, and useless logomachies . . . The most profitable and philosophical speculations of Political Economy are however of a different kind: they are those which are employed not in reasoning *from* principles, but *to* them: in extracting from a wide and patient survey of facts the laws according to which circumstances and conditions determine the progress of wealth, and the fortunes of men.[14]

This plea for induction was characteristic of Whewell, whose greatest works were on the history and philosophy of the inductive sciences, and who enjoyed a long friendship with the leading 'inductive' and historical political economist, Richard Jones.[15]

Another reason that it was a Frenchman who pioneered the mathematical representation of competitive behaviour may have been that the legal background to competition and combination took a very different form in France from that which was to be found in England, at least from the 1820s. Revo-

13. William Whewell, 'Mathematical Exposition of some of the Leading Doctrines in Mr. Ricard's "Principles of Political Economy and Taxation"', *Transactions of the Cambridge Philosophical Society* 4 (1833): 167–168.

14. Ibid., p. 197.

15. See Menachem Fisch, *William Whewell, Philosopher of Science* (New York: Oxford University Press, 1991).

lutionary France had not merely destroyed the *ancien régime* corporations, but had also outlawed all partial associations (to use the Rousseauian term), including trades unions. The famous Le Chapelier law of 14 June 1791 proclaimed that

> [i]t must not be permitted to citizens of certain professions to assemble for their supposed common interests. There are no longer corporations in the State; there is no longer anything but the particular interest of each individual, and the general interest. It is permitted to no one to inspire an intermediary interest in citizens, to separate them from the public interest [*chosen*] by a spirit of corporation. . .
>
> If, against the principles of liberty and the constitution, citizens attached to the same professions, arts and trades, should make deliberations, should make agreements among themselves tending to refuse in concert, or to accord only at a determined price the aid of their industry or their labours, the said deliberations and agreements . . . are declared unconstitutional and an assault against liberty and against the declaration of the rights of man, and of null effect.[16]

The restoration left these principles on the statute book, and they remained enshrined within French law for another seventy years; not until 1864, after a plebiscite called by Napoleon III, was any form of combination legal in France. Consequently the French of the early and mid-nineteenth century (like, as we shall see, the Americans of the early twentieth century, after the passage of the Sherman Act) could simply assume a legal background in which organised and overt co-operative activity in the economy was impossible. This obviously simplified analysis of competitive behaviour, though at the cost of losing the realism and complexity of what had hitherto been the classical theory.

With these two simplifying assumptions in place—that we can have continuous functions representing choices between goods, and that collaboration is not an option—Cournot was able to develop his mathematical model of competition. It took the form of an analysis of the appropriate strategies available to producers (he imagines proprietors of identical springs of mineral water) on the assumption that they all faced a particular demand curve for their product (that is, that there was a given amount which the market as

16. William H. Sewell, Jr., *Work and Revolution in France* (Cambridge: Cambridge University Press, 1980), pp. 88–89.

a whole would purchase at any given price). It was usual to suppose that in this situation a monopolist would adjust the amount he put on the market in order to raise the price and give himself maximum profits; the most vivid example of this, for late seventeenth-, eighteenth- and nineteenth-century writers, was the practice of the Dutch in destroying some of the spice crop of the East Indies in order to maintain high prices for spices in Europe.[17] This was a particularly graphic illustration both of the strategy used by monopolists to manipulate prices and of the fact that monopolised production was supposedly inefficient—a world in which a useful commodity was destroyed could not on the face of it be better for anyone at all than an alternative in which the spices were preserved and distributed in some fashion which would leave the East India Company at least as well off as it was under its destructive policy, but which would add to the commodities available to everyone.

Cournot argued that the right way to think about two or more producers competing with one another was to attribute the monopolist's strategy to each of them: that is, each one would adjust his supply to produce the greatest profit for himself, given the amount being put on the market by his rivals and the resulting price for the commodity in the general market. The oddity of Cournot's theory, it should be noted, was that he stipulated that there was only one price for mineral water at any one time in the market, even when there was a small number of producers, and thereby he ruled out the traditional supposition that a competitive producer would undercut his rivals' prices and seize most of the market for himself. His motive for making this assumption was largely its greater analytical simplicity: he was able to view the price structure for oligopoly as identical to the price structures under both monopoly (for a monopoly has only one price for the product, determined by the amount the monopolist wishes to sell) and perfect competition, in which the nature of the market ensures that there is only one price at any one time. This in turn allowed him (as we shall see) to treat the transitions from what we would call monopoly to oligopoly and from oligopoly to perfect competition as gradual and continuous. It also simplified his exposition, as he was able to disregard the complexities introduced into the account by consumers choosing between the different prices on offer from dif-

17. See, for example, Samuel Pufendorf, *De Iure Naturae et Gentium,* trans. as *The Law of Nature and Nations* by J. Barbeyrac (London, 1749), V.I.6, p. 462; Smith, *Wealth of Nations,* I.xi.b.33, IV.v.b.4 and IV.vii.c.101 (Glasgow ed., pp. 175, 525 and 636); Mill, *Principles of Political Economy* III.ii.5 (Toronto ed., II, p. 468).

ferent producers. In a sense, his model was strictly a game played among the producers, rather than one among the producers and the consumers, as a model with differential prices would have been.[18]

Having discussed monopoly, Cournot posed the question of what was later called duopoly, with competition between two independent producers. Independence here means that there was no formal agreement between the producers of the kind banned by the Le Chapelier law, and that neither had any 'direct' influence over the other's production strategy—'all [Proprietor 1] can do, when [the output of Spring 2] has been determined by Proprietor 2, is to choose for [the output of Spring 1] the value which is best for him'.[19] This point needs a certain amount of discussion, as it has often led to some confusion in the discussion of these matters; non-collusion can be understood in a variety of different ways. What Cournot envisaged was that there would be, so to speak, a series of rounds in the competitive game played between the two proprietors. In each round one producer would respond to the level of production set by his opponent, or rather to the price set in the market for the water as a result of his opponent's production decision, *as if there were going to be no more play after his own level had been set;* that is, each producer would simply do the best he could in the circumstances created by his opponent's last move. He would not consider the indirect or long-term implications of his decision. His decision then constituted the new environment for the other player in the next round, and so on. At some point there would be no need for any new response by either producer, and that would be the 'equilibrium'. It is important to stress what is seldom recognised, that Cournot's argument was *hypothetical:* he was merely postulating that competitors would not think at all about the indirect or long-term consequences of their actions, and he explicitly recognised that they might well act irrationally or imprudently by not doing so. Not until it came to be believed that imprudent action of this kind in fact made sense was Cournot's argument taken to be an account of *rational* conduct.

Chamberlin later produced a useful simplified version of Cournot's argument using the diagram in Figure 5.1. In it, OY represents the price of the water and OX the quantity put on the market. The demand curve for the water is DB. What on an ordinary diagram of supply and demand curves

18. This is a point made by Andrew Daughety in his introduction to the essays on Cournot oligopoly which he edited, *Cournot Oligopoly: Characterization and Applications* (Cambridge: Cambridge University Press, 1988), pp. 18–25.

19. Cournot, *Researches into the Mathematical Principles*, p. 80.

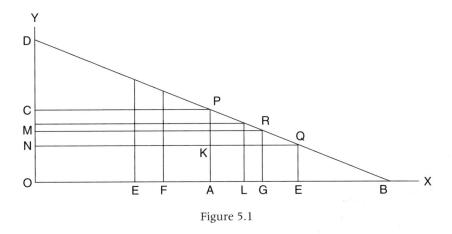

Figure 5.1

would be the supply curve is here represented by OB—that is, for the sake of clarity we presume that there are no expenses of production. The optimum production level is OA (= AB): at that point the total profits of the industry are maximised (the rectangle OAPC is the largest in area which can be fitted in the triangle OBD). If one of the producers sets his production level at OA, his rival can do best (on Cournot's assumptions) by setting his level at AH (AHQK is the largest rectangle which can be inscribed in the triangle ABP, where the line PB represents the remaining set of possible sales which are available to the second producer; AH = HB). The first producer's profits are now reduced to OAKN (what he will earn if the new price at which both springs' production is sold is HQ and he continues to put on the market an amount equivalent to OA). He can now maximise his profits, given the current state of affairs, by performing the same calculation as his rival in the first round, that is, by moving to a level of production which would enable him to make half the remaining possible sales. Each of the producers in turn performs these calculations, and the end result is that they eventually come to an equilibrium where they alight on the same price. What intrigued Cournot, and has intrigued his subsequent readers, is that this equilibrium will not be ½ OB, as it would have been for a monopolist, but ⅔ OB (= OG), with each proprietor settling on a production level equivalent to OF (= FG). The total profits (now to be divided in half) are OGRM—less than the monopoly profit.[20]

20. Edward Hastings Chamberlin, *The Theory of Monopolistic Competition*, 5th ed. (Cambridge, Mass.: Harvard University Press, 1947), pp. 32–33.

By stipulating the players' assumptions in this way and showing their implications, Cournot had in effect formalised for the first time the equivalent of a one-shot prisoners' dilemma. He expressed it in terms of an equilibrium point on the intersecting schedules of production of the two proprietors, but this difference in presentation should not blind us to the identity of the two situations—though Cournot's method is more appropriate to a case like the production of mineral water, where there is theoretically an infinite set of possible levels of production for each proprietor. It was the equivalent of a one-shot dilemma because Cournot stipulated that his producers would use the same strategy in each round and would not alter it in light of what their rival might do; as a consequence, one could construe it as a single game, in which the final payoffs for the game were those associated with each strategy at the equilibrium point, when play (according to Cournot) would come to an end. In the last round, let us say that each proprietor has a choice of implementing the general strategy assumed in this example—that is, to set his production at ½ (OB less the previous proprietor's production level)—or to move to a production level equivalent to half the monopoly level. At this stage, the former strategy (which I will call the Cournot strategy), applied by both proprietors, leads to Proprietor 1's setting OF and Proprietor 2's setting FG. If Proprietor 1 instead used the latter strategy (which I will call the collaboration strategy), he would set his level at OE (= EA); Proprietor 2 could either do the same or use the Cournot strategy, which would lead him to set his production at ½ (OB − OE), that is, EL. Given these possibilities, we can construct a symmetrical matrix to illustrate the alternatives in this final round (see Figure 5.2). (I will term the first proprietor 'Roman' and the second proprietor 'Arab', as in Chapter One). A reasonably straightforward calculation can then give the relative profits for each proprietor under these circumstances (see Figure 5.3).[21] It will immediately be seen that this is indeed a prisoners' dilemma: whatever the other proprietor does, the Cournot strategy dominates, but the Cournot equilibrium is Pareto-inferior to the joint collaborative outcome.

Having established this result in the two-person case, Cournot proceeded in the next chapter to extend it to a multi-person case. Given that the basic assumption of his analysis was that the proprietors would take as the environment for their decision whatever features of the market had been pro-

---

21. Each numeral is given by the following calculation. The profit for a proprietor in each situation is calculated as a fraction of the area of OB multiplied by OD, and then expressed as a numerator with the lowest common denominator (576).

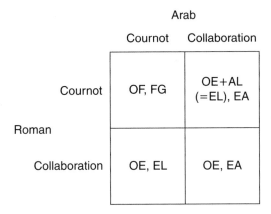

Arab

	Cournot	Collaboration
Cournot	OF, FG	OE+AL (=EL), EA
Collaboration	OE, EL	OE, EA

Roman

Figure 5.2

Arab

	Cournot	Collaboration
Cournot	lxiv, 64	lxxxi, 54
Collaboration	liv, 81	lxxii, 72

Roman

Figure 5.3

duced by the decisions of their fellow competitors, he easily showed that as the numbers increased, the equilibrium tended towards the perfectly competitive point. In terms of the diagram above, if the first two proprietors had settled on OG as their joint production, a new proprietor (working still with the same potential output of the springs) would do best by setting his production at ½ GB; the first two would have to respond accordingly, and the new equilibrium would be ¾ OB rather than ⅔ OB. We now have a series: one producer implies equilibrium at ½ OB, two at ⅔ OB, three at ¾ OB, four at ⅘ OB, and so on. As the number of proprietors grows, the equilibrium point tends to OB, which is the perfectly competitive equilibrium.

As far as Cournot was concerned, we should recognise, there was no difference in character between the competitive behaviour displayed by large groups and that displayed by small ones. Since in both cases he presumed that producers would not act strategically, the question of the circumstances in which strategic interaction would make sense simply did not come up. He did not commit himself to the later view that it is rational to be a price-taker where there are large numbers but not where there are small numbers; nor, indeed, as I have said, did he even commit himself to the view that it is rational to be a price-taker at all. The reason that a multiplicity of producers would not simply alight on the monopolistic equilibrium, he thought, was that 'in the moral sphere men cannot be supposed to be free from error and lack of forethought any more than in the physical world bodies can be considered perfectly rigid, or supports perfectly solid, etc.'[22] So a failure of collaboration for Cournot was still an 'error' or a mistake of prudence, just as it had been for his eighteenth-century predecessors.

Cournot's model offered to his successors both a tantalising, plausible way of representing economic choice mathematically and a deeply implausible set of assumptions and conclusions. As interest in developing a properly mathematical economics grew in the late nineteenth century, the discussion of competitive behaviour and its rationality in different circumstances took place largely in the context of criticising and correcting Cournot—whom all the great theorists of 'marginalist' economics had read closely, and whom at least the founding generation followed in their theoretical premises.[23] The first marginalists, like most of Cournot's subsequent readers, found his account of the specificities of competition unconvincing, and in general presumed that what we might call the 'classical' theory was correct—that is, if competition occurs, it takes the form of price-cutting in which eventually,

22. Cournot, *Researches into the Mathematical Principles,* p. 83.
23. See, for example, W. S. Jevons's remarks in *The Theory of Political Economy* (1871):

> I must here point out that, although the theory presumes to investigate the condition of a mind, and bases upon this investigation the whole of Economics, practically it is an aggregate of individuals which will be treated . . . [I]t is quite impossible to detect the operation of general laws of this kind in the actions of one or a few individuals. The motives and conditions are so numerous and complicated, that the resulting actions have the appearance of caprice, and are beyond the analytic powers of science. With every increase in the price of such a commodity as sugar, we ought, theoretically speaking, to find every person reducing his consumption by a small amount, and according to some regular law. In reality, many persons would make no change at all; a few, probably, would go to the extent of dispensing with the use of sugar alto-

whatever the numbers involved, the greatest feasible level of production in an industry would be reached.[24] Consequently, they also presumed that although one could analyse a competitive equilibrium of this kind as a situation in which the participants were price-takers,[25] the number of people involved was not a particularly relevant consideration—if competitive behaviour was to be assumed, then it would be a type of behaviour evinced by any number of people, and its results would be the same whatever the number. But, also like the classical writers, they were in fact far from persuaded that competitive behaviour among an existing group of producers would be rational; thus Jevons, despite a high degree of scepticism about the efficacy of trades unions in raising real wages, was rather keen on workers' co-operatives and looked forward to the day when workers would act as 'their own capitalists'.[26] In the end their accounts of the competitive market were simply hypotheses to demonstrate what would happen if (for some unspecified reason) people forbore from collaborating. The mechanism by which competition might be secured, other than by removing barriers to entry, was left

---

gether as long as its cost continued to be excessive. It would be by examining the average consumption of sugar in a large population that we might detect a continuous variation, connected with the variation of price by a constant law.

The same idea is to be found in his first essay on mathematical economics; see n. 35 below. This may be a case of intellectual convergence—Jevons claimed in the second edition of *The Theory of Political Economy* that he had not read Cournot before writing the first edition. See also Léon Walras's remarks about his relationship to Jevons and Cournot in the preface to the fourth edition of his *Eléments d'économie politique pure* (*Elements of Pure Economics*), trans. William Jaffé (London: Allen & Unwin, 1954), pp. 35–37, and his use of the 'law of large numbers' to smooth out discontinuities (p. 95).

24. Feasible, that is, in the sense that it is the lowest level of profits before capital would begin to migrate to another industry.

25. '[A] single trader . . . must buy and sell at the current prices, which he cannot in an appreciable degree affect'; Jevons, *The Theory of Political Economy*, 1st ed., p. 111. See also Walras, *Elements of Pure Economics*, p. 92 ff.

26. See his letter to the *Manchester City News*, 3 November 1866, in *Papers and Correspondence* (London: Macmillan, 1977), III, pp. 137–138, and his remarks on the subject in *The State in Relation to Labour* (London: Macmillan, 1882). In this book he explicitly followed Edgeworth in arguing that workers will tend to form cartels and that there will be no natural solution to the bargaining problem; instead, utilitarian arbitration will be needed; see pp. 154–155. (For Edgeworth, see below, pp. 181–183.) It is worth noting that in *The State in Relation to Labour*, Jevons also expressly dealt with the sorites (in the context of a discussion about the problems raised by questions of degree in legislation), and concluded that 'at some point . . . an infinitesimal difference lies between crime and innocence' (pp. 21–22).

unspecified. We could summarise the position for these early marginalists by saying that they possessed one key element in the modern theory, the idea that if producers discounted the effect of their actions on the market price, they would behave in such a way that a competitive equilibrium would result. But they lacked the other key element, the claim that individuals in this situation would not form cartels in order to prevent this result. This was the idea which, as we shall see, was not clearly stated until the first half of the twentieth century. From the early marginalists' point of view, the very fact that behaving in this fashion would produce an adverse result for the producers was in itself a good reason for the producers to band together.

This view continued to be regarded as common sense; it was, for example, substantially the point made in his explicit critique of Cournot by Joseph Bertrand, 'the first mathematician of France',[27] who remarked in an influential essay of 1883 that Cournot's solution to the problem of duopoly was clearly false, as either the duopolists would collaborate or (if for some reason they did not do so) they would compete by price-cutting until the minimum-profit equilibrium was reached. It was also the conclusion reached by Henry Sidgwick in his *Principles of Political Economy* (also 1883), the first philosophically sophisticated version of post-Jevons economics, though he reached it for distinctive reasons of his own. He argued that if 'a commodity . . . is sold by a number of persons who do not combine', then

> generally speaking, the amount of supply will be practically settled by the dealers selling all that they can bring to market. But it may happen here— just as in the case of strict monopoly,— that if each individual seller aimed intelligently at obtaining the greatest possible profit, and were able to rely on an equal exercise of self-regard on the part of all the rest, each would artificially limit his supply.

Sidgwick recognised that

> a point at which it would be the combined interest of the sellers to stop the supply, if only each could rely on all the others doing the same, will generally be a point at which it would be any individual seller's immediate interest to add to his supply; since the fall in the price of his commodity caused

27. Henry L. Moore, 'Paradoxes of Competition', *Quarterly Journal of Economics* 20 (1908): 218.

by this addition would generally be more than compensated by the profit on the extra amount that he would sell; . . . self-interest without concert would prompt each and all to enlarge the supply until it reached the point at which each would immediately lose by going further.[28]

Although he agreed that in theory this might be the Cournot duopolistic equilibrium, he observed that

the determination of this point has, I conceive, hardly any practical interest; since in practice such sellers—if combination were for some reason impracticable—would be almost certain to go beyond this point, and to sell as much as they could.[29]

But the reasoning he employed to show this went well beyond Cournot's assumptions. In effect, Sidgwick supposed that the players in a prisoners' dilemma would think strategically about the harm they were doing to their rivals as well as the benefits they themselves received from their action, and would choose the strategy which did most short-term damage to their competitors. Thus the sellers would go beyond the Cournot point, because

though each would immediately lose somewhat by so doing, his own loss would be much less than the loss he would inflict on the rest; since the price would fall for all alike, while he alone would be partly compensated by his profit on the extra amount he sold. On the other hand, if one seller were mistakenly to limit his supply, he would injure himself alone, while slightly benefiting his rivals. Under these conditions the coolest self-interest would prefer to err in the direction of extending supply; so that each would find it better on the whole to guard against the danger of such error on the part of others, by extending his own supply.[30]

Adjusting supply thus turned out (on Sidgwick's view) to have the same result as adjusting price; but he believed this because he introduced into the considerations applicable to supply adjustment a form of strategic thinking

28. Sidgwick, *The Principles of Political Economy,* pp. 194–195. Compare the second edition (1887), pp. 183–184, in which the passage is slightly revised but not materially altered (though Sidgwick inserted an acknowledgement that he had borrowed the argument from Cournot, which he had omitted in the first edition).

29. Ibid., 2d ed., pp. 183–184; see 1st ed., p. 195.

30. Ibid., 1st ed., p. 195; 2d ed., pp. 184–185.

about the position of one's rival vis-à-vis the wider market which was comparable to the strategic thinking involved in price-cutting.[31]

But Sidgwick never lost sight of the fact that competition of this kind was 'unintelligent', and that co-operation would be an instance of 'enlightened self-regard'. Like the earlier utilitarians, he understood that '[c]ombination is no doubt often tacitly excluded in the reasoning by which it is argued that the most economic production tends to result from the play of individual self-interest. But I do not see how it is legitimately to be excluded'.[32] This remark, indeed, went to the heart of the matter. No one (in this genre) questioned the priority of self-interest; the questions were, what *counts* as self-interest, and why does collaboration in furtherance of our ends not count? In the second edition of *The Principles of Political Economy*, Sidgwick inserted a passage explaining (in ways reminiscent of Mill) why an element of enforcement might be needed in socially beneficial co-operative action such as the protection of land from flooding.

> In a perfectly ideal community of economic men all the persons concerned would no doubt voluntarily agree to take the measures required to ward off such common dangers: but in any community of human beings that we can hope to see, the most that we can reasonably expect is that the great majority of any industrial class will be adequately enlightened, vigilant, and careful in protecting their own interests; and where the efforts and sacrifice of a great majority are liable to be rendered almost useless by the neglect of one or two individuals, it will always be dangerous to trust to voluntary association.[33]

This was an extremely clear statement of the classical view, that collaboration (even of large numbers) is ideally rational, that when it fails it does so because of ordinary human fallibility, and that compulsion is a *pis aller*: precisely Hume's idea, and more or less the exact reverse of Olson's. Like his predecessors, Sidgwick believed that it would be 'palpably rash' to rely on voluntary co-operation, especially in cases such as fisheries, where great re-

31. To care about the greater harm done to one's rival than to oneself as a result of a process of mutual impoverishment is to be thinking in terms of positional goods: it is better to be stronger than my competitor even if neither of us is as strong as we were. This, of course, makes sense if the game is not one-shot and strategic thinking about future contests is allowed.

32. Ibid., 1st ed., p. 415 n. 1; 2d ed., p. 409 n. 1.

33. Ibid., 2d ed., p. 410; compare 1st ed., p. 414.

wards might be enjoyed by those people who did not comply with rules limiting over-fishing; but that was because people are *not* 'perfectly ideal . . .
economic men', rather than because they *are*. Sidgwick's economics thus
meshed exactly with his moral philosophy, as I depicted it in Chapter Four: it
is rational for agents who share a common purpose to collaborate, at least up
to a certain point, though one can never entirely rely on people to be rational and one must guard against the damage done by short-sighted defections.

The same conviction, that collaboration or combination is rational for self-
interested agents, still governed the next generation of writers on economics, which included perhaps the most creative figures in the history of marginalism, F. Y. Edgeworth and Vilfredo Pareto. As we saw in Chapter Four,
Edgeworth was an enthusiastic reader of Sidgwick's *Methods of Ethics,* and in
his own *New and Old Methods of Ethics* (1877) he took Sidgwick's ideas and
systematised them into what he termed 'exact utilitarianism', in which distributional questions were largely disregarded, or at least not treated as at all
fundamental; aggregate utility, assuming comparability between persons,
was what was to be maximised. Accordingly, Edgeworth developed in this
book the first genuinely mathematical model for utilitarianism. But Edgeworth was also well aware, as Sidgwick had been, that interpersonal comparability was merely an assumption, necessary if one was to be a utilitarian,
but hard to justify against a critic of utilitarianism. This (as we saw) was a
point which had been stressed in the 1860s by John Grote, and it had been
taken up very quickly by the early marginalists; Jevons, for example, remarked in *The Theory of Political Economy* (1871) that

> [t]he reader will find . . . that there is never, in any single instance, an at-
> tempt made to compare the amount of feeling in one mind with that in an-
> other. I see no means by which such comparison can be accomplished. The
> susceptibility of one mind may, for what we know, be a thousand times
> greater than that of another. But, provided that the susceptibility was differ-
> ent in a like ratio in all directions, we should never be able to discover the
> difference. Every mind is thus inscrutable to every other mind, and no com-
> mon denominator of feeling seems possible.[34]

34. W. S. Jevons, *The Theory of Political Economy,* 3d ed. (London: Macmillan, 1888),
p. 14. See the same sort of idea, less philosophically expressed, in Walras's *Elements of Pure
Economics,* in his exposition of his notion of *rareté,* or the value for any consumer of a particular commodity. Each commodity, he argued, has a determinate *rareté* for each of its hold-

This was to be the central plank of marginalist economics, and the thing that differentiated it fundamentally from its classical predecessor. For the classical political economists, interpersonal comparisons of utility were clearly possible, and the basic question to ask about economic activity was a distributional one: were the benefits of exchange equally distributed among the participants, in the sense that their utilities measured against some common scale were equal? (This was the point of the so-called labour theory of value.) But for their successors, that kind of question could not be asked; instead, social arrangements could be justified only if they were in some sense unanimously agreed on by the participants and no interpersonal comparisons were required.

Edgeworth understood the importance of this theory, and in a book published four years after *New and Old Methods of Ethics,* entitled *Mathematical Psychics,* he produced an astonishing tour de force of an argument designed to combine modern economics and modern utilitarianism. In the first half of the book he presented what was in effect the principle of Pareto optimality, and in the second half he showed why the principle had to be supplemented with utilitarianism, though the two principles had to be taken in what is now called lexical order, with the Pareto principle applied first and the utility principle applied second. The first half was based on a general theory of bargaining; as he remarked later, '[I]t may be said that in pure economics there is only one fundamental theorem, but that is a very difficult one: the theory of bargain in a wide sense'.[35] Just as the one-shot prisoners' dilemma

---

ers: 'I say for each of the holders of this commodity—and I wish to emphasize this point—because there is no such thing as *the rareté* of commodity (A) or *the rareté* of commodity (B) . . . ; there are no other *raretés* than the *raretés* of (A) or (B) for holders (1),(2),(3) . . . of these commodities . . . *Rareté,* one might say, is *individual.*' In later editions this last sentence reads, '*Rareté* is *personal* or *subjective;* value in exchange is *real* or *objective*'; pp. 146, 572. Jevons's earlier forays into mathematical economics had not involved a denial of interpersonal comparability: see the paper he read at the 1862 meeting in Cambridge of the British Association for the Advancement of Science, entitled 'A Brief Account of a General Mathematical Theory of Political Economy' (summarily reported on in the *Report of the Thirty-Second Meeting* (London, 1863), Part 2, pp. 158–159, and published in its entirety four years later in the *Journal of the Statistical Society of London* 29 [1866]: 282–287). It seems to have been his awareness of the views of Grote or Sidgwick which led him into the position voiced in *The Theory of Political Economy.*

35. From his address to the British Association in 1889, 'On the Application of Mathematics to Political Economy', in F. Y. Edgeworth, *Papers Relating to Political Economy* (London: Macmillan, 1925), II, p. 288.

was first formalised by Cournot, though not in the language of game theory, so Edgeworth was the first person to formalise bargaining and draw the conclusions which reappeared (often in ignorance of his work) in the game theory of the 1950s. *Mathematical Psychics* is a strange and difficult work, and here I do not want to go into the technical details of his argument, but basically it went as follows. In a setting in which there are two commodities to be exchanged in different amounts between two traders, there will be a set of possible trades—say, four apples for two nuts, five apples for three nuts and so on. Among these trades there must be some which are better for both participants than some alternatives; plotted on the graphs which Edgeworth used to illustrate his theory, this subset was represented by what Edgeworth termed a 'contract curve'. Any bargain or contract between rational traders must be somewhere on the curve, since any bargain off it must be inferior for both of them to a bargain on it.

For two traders, that leaves a wide variety of possible trades, ranging from the most preferred for the holder of apples (getting all the nuts in exchange for no apples) to the most preferred for the holder of nuts (the opposite). Edgeworth was clear that in the situation of pure bargaining, there was no means of determining where on the contract curve an actual trade—what he termed a 'final settlement'—would take place.

> It is the interest of both parties that there should be *some settlement*, one of the contracts represented by the contact-curve between the limits. But *which* of these contracts is arbitrary in the absence of arbitration, the interests of the two *adversa pugnantia fronte* all along the contract-curve . . . An accessory evil of indeterminate contract is the tendency . . . towards dissimulation and objectionable arts of higgling.[36]

The traders were like opposing armies, seeking to acquire territory at the expense of their rival, an analogy Edgeworth was well aware of—'"Is it peace or war?" asks the lover of "Maud", of economic *competition*, and answers hastily: It is both'.[37] The settlement depended on the relative power of the participants to force a bargain most favourable to themselves, and this was a contingent matter dependent on all sorts of facts about the social and psychological circumstances of the two agents. It was, in Edgeworth's terminology, *indeterminate*. He did not mean by this that no kind of account could

36. F. Y. Edgeworth, *Mathematical Psychics* (London: C. K. Paul, 1881), pp. 29–30.
37. Ibid., p. 17.

be given of where the final settlement would be, but that it could not be determined purely by looking for a settlement which was superior to its alternatives and easily agreed on by both parties. It was, we might say, *morally* indeterminate—someone had to be the loser, and there was (at this stage of Edgeworth's argument) no way of deciding morally who the loser should be.

However, Edgeworth observed that if there was, so to speak, internal competition within one trader, the advantage in the negotiation would necessarily shift to the other one. If we imagine cartels rather than natural individuals, we can see this easily. Edgeworth himself proved it geometrically, but it is basically the familiar idea that if a cartel produces a commodity at a certain price (that is, the ratio of apples to nuts), there will at that price be an incentive for part of the cartel to break away and produce somewhat more than its quota, in order to increase its profits. The rest of the cartel will have to react by increasing its production; the price of the commodity will then fall. In Edgeworth's terms, the contract curve will have been 'shortened' by losing some of the settlements which would have been most favourable to the former cartel. If the numbers competing increase, the price will continue to fall and the curve will become shorter, until a point is reached where *through this process* the price cannot fall any further.

It is important to stress something, however, which is usually neglected in accounts of Edgeworth: that this is not a process which determines an *actual* price or production level. Though the contract curve is shortened, it does not diminish to a *point* unless there is competition at *both* ends. If a monopolist faces a competitive market of consumers, there is still (on Edgeworth's account) a substantial stretch of untouched contract curve, ranging from the monopolist's getting all the consumers' holdings in return for providing virtually nothing, up to his providing the commodity at the price determined by the consumers' internal competition. Many readers of Edgeworth assumed that he was analysing the process whereby price is determined in a market, as Cournot had tried to do, but actually he was analysing the *moral* basis of price: the price which a monopolist might set for his product could be justified if it was somewhere on the remaining contract curve, but to narrow it down beyond that, 'dissimulation and objectionable arts of higgling' must once again come into play. The moral scientist (at this phase of the argument) could only be neutral between the remaining options. Interestingly, Edgeworth observed *inter alia* that in practice the price on which a monopolist and a competitive group of consumers would agree might depend on whether the parties were (as he put it) 'working up' or 'working down' the contract curve. For example, it might depend on whether a competitive group of producers were forming a cartel against a continuingly competitive group of consumers, or whether a cartel of producers was breaking up in the face of a monopsonist.

> Going beyond Cournot, not without trembling, the present inquiry finds that, where the field of competition is sensibly imperfect, an indefinite number of *final settlements* are possible; that in such a case *different* final settlements would be reached if the system should run down from different *initial positions* or contracts. The sort of difference which exists between Dutch and English auction, theoretically unimportant in *perfect competition,* does correspond to different results, *different final settlements* in imperfect competition.[38]

Edgeworth had thus invented not only the modern theory of bargaining, but also the currently fashionable idea of 'path-dependence'.

But Edgeworth did not end his argument at this point, as one might imagine a modern economist would have done. Instead, he turned quite explicitly, like Sidgwick, to what from my point of view is the important question: given this analysis, is it rational for economic agents to compete with one another? His answer to this was quite clear, and was the basis of the second half of the book. Competition, he had shown, reduced indeterminacy (in his sense), and combination increased it; but combination always increased it in the interests of the combiners, that is, it extended the contract curve in a direction which was favourable to them, and thereby offered the prospect of a better deal. Edgeworth in fact believed that his book was a defence of combination, not of competition.

> As far as the writer is aware, a straightforward answer has never been offered to the abstract question, What is the effect of combinations on *contract* in an otherwise *perfect* state of competition, as here supposed? Writers either ignore the abstract question altogether . . . Or, while they seem to admit that unionism would have the effect of raising the *rate of wages,* they yet deny that the *total remuneration* of the operatives, the *wage-fund* (in the intelligible sense of that term), can be increased. But if our reasonings be correct, the one thing from an abstract point of view visible among the jumble of cattalactic molecules, the jostle of competitive crowds, is that those who

38. Ibid., pp. 47–48.

form themselves into compact bodies by *combination* do not tend to lose, but *stand to gain* in the sense described, to gain in point of utility, which is a function not only of the (objective) remuneration, but also of the labour, and which, therefore, may increase, although the remuneration decrease ... And if, as seems to be implied in much that has been written on this subject, it is attempted to enforce the argument against Trades Unionism by the consideration that it tends to diminish the *total national produce*, the obvious reply is that unionists, as 'economic men', are not concerned with the *total produce*. Because the total produce is diminished, it does not follow that the labourer's share us diminished ... ; much less does it follow (as aforesaid) that there should be diminished that quantity which alone the rational unionist is concerned to increase—*the labourer's utility*. If this view be correct, it would seem as if, in the matter of *unionism*, as well as in that of the predeterminate *wage-fund*, the 'untutored mind' of the workman had gone more straight to the point than economic intelligence *misled by a bad method*, reasoning without mathematics upon mathematical subjects.[39]

Edgeworth went on to argue that the modern world is particularly marked by the growth of combinations of one kind or another—trades unions or workers' co-operatives—and that 'it does not seem very rash to infer, if not for the present, at least in the proximate future, a considerable extent of indeterminateness'. As a consequence, 'the whole creation groans and yearns, desiderating a principle of arbitration, an end of strife'.[40] So Edgeworth was very clear that his analysis of competitive behaviour showed that it was rational *not* to compete but instead to form combinations, cartels and trades unions: the idea that generalised competition would magically solve distributive questions, on his account, was a fantasy.[41]

39. Ibid., pp 43–45.

40. Ibid., pp. 50, 51.

41. It would have surprised Edgeworth that Kenneth Arrow and Frank Hahn used his theory to argue the *reverse* of his conclusions: in their *General Competitive Analysis* (San Francisco: Holden-Day, 1971), they remarked that Edgeworth's idea of the 'core' (that is, the contract curve) suggests that 'competitive equilibrium is very sturdy ... This is contrary to the view sometimes expressed that competitive equilibrium has an inherent instability in that it would pay, for example, the owners of some one commodity to form a cartel and exploit their monopoly power. The theorems on the relation between competitive equilibria and the core suggest that any such attempt would be broken up by the formation of coalitions involving some buyers and some sellers of that commodity' (p. 186).

The solution instead lay with the second principle which I mentioned at the start of my discussion of Edgeworth. The first principle, that a settlement must be on the contract curve, was, of course, in essence the principle of Pareto optimality, which in its modern form goes as follows (after Sen, *Collective Choice and Social Welfare*, p. 21): (a) if everyone in the society is indifferent between two alternative social situations *x* and *y*, then the society should be indifferent too; and (b) if at least one individual strictly prefers *x* to *y*, and every individual regards *x* to be at least as good as *y*, then the society should prefer *x* to *y*. But the second principle was Edgeworth's 'exact utilitarianism'.

> It is a circumstance of momentous interest—visible to common sense when pointed out by mathematics—that *one* of the in general indefinitely numerous *settlements* between contractors is the utilitarian arrangement of the articles of contract, the contract tending to the greatest possible total utility of the contractors. In this direction, it may be conjectured, is to be sought the required principle. For the required basis of arbitration between economical contractors is evidently *some* settlement; and the utilitarian settlement may be selected, in the absence of any other principle of selection, in virtue of its moral peculiarities: its satisfying the sympathy (such as it is) of each with all, the sense of justice and utilitarian equity.[42]

(Edgeworth added a characteristic footnote to explain the last phrase: 'whereof the unconsciously implicit first principle is: Time-intensity units of pleasure are to be equated irrespective of persons'!) So the point on the contract curve at which there is a utilitarian optimum is to be selected as the socially desirable allocation of resources.[43]

Later economists, beginning with Pareto, would have a different answer: they pointed out that the fully competitive equilibrium (that is, the point reached when both sides of the trade were competitive and there were no combinations) was also a special point on the contract curve. It was Pareto-superior to all other points, in the sense that if (for example) a monopolist was forced to give up his dominant market position, he could be compensated out of the extra commodities generated at the competitive equilibrium, while his former trading partners would be better off—a more formal

---

42. Edgeworth, *Mathematical Psychics*, p. 54.

43. Compare Nash's solution to the bargaining problem: R. Duncan Luce and Howard Raiffa, *Games and Decisions* (New York: Wiley, 1957), pp. 126–127.

version of the idea which the first thinkers about monopoly had had (see above, p. 167).[44] Edgeworth was, of course, perfectly well aware of this, but from his point of view a 'compensation principle' of this kind was of little interest, for familiar reasons: to be in a position to receive compensation, one must already have succeeded in establishing oneself as a monopolist. One would still do best by winning the 'war' between the traders. The compensation principle gives no reason to individual agents to refrain from the kind of struggle in which Edgeworth was interested, and (given his ethical views) it had no particular advantage over exact utilitarianism as a principle of arbitration. Its merit was to be that it allowed Pareto and his successors, who did not share those views, to have a principle of social decision without endorsing interpersonal comparison of utility; it could then in effect replace utilitarianism as the principle that decided which of the points on Edgeworth's contract curve should be chosen as the social arbitration. This idea became very popular with both the left and the right in the first part of the twentieth century, and I shall have more to say about this in the Conclusion to Part II.

It should be stressed that his principle was for Pareto a principle of *social* choice, to be enforced in some way upon a population, not an account of how individuals would actually behave in a competitive market. When he came to give that account, in his *Cours d'économie politique* (1896) and in his *Manuel d'économie politique* (1909), Pareto continued to allow for the formation of monopolistic or oligopolistic combinations and cartels, though he did put forward a different kind of theory about competitive behaviour from Edgeworth's. According to Pareto, competitors and monopolists behaved as they did because they had two quite different 'Types' of psychology, one ('Type I') being a price-taker, and the other ('Type II') a price-manipulator. Price-taking, he accepted, was more common where large numbers were involved:

> It is precisely because there are many people who buy and sell French rentes each day on the Paris Bourse, that it would be foolish to try to modify the conditions of that market by buying or selling a few francs of rentes. Obviously, if all those who are selling (or buying) were to enter into an agreement, they could actually modify these conditions to their profit; but they do not know one another, and each acts on his own behalf. Amid this con-

44. See the useful article on 'The Compensation Principle' by John Chipman in *The New Palgrave: A Dictionary of Economics* ed. John Eatwell, Murray Milgate and Peter Newman (London: Macmillan, 1987), I, pp. 524–531.

fusion and competition, each individual can do no more than handle his own affairs and seek to satisfy his own tastes, in accordance with the different conditions which may appear on the market. All the sellers (or buyers) of rentes clearly modify the prices, but they modify them without previous design; it is not the purpose, but the effect of their actions.[45]

But Pareto, as this passage illustrates, was not very far removed even from Smith in his explanation of competitive behaviour, namely, that the competitors do not know each other. And he fully recognised that 'it often happens that a certain number of individuals join together precisely so that they can dominate the market; in this case we still have Type II, since, from certain points of view, the association can be considered as comprising only one individual'. Indeed, he understood socialism itself as the ultimate expression of a Type II personality.[46] If on the one hand many individuals could form a combination, on the other hand a few individuals could compete with each other down to the perfectly competitive equilibrium.[47] Following Bertrand, Pareto believed that Cournot had been wrong in his account of duopoly, and that two Type I (competitive) individuals would end up cutting their prices down to the minimum, while two Type II individuals would collaborate.

Edgeworth also turned his attention to Bertrand's argument about duopoly in the 1890s, and claimed that even with price-cutting the duopolistic solution is indeterminate, if the producers are able to sell their goods sequentially rather than simultaneously (for then the first producer to lower his price to the perfectly competitive level will sell all his stock, leaving his competitor free to raise his price for the remaining customers).[48] Essentially, Edgeworth converted Cournot's one-shot duopolistic prisoners' dilemma into a game which involved strategic thinking, rather as Sidgwick had done fourteen years earlier, and (as one would expect) he drew the

45. Vilfredo Pareto, *Manual of Political Economy,* trans. Ann S. Schwier (London: Macmillan, 1972), p. 116.

46. 'It is the one which occurs when one wishes to arrange the entire economic phenomenon in such a way that maximum welfare [that is, Pareto optimality] is obtained for all those who participate . . . [This species of Type II] corresponds to the collectivist organization of society'; ibid., pp. 117–118.

47. Vilfredo Pareto, *Cours d'économie politique professé à l'université de Lausanne* (Lausanne: F. Rouge, 1896), pp. 67–68.

48. Francis Edgeworth, 'La Teoria Pura del Monopolio', *Giornale degli Economisti* 15 (1897): 13–31, 307–320, 405–414, partially translated in his *Papers Relating to Political Economy* (London: Macmillan, 1925), I, pp. 111–142.

same conclusion as many modern game theorists: that the result was inde-terminate. He was praised for this the following year by Irving Fisher, who pointed out that both Cournot and Bertrand had assumed no strategic think-ing on the part of the duopolists—the former presumed that each duopolist would take his rival's *production* as given, and the latter that each duopo-list would take his rival's *price* as given.

> But, as a matter of fact, no business man assumes that his rival's output or price will remain constant any more than a chess player assumes that his opponent will not interfere with his effort to capture a knight. On the con-trary, his whole thought is to forecast what move the rival will make in re-sponse to one of his own. He may lower his price to steal his rival's business temporarily or with the hope of driving him out of business entirely. He may take great care to preserve the *modus vivendi,* so as not to break the market and provoke a rate war. He may raise his price, if ruinously low, in hopes that his rival, who is in the same difficulty, may welcome the change, and follow suit. The whole study is a 'dynamic' one, and far more complex than Cournot makes it out to be. The completest treatment of this intricate and neglected problem is contained in Professor Edgeworth's brilliant arti-cles in the *Giornale degli Economisti.*[49]

The end result of the labours of both Edgeworth and Pareto was thus an emphasis on the psychological and social complexity of both competitive and collaborative behaviour. *If* people chose to compete, then (where their individual contributions were relatively small) they would end up at the competitive equilibrium; but the same might be true if their individual con-tributions were quite large. And, above all, there was as yet no idea that it would be more *rational* for the small contributors to compete than for the large ones to do so: for Pareto, it was a matter of psychological type, while for Edgeworth it was clearly rational even for trades unionists (pre-emi-nently 'small' contributors) to combine and benefit themselves. This accep-tance of the force of combination was widespread in the late nineteeenth century. Alfred Marshall, for example, consistently stressed the benefits of combination, particularly through the phenomenon of increasing returns to scale. Indeed, he took the view that duopoly would normally contract to monopoly because of this: '[I]f any one of the rivals got an advantage, and

49. Irving Fisher, 'Cournot and Mathematical Economics', *Quarterly Journal of Economics* 12 (1898): 126–127.

increased his scale of production, he would thereby gain a further advantage, and soon drive all his rivals out of the field. Cournot's argument does not introduce the limitations necessary to prevent this result.'[50] He defined free competition as when 'a man competes freely when he is pursuing a course, which without entering into any combination with others, he has deliberately selected as that which is likely to be of the greatest material advantage to himself and his family'; but he also remarked of combinations that, 'themselves the product of firm resolve and deliberate enterprise', they were 'the principal force in the modern world that might check the onrush of competition'.[51] In a note to his Mathematical Appendix, he took as 'normal' the case of a producer who makes a negligible contribution to the market; but he did not justify this, nor explain why it might be worthwhile to consider what 'deliberately enterprising' men would do under the arbitrary limitation that they should not enter into combination with others to secure their objectives.

The economists of Marshall's generation were, of course, living in a world which seemed to be increasingly dominated by cartels of one kind or another. The two most dynamic economies of the late nineteenth century, those of the United States and Germany, were also the economies most characterised by trusts, monopolies or Kartels. Kartels were declared legal by a decision of the Imperial Supreme Court in 1897, and by 1907 they were controlling more than half the production in most important German industries; indeed, a potash Kartel was made legally compulsory in 1910. The German readiness to work with Kartels was not (as is well known) paralleled in the United States; there, the great trusts and monopolies (particularly in railroads, oil and sugar) were fiercely attacked in the course of the 1880s and 1890s. In late nineteenth-century North America, as in eighteenth-century Europe, it was farmers who suffered most from the existence of monopolised industries, and it was their complaints which were listened to in the Fifty-first Congress, which passed the famous Sherman Act in 1890—the major trust-busting legislation which began the process of dismantling the monopolies in theUnited States.[52] The debates on the bill reflected the difficulty the congressmen felt in discriminating between trades unions and industrial monopolies, with a number of speakers expressing

---

50. Alfred Marshall, *Principles of Economics*, ed. C. W. Guillebaud (London: Macmillan, 1961), II, p. 452.

51. Ibid., II, pp. 155, 575.

52. Hans B. Thorelli, *The Federal Antitrust Policy* (London: Allen & Unwin, 1954), p. 143.

alarm that it might be used against farm and labour organisations;[53] in the end, proposals specifically to exempt such organisations were dropped, though the act was not in fact used against them. Only one speaker defended combinations in the kind of terms that Edgeworth was using in England, with a call for countervailing combinations of the public; and no one defended the free activity of the market. American farmers had learned to their cost that competitive behaviour was not spontaneously generated by the market, but they did not wish to fight combination with combination, as the trades unionists of Europe did; instead, they wanted to impose the competitive equilibrium through state action, something which in its essentials (though not, of course, in its actual mechanism) was not so far removed from the central planning of Pareto or Barone!

Confirmation that members of this late nineteenth-century generation of economists were not inclined to think in terms of the modern theory of competition comes from the continental discussion of public finance. From the 1880s down to the 1920s, a number of writers (particularly in Italy) tried to extend the ideas of the marginalists into the area of taxation policy; they are often termed the 'voluntary exchange' theorists of public finance.[54] It was within this tradition that the term 'public goods' was coined, to differentiate the goods (and services) provided by the state from the 'private goods' provided by the market.[55] They believed that it ought to be possible to view taxes as payments for the services provided by the state, payments which in principle would be made voluntarily if the tax on each individual corresponded to the value set by him on the service compared to all the other outlets for his purchasing power available, both public and private. A good summary of the basic idea was provided by one of the earliest figures in the tradition, the Austrian Emil Sax:

[E]veryone contributes for his share of benefit the full measure of goods he would use in his own economic unit [that is, not as part of the collectivity] in equal circumstances, that is, what he would be prepared to spend

53. Ibid., p. 190.

54. See, for example, Richard Abel Musgrave, 'The Voluntary Exchange Theory of Public Economy', *Quarterly Journal of Economics* 53 (1939): 213–237; p. 214 n. 2 lists the principal figures in the tradition.

55. It was, for example, extensively used in Ugo Mazzola's *I dati scientifici della finanza pubblica* (Rome: Ermanno Loescher, 1890); see Chapter 9, translated in Richard A. Musgrave and Alan T. Peacock, eds., *Classics in the Theory of Public Finance* (London: Macmillan, 1958), pp. 37–47.

according to his individual valuation. This is indeed what happens in free 'mutalistic' associations. Thus the members' relative interests find expression in the fact that each contributes to the cost according to his individual valuation. Joint action on the basis of this principle also ensures that the purpose is achieved in the most economical manner, which is everybody's intention.[56]

Ugo Mazzola, similarly, writing in 1890, concluded that the 'price' of a public good—that is, the tax—had to be fixed 'in accordance with the maximum [a citizen] can pay as determined by the degree of final utility the goods have for him'.[57]

The writers concerned were well aware that public goods are 'indivisible' (another term they coined) and non-excludable—that is, as Mazzola recognised, 'if public goods had a price exceeding their final utility for some classes of consumers, these latter's inability to pay the price would not debar them from using the goods'—and they understood that as a consequence, a wholly free tax regime would be unreliable. But they still took the free mutualistic association to be a model, and citizens who did not wish to collaborate under such arrangements might even be described as (in the words of another Italian theorist, Antonio De Viti De Marco) 'a pathological group against which society must defend itself'.[58] The fundamental assumption was still that if it was clear that a particular public good represented a benefit for the individual citizen, compared with the tax levied on him as part of the funding of the project, then the citizen had a good reason to pay the tax, just as he had a good reason to pay the appropriate price for a private good; and this remained the assumption of writers in this tradition down to the 1930s. The idea that collaboration was irrational even where the participants received clear individual benefits from the collaborative activity was not one that had yet fully occurred to anyone, any more than it had occurred to the marginalist writers on the theory of competition.

There is one apparent exception to this among the theorists of public goods. In the 1950s the modern theorists of public finance, whose ideas

56. Emil Sax, 'The Valuation Theory of Taxation', a translation of 'Die Wertungstheorie der Steuer', *Zeitschrift für Volkwirtschaft und Sozialpolitik* n.s. 4 (1924), in Musgrave and Peacock, eds., *Classics in the Theory of Public Finance*, p. 181. The essay summarises Sax's *Grundlegung der theoretischen Staatswirtschaft* (Vienna: A. Hölder, 1887).

57. In Musgrave and Peacock, eds., *Classics in the Theory of Public Finance*, p. 42.

58. De Viti De Marco, *First Principles of Public Finance*, trans. Edith Pavlo Marget (London: Jonathan Cape, 1936), p. 114.

Olson developed, frequently cited a passage in the works of one of these voluntary exchange theorists, the Swede Knut Wicksell, as a clear statement of the free-rider problem. Wicksell had remarked in his 1896 essay 'A New Principle of Just Taxation' that Mazzola's idea 'is really meaningless', as

> if the individual is to spend his money for private and public uses so that his satisfaction is maximised, he will obviously pay nothing whatsoever for public purposes (at least if we disregard fees and similar charges). Whether he pays much or little will affect the scope of public services so slightly, that for all practical purposes he himself will not notice it at all. Of course, if everyone were to do the same, the State would soon cease to function. The utility and the marginal utility of public services (Mazzola's public goods) for the individual thus depend in the highest degree on how much the others contribute, but hardly at all on how much he himself contributes.[59]

Clearly Wicksell was close here to the later idea, and it is not at all surprising that the modern theorists should have quoted him with reverence—Buchanan indeed later declared himself to be a 'Wicksellian'.[60] But Wicksell (as Paul Samuelson understood)[61] was in reality making a more limited point. His criticism of Mazzola was a criticism of the fact that Mazzola apparently supposed that an optimal distribution of the tax burden could be achieved in some unspecified way similar to a private market, rather than through a collective *political* process; as Wicksell continued,

> Equality between the marginal utility of public goods and their price cannot . . . be established by the single individual, but must be secured by consultation between him and all other individuals or their delegates. How is such consultation to be arranged so that the goal may be realized? On this point Mazzola does not say a word, but, as I see it, this is precisely the question which ought to be decided.[62]

59. 'Ein neues Prinzip der gerechten Besteuerung', in Knut Wicksell, *Finanztheoretische Untersuchungen* (Jena: G. Fischer, 1896), translated in Musgrave and Peacock, eds., *Classics in the Theory of Public Finance*, pp. 81–82.

60. James M. Buchanan, 'The Constitution of Economic Policy', Nobel Lecture, 8 December 1986, in *Economic Sciences 1981–1990*, ed. Karl-Göran Mäler (Singapore: World Scientific, 1992), p. 180.

61. Paul A. Samuelson, 'Wicksell and neoclassical economics', in *The New Palgrave: A Dictionary of Economics*, ed. John Eatwell, Murray Milgate, and Peter Newman (London: Macmillan, 1987), IV, pp. 908–910.

62. In Musgrave and Peacock, eds., *Classics in the Theory of Public Finance*, p. 82.

And he concluded that one should think about the supply of public goods as if the state were a voluntary association in which everyone had to agree on the distribution of the burden; indeed, he was an enthusiast for such associations, remarking that voluntary collaboration

> has been adopted on a large scale even in spheres which are normally regarded as properly belonging to the competence of the State. Side by side with the national army, many countries have voluntary rifle clubs and similar institutions which sometimes constitute no mean military force; or quite considerable means of warfare are sometimes raised privately and placed at the disposal of the State.

Coercion, he said, 'is always an evil in itself and its exercise, in my opinion, can be justified only in cases of clear necessity', and such cases did not in general include the provision of public goods.[63]

Accordingly, he proposed that taxation and public expenditure should be decided *unanimously* (by delegates, rather than the whole population, though in principle he obviously would have liked universal unanimity). It was this, together with his remark about the negligible character of any one citizen's contribution to a large-scale collaborative enterprise, which was picked up by writers in the 1950s and 1960s and treated as the first modern theory of public goods. But it was an important feature of Wicksell's discussion that he did not consider the strategic questions opened up by a principle of unanimity. As we saw in the Introduction, if the participants in a collective enterprise are thinking strategically, then a unanimity rule raises possibilities for them of bargaining and holding out, and its enforcement will require coercion in order to stop subgroups from securing better arrangements for themselves than they would be obliged to make under the condition of unanimity. The fact that Wicksell was so confident that 'voluntary consent' and 'unanimity' went together[64] suggests that he did not suppose that his citizens (or their delegates) would be thinking strategically, and his discussion of the ways in which unanimity would operate presumes (for example) that people would be honest in expressing their preferences between options and would in effect treat their deliberations as a means to the collaborative construction of a common goal.

Moreover, Wicksell's ideas in this essay were not treated by his contemporaries as at all extraordinary; he was seen as a contributor to the continen-

63. Ibid., p. 90.
64. See, for example, his remarks on p. 91.

tal tradition of voluntary exchange theory, and indeed the essay (as Erik Lindahl, his principal early follower, said) 'does not seem to have attracted a great deal of attention'.[65] Lindahl himself was inspired by it in the second decade of the twentieth century to produce his own theory of 'just taxation', in which bargaining was made part of the model—but it was bargaining within substantial limits, in particular with no attempt by the participants to mislead or outwit their partners. And when, towards the end of this tradition's life, an English admirer of it discussed the principle of unanimity, he revealed that as far as he was concerned, it presupposed the rationality of voluntary collaboration:

> The postulate of unanimous agreement appears to break down if some persons declare themselves unwilling to contribute anything towards collective services. It is no solution to exempt them from all taxation. They could not be prevented from sharing the indivisible benefits; and others would be tempted to feign a like unwillingness. De Viti de Marco declares that they must be regarded as pathological cases against whom the State should defend itself. Certainly they are inconsistent. They apparently desire to live: the poet's statement:
>
> > And if you would not this poor life fulfill,
> > Lo! it is yours to take it when you will'
>
> remains true. Yet they refuse to contribute towards services which assist them to obtain and enjoy the means to life, services which would not exist without the State. They are a problem. The problem can be evaded by assuming that all men act consistently; or it can be handed to the social philosopher for his discussion; or it can be dismissed by pointing to the relatively negligible numbers of such persons.[66]

So as late as 1934 it still seemed obvious to economists in the marginalist tradition that it was 'inconsistent' to value an outcome and not to wish to contribute towards it.

The movement away from this view had, however, already begun, led as one would expect by theorists of competition. The first clear statement of something like the modern theory of perfect competition had come in

---

65. Knut Wicksell, *Selected Papers in Economic Theory*, ed. Erik Lindahl (London: Allen and Unwin, 1958), p. 18.

66. F. C. Benham, 'Notes on the Pure Theory of Public Finance', *Economica* n.s. 1 (1934): 453–454.

1906—though it was not to be fully accepted by the leading economists for another twenty years. It was in an article by a young economist, Henry L. Moore of Columbia University, in the *Quarterly Journal of Economics*, revealingly entitled 'Paradoxes of Competition'. Moore had projected a book on Cournot, and had been led to think hard about Cournot's assumptions.[67] Accordingly, he argued that properly speaking, competition 'is a blanket-term covering more or less completely at least the following implicit hypotheses'. These were:

> I. Every economic factor seeks a maximum net income. This is the essential meaning of the term . . . II. There is but one price for commodities of the same quality in the same market . . . III. The influence of the product of any one producer upon the price per unit of the total product is negligible . . . IV. The output of any one producer is negligible as compared with the total output . . . V. Each producer orders the amount of his output without regard to the effect of his act upon the conduct of his competitors. Where III. and IV. coexist, V. is a simple corollary, otherwise it is an independent and inadmissible hypothesis. This fact should be carefully observed . . . In most systems of economics a theory of distribution is developed by reasoning consciously from hypotheses I. and V. It is not, however, by any means always perceived that the truth of the theory is further limited by the implicit assumption of hypotheses II., III., and IV. This loose method of procedure entails no necessary harm so long as the investigation is confined to a simplified hypothetical state, but great harm is done when, in approaching the problems of actual industry,— which, to a large extent, is in a state intermediate between perfect monopoly and perfect competition,— the economist flings the inquirer into the vague with the assurance that static standards will tend to prevail. In this intermediate state between perfect monopoly and perfect competition, hypotheses III. and IV. are never true, and hypothesis II. is frequently untrue.

Moore concluded '(1) That the term "competition" undergoes a change of meaning according as competition is between many or a few competitors; (2) That there is needed a very careful study of the number of competitors that will render fallacious the usual form of treating economic equilib-

67. The previous year he had published an article on 'The Personality of Antoine Augustin Cournot', *Quarterly Journal of Economics* 19 (1905): 370–399. For Moore's life, see George J. Stigler, 'Henry L. Moore and Statistical Economics', *Econometrica* 30 (1962): 1–21.

rium'.[68] So the modern idea of perfect competition had at last been voiced: *if* one's contribution is negligible, one will have no regard for the effect of one's act on one's competitors, but if *not*, then (in most cases) one will. It is in itself revealing that Moore presented this insight as new, and neglected by all his contemporaries; as far as he was concerned, this neglect had simply been the result of fallacious reasoning, but as we can now see, it is more likely to have been the result of a pervasive sense that even negligible contributions must be supposed to have some kind of effect on an outcome.

And that sense, unsurprisingly, continued for some years after Moore's article. Moore himself moved sideways into developing the study of econometrics, and in particular into reviving and making more sophisticated an old idea of Jevons's that sun-spots and other global climatic influences determine the business cycle; meanwhile, the leading American economists in the years after the First World War continued to be highly sceptical about the rationality of competitive behaviour. John Maurice Clark, for example, in *The Economics of Overhead Costs* (1923), was particularly interested in the tacit conventions which governed competition, such as the prejudice among producers about 'spoiling the market' (a convention to which, it will be remembered, Irving Fisher had referred).

> Granted a surplus of productive capacity, if a producer can cut prices and thereby secure a part of all his competitors' business or the lion's share of the increased business which his reduction of prices brings forth, he can make an immediate gain by cutting, regardless of whether prices cover total expenses or not, provided only they yield something above differential cost. One of the commonest ways of expressing the forces which restrain competitors from carrying price-cutting to the limit is to say that they are held back by a sentiment against 'spoiling the market'.[69]

Elsewhere, Clark argued that a competitive market must display price differentials, rather than being marked (as the traditional view had it) by uniformity of price, since competitive price-cutting required a short period during which the competitor's prices were lower than those of his fellow producers.

68. Henry L. Moore, 'Paradoxes of Competition', *Quarterly Journal of Economics* 20 (1906): 213–215.

69. John Maurice Clark, *Studies in the Economics of Overhead Costs* (Chicago: University of Chicago Press, 1923), p. 439.

If all the competitors followed suit instantly the moment any cut was made, each would gain his quota of the resulting increase in output, and no one would gain any larger proportion of his previous business than a monopoly would gain by a similar cut in prices. Thus the competitive cutting of prices would naturally stop exactly where it would if there were no competition.[70]

Clark's famous protégé Frank Knight, in his *Risk, Uncertainty, and Profit* (1921), went even further. He argued that if organisation costs were 'absent or small', there was a necessary tendency under perfect competition for agents to combine in order to increase their profits.

Therefore, under perfect competition, they will combine and bargain as a unit; and the same incentive will urge them to keep on combining until a monopoly results . . . It need not be remarked that this process would not go far in fact until something would have to be done to stop it. There does seem to be a certain Hegelian self-contradiction in the idea of theoretically perfect competition after all. As to what the end would be, it is fruitless to speculate, but it would have to be some arbitrary system of distribution un-der some sort of social control, doubtless based on ethics or political power or brute force, according to the circumstances—providing that society or somebody in it had sufficient intelligence and power to prevent a reversion to the *bellum omnium contra omnes*. Competitive industry is or hitherto has been saved by the fact that the human individual has been found normally incapable of wielding to his own advantage much more industrial power than, aided by legal and moral restraints, society as a whole can safely per-mit him to possess. How long this beneficent limitation can be counted upon to play its saving role may in the light of current business develop-ment occasion some doubt. With this subject we are not here particularly concerned, but it has seemed worth while to point out, in connection with the discussion of an ideal system of perfect competition, that such a system is inherently self-defeating and could not exist in the real world. Perfect competition implies conditions, especially as to the presence of human limi-tations, which would at the same time facilitate monopoly, make organiza-tion through free contract impossible, and force an authoritarian system upon society.[71]

70. Ibid., p. 417.

71. Knight, *Risk, Uncertainty, and Profit* (Boston: Houghton Mifflin, 1921), pp. 192–193. He made the same point in his 1923 article 'Ethics of Competition', reprinted in his collec-tion of essays of the same name (London: Allen & Unwin, 1935), p. 52.

So, surprising as it may seem, it was not until the *1930s* that the modern theory of the rationality of perfect competition, oligopoly and monopoly came to be systematically developed. To contemporaries, this seemed part of the *Zeitgeist*—as K. W. Rothschild pointed out a few years later,[72] the terminology of military affairs had invaded economics, nowhere more obviously than in a book by the Danish economist F. Zeuthen, *Problems of Monopoly and Economic Warfare* (1930). But it was Zeuthen's American counterpart, Edward Chamberlin, who was the key figure, and it was his analysis and terminology which became the standard theory for the remainder of the twentieth century. The analysis appears in *The Theory of Monopolistic Competition* (1933, but based on a Ph.D. thesis of 1927), which was in part a notable discussion of the idea of 'product differentiation'—that producers will compete by differentiating their product from another's rather than simply by competing on the price of identical articles. But the book began with a general theory of competition, of great clarity and interest.[73] Chamberlin first asserted plainly that

> the dominant force in a competitive market is [not] of a different order from that in a monopolistic one. The competitor is in no respect a different sort of person economically from the monopolist. He does not 'compete' and cut prices, by contrast with the monopolist who holds them up in order to maximise his profit. He is, presumably, as much bent upon maximising his profit as is the monopolist, and pursues this end with equal intelligence and foresight.[74]

In other words, if a coherent account of competitive behaviour was to be given, it had to explain why a rational self-determining individual of this kind would compete with his economic rivals and not collaborate with them.

This was a particularly urgent question for Chamberlin, given that his own solution to the problem of duopoly was a very pellucid statement of the rationality of collaboration. In his discussion of this issue, he first explained what should be meant by the 'independence' of the duopolistic competitors.

---

72. Rothschild, 'Price Theory and Oligopoly', *Economic Journal* 57 (1947): 305–307.

73. Chamberlin himself said that it was his investigation of oligopoly that came first, and the discussion of product differentiation followed—his theory was 'born out of oligopoly'; *Towards a More General Theory of Value* (New York: Oxford University Press, 1957), p. 32 n. 3.

74. Edward Chamberlin, *The Theory of Monopolistic Competition*, 6th ed. (Cambridge: Harvard University Press, 1948), p. 16.

One of the conditions of the problem must be the complete independence of the two sellers, for obviously, if they combine, there is monopoly. This independence must, however, be interpreted with care, for, in the nature of the case, when there are only two or a few sellers, their fortunes are not independent. There can be no actual, or tacit, agreement—that is all. Each is forced by the situation itself to take into account the policy of his rival in determining his own, and this cannot be construed as a 'tacit agreement' between the two.

This is true, no matter how complex the manner in which his competitor's policies figure in the determination of his own. A certain move, say a price cut, may be advantageous to one seller in view of his rival's present policy, i.e., assuming it not to change. But if his rival is certain to make a counter move, there is no reason to assume that he will not; and for the first seller to recognize the fact that his rival's policy is not a datum, but is determined by his own, cannot be construed as a negation of independence. It is simply to consider the indirect consequences of his own acts—the effect on himself of his own policy, mediated by that of his competitor. Of course, he may or may not take them into account, but he is equally independent in either case.[75]

Chamberlin went on to argue that if the duopolists did not consider the indirect consequences of their policies, the result would be either the Cournot or the Bertrand, or (he believed, arguably mistakenly) the Edgeworth solution; but if they did consider the indirect consequences, the result would be the monopoly price—that is, the producers would behave like an informal cartel. This is so, Chamberlin claimed, whether the duopolists adjust the amount they produce (as in Cournot) or the price (as in Bertrand). He put the matter clearly when discussing the latter case. Suppose the price of the commodity rests temporarily at the monopoly level, that is, at the level which gives the highest profit to the industry as a whole. If either one of the producers cut below this price,

> he would, by the incursions made upon his rival's sales, force him at once to follow suit. To the argument that if he did not cut his rival would, the answer is that his rival would not for the same reason that he does not. If each seeks his maximum profit rationally and intelligently, he will realize that when there are only two or a few sellers his own move has a considerable

75. Ibid., p. 31.

effect upon his competitors, and that this makes it idle to suppose that they will accept without retaliation the losses he forces upon them. Since the result of a cut by any one is inevitably to decrease his own profits, no one will cut, and, although the sellers are entirely independent, the equilibrium result is the same as though there were a monopolistic agreement between them.[76]

So Chamberlin was clear that if one producer has 'a considerable effect' on his rival, there will be an incentive for his rival to strike back in some fashion, with the result that it is possible for them together to maintain a monopoly production level. This is, of course, precisely the point that we looked at in Chapter One: a prisoners' dilemma with strategic interaction may lead to the maintenance of the co-operative outcome. Any situation where there is a 'considerable effect' of this kind would in principle generate collaboration, and Chamberlin coined the term 'oligopoly' to describe such a situation.[77]

Accordingly, truly competitive behaviour occurred only when the effect of one person's actions on another was inconsiderable. Chamberlin very precisely defined perfect (or, the term he preferred, 'pure') competition as involving

(1) a relatively large number of buyers and sellers of (2) a perfectly standardized product. The first diminishes the influence of any one in the general market situation to negligibility; the second, by identifying completely the product of a single seller with those of his competitors, denies him any measure of control over his own price as distinct from the general market price, which control might exist by reason of buyers" preferences for one variety of good over another.[78]

He then summarised his idea. If one assumes that each participant 'seeks independently to maximize his profit', then one will conclude that there will be

76. Ibid., pp. 47–48.

77. See 'On the Origin of "Oligopoly"' in his *Towards a More General Theory of Value*. His invention of the word (or, strictly speaking, his re-invention of it, or his introduction of it into English—it can be found in the Latin text of More's *Utopia!*) is a neat illustration of how recent a clear theory of competition, oligopoly and monopoly was, and how late in the history of modern economics anyone looked seriously at the problem of small or large numbers of agents.

78. Chamberlin, *The Theory of Monopolistic Competition*, p. 16.

a monopoly price for any fairly small number of sellers. No one will cut from the monopoly figure because he would force others to follow him, and thereby work his own undoing. As their numbers increase, it is impossible to say at just what point this consideration ceases to be a factor. If there were 100 sellers, a cut by any one which doubled his sales would, if his gains were taken equally from each of his competitors, reduce the sales of each of them by only 1/99, and this might be so small as not to force them, because of the cut, to do anything which they would not do without it. At whatever point this becomes true, the barrier to the downward movement of price from the point which will maximize the joint profits of all is re-moved. No one seller will look upon himself as causing the dislodgement, since he secures his gains with comparatively little disturbance to any of his rivals. Under these circumstances there is no reason for him to withhold a shading of his price which is to his advantage, and which has no repercus-sions. Nor is there any reason for the others not to do likewise, and the price becomes the purely competitive one.[79]

These pages of Chamberlin's *Theory of Monopolistic Competition* represent, extraordinary as it might seem, the first wholly clear and consistent state-ment of the modern theory of monopoly, oligopoly and perfect competition. And yet precisely because of their clarity we can see some of the obvious problems about the theory, and why his predecessors had kept their distance from such a schematic account. First, Chamberlin, as we have seen, insisted on many occasions that he was not talking about tacit agreement between oligopolists to keep a monopoly price level; and yet there is one perfectly straightforward tradition of discussing tacit agreements or conventions in which the behaviour of the oligopolists would immediately be construed as an agreement—that is, of course, the tradition going back to Hume's re-marks in the *Enquiries* about the two men rowing a boat together.

Thus, two men pull the oars of a boat by common convention for common interest, without any promise or contract: thus gold and silver are made the measures of exchange; thus speech and words and language are fixed by human convention and agreement. Whatever is advantageous to two or more persons, if all perform their part; but what loses all advantage if only one perform, can arise from no other principle.[80]

79. Ibid., p. 49.
80. Ibid., p. 306.

It is true that, as Hume says, this is not a promise, but it is a convention, and the notion of tacit agreement is very close to that of convention. Chamberlin later expressed himself puzzled by commentators on his work who insisted on treating his indirect consequences as examples of co-operation,[81] and yet the distinction which he insisted on is not at all clear.

Nor is the related distinction between retaliation by price-cutting and retaliation by other means. Suppose there were some more or less formal agreement between the firms, breach of which was punished in some way: since the point of the agreement would be to maximise the profits of each firm, making the agreement and policing it would both be means towards the goal of each 'independently' maximising its profits. The only reason on the face of it for selecting the means of retaliation which Chamberlin did—price-cutting or increasing the amount produced—is that they are the ones permitted under some (though not all) legal anti-trust regimes. This artificial restriction on the forms of collaboration and retaliation would not have seemed so plausible to an economist writing at the beginning of the anti-trust era rather than some thirty or forty years into it.

And, above all, there is a major puzzle (to which my discussion in Chapter Three will have alerted us) in Chamberlin's account of the transition from oligopoly to a regime of perfect competition. 'At whatever point this becomes true [that no one is significantly affected by a rival's action], the barrier to the downward movement of price from the point which will maximize the joint profits of all is removed. No one seller will look upon himself as causing the dislodgement, since he secures his gains with comparatively little disturbance to any of his rivals.' If there genuinely *is* such a point, then however small the contribution which any individual makes, it is still *that* contribution which crosses the threshold. What Chamberlin in fact had in mind, almost certainly, was a situation where there is no such threshold: whether or not something makes a discernable or appreciable difference is a classic sorites question. If something either is or is not appreciable (which seems plausible), it does not follow, as we have repeatedly seen, that we can determine the precise point at *which* it becomes appreciable. Only in such a situation would it be reasonable to conclude of our contribution that it had not 'caused the dislodgement'; but the paradoxical quality of such reasoning

81. See his 'On the Origin of Oligopoly', *Economic Journal* 67 (1957): 216–217; *Towards a More General Theory of Value*, p. 42.

ought to have alerted Chamberlin (as it might have alerted his predecessors) to the difficulties of his argument.

Nevertheless, this part of Chamberlin's discussion became immensely influential. He had made the all-important distinction between situations where one person's actions had real consequences on another's well-being and there were therefore good reasons for the sufferer to take action against the cause of his suffering, and situations where this was not so because of the negligibility of the experienced effect. As a result, he had given an explanation of why producers in a competitive situation would not band together which went far beyond the vague notions of earlier writers that they would find it practically difficult to do so, through inability to communicate and so on; though it might be worth remarking that even Paul Samuelson, writing about Chamberlin in the 1960s, argued that it was only the costs of communication which stopped large numbers of people from colluding in informal cartels: '[P]erhaps we are lucky that people are so dispersed, perverse, cantankerous and deaf to communication, for otherwise our world of not-very-workable competition could be far more imperfectly competitive indeed.'[82] The implications of Chamberlin's ideas began to be drawn by various economists in the 1940s and 1950s, as they started to investigate more fully the difficulties inherent in a wide variety of co-operative enterprises. Ironically, in view of the fact that his theories of product differentiation and of prevalent monopoly came under their most bitter attack from economists at the University of Chicago,[83] it was writers in the so-called Chicago School who insisted most vehemently on analysing perfect competition and monopoly in Chamberlinian terms. An early example of this was an article by Don Patinkin analysing cartels and arguing that they would always have a tendency to fall apart as the number of participants increased.[84] But the most important example was the extremely influential textbook by George Stigler called *The Theory of Price*, which was rewritten several times from its first appearance in 1942 to its last in 1987.[85] The 1946 edition used Chamberlin's

82. Paul Samuelson, 'The Monopolistic Competition Revolution', in R. E. Kuenne, ed., *Monopolistic Competition Theory: Studies in Impact* (New York: Wiley, 1967), p. 120.

83. See, for example, Chamberlin, *Towards a More General Theory of Value*, pp. 296–306.

84. Patinkin, 'Multiple-Plant Firms, Cartels, and Imperfect Competition', *Quarterly Journal of Economics* 66 (1947): 173–205.

85. Published as *The Theory of Competitive Price* (New York: Macmillan, 1942); this was much augmented and given the new title *The Theory of Price* in 1946 (New York: Mac-

analysis, and terminology, of oligopoly and monopoly, while Stigler's discussion of cartels in the 1966 edition effectively introduced the term 'free rider' into academic discourse, though it was a term which had long been used among trades unionists.[86]

> Suppose $(n - 1)$ firms join the cartel, but one firm remains outside. So far as the members of the cartel are concerned, the situation is not very different. Each gets a quota of $1/(n - 1)$ of total sales by the cartel. The firm remaining outside the cartel is not large enough to have much influence on price . . .
>
> If the cartel members are not much influenced by the recalcitrant firm, its owner is much altered in circumstances. He obtains a profit . . . in excess of that of a cartel member, per unit of time. After all he is getting the full benefit of the higher price without paying any of the cost by way of reduced output. In labor union language he is a free rider.
>
> And this is the first difficulty in forming a cartel. Every firm would prefer to be the outsider, and yet if enough stay outside the cartel becomes futile: a large group of free riders will find that the streetcar won't run. In general the cartel becomes feasible only if the number of firms is not very large, and (what is then usually the case) a few firms are so large relative to the industry that they cannot individually abstain from the cartel or it will not be formed.[87]

At the same time writers on public finance were developing similar ideas in their field. The process began with an article by the young Richard Musgrave in 1938, in which he called into question the reasoning of Sax, De Viti De Marco, Wicksell and Lindahl. Citing the new ideas of Chamberlin about competition and collusion in the economy of private goods, he stressed the

millan), which in turn was issued in a revised edition in 1952, a third edition in 1966, and a fourth edition in 1987.

86. It was first used, in its literal sense, in late nineteenth-century American slang to describe the practice of riding on trains without paying (like the hobos of the Depression); it had then found its way into American trades union parlance by the time of the Second World War. See the *Oxford English Dictionary*, where the first example of its use in its modern sense is from an article on cartels of 1941 (Robert A. Brady, 'Policies of National Manufacturing Spitzenverbande I', *Political Science Quarterly* 56 [1941]: 222). So not only the idea but also the terminology was surprisingly late.

87. Stigler, *The Theory of Price*, 3d ed., p. 233.

fact that compulsion had proved absolutely necessary for the provision of public goods:

> [I]ndirectly the element of compulsion affects the behavior of individuals in the formulation of collective decisions. In attempting to minimize their own contributions, political groups are concerned with the task of *forcing* a maximum contribution upon others, rather than with accepting the latter's voluntary offers.[88]

And in a footnote he broached the central idea of the new approach to public finance.

> We note the theoretical difficulty which arises for the voluntary exchange theory in the event that some of the members of the community should attempt to benefit from public services without in turn being eager to contribute their share. While recognized as constituting a 'pathological group' and a 'problem,'[89] they are ruled out by the assumption of purely voluntary action. Assuming, however, for the sake of argument that all people act in the precribed 'pathological' manner, the following problem arises: if the total cost of public services is covered by a large number of contributors, a reduction in the contribution of any one contributor will fail to affect notably the total supply of public services—either from the point of view of this contributor or in the eyes of other contributors who join in the consumption of the same indivisible services. Hence the reduction will result in a gain for the contributor in question without leading to reprisals. If all contributors should accordingly decide to reduce their contributions, the volume of public services will tend to shrink, and an unstable situation will result.[90]

This thought was picked up after the war by Paul Samuelson in a well-known article on 'The Pure Theory of Public Expenditure', in which he observed that because of this one could never determine an optimal level of collective consumption, in the way that the competitive market determined

88. Musgrave, 'The Voluntary Exchange Theory of Public Economy', *Quarterly Journal of Economics* 53 (1939): 224–226, 220.

89. References respectively to De Viti De Marco and Benham. It should be noted that Musgrave, like Benham, assumed that Wicksell was committed to the voluntary exchange theory, and that his own remarks in this footnote were as much a criticism of Wicksell as of the rest of the voluntary exchange theorists.

90. Musgrave, 'The Voluntary Exchange Theory of Public Economy', p. 219 n. 5.

it for private goods, as 'now it is in the selfish interest of each person to give *false* signals, to pretend to have less interest in a given collective consumption activity than he really has, etc'.[91] Musgrave adopted this version of his original point when he returned to the question in his 1959 book on *The Theory of Public Finance*. This then became the background against which Olson wrote *The Logic of Collective Action*, and the ideas developed which I traced in the course of Part I of this book.

91. Samuelson, 'The Pure Theory of Public Expenditure', *Review of Economics and Statistics* 36 (1954): 387–389.

Conclusion to Part II

Although, as in any historical narrative, there have been many false starts and dead ends, a reasonably consistent story has emerged from the account which I have given in the previous two chapters. Over the past two hundred and fifty years, ideas about co-operation remained fairly stable until the early twentieth century. On the whole, philosophers until then were impressed by the propensity of human beings to co-operate on common enterprises even in quite large numbers, and indeed they often saw that propensity as something to beware of rather than something to encourage—as in the case of the conspiratorial producers anathematised by Adam Smith, and, more generally, the fear of powerful 'partial associations' manifested by Hobbes, Hume, Rousseau and Bentham (and, indeed, Marx). They were also aware that it was by no means an entirely reliable propensity, and that some people would always fail to see that their interest lay in collaboration. They tended to give two explanations for this. One was that it was not always clear to people that they did share a common interest with their collaborators, and the other was that even when they were aware of the shared objective, they could simply be imprudent about the means to achieve it, just as they could be imprudent about any other long-term or distant goal. These philosophers did not believe that failure to collaborate could be regarded as rational, as long as it was the case that the collaboration would indeed be effective at securing the goals of the participants. Their chief concern was usually to demonstrate that underlying the apparent welter of particular interests and conflicting beliefs lay certain common goals which all men would share, and that, understood properly, politics and ethics could be the pursuit of individual self-interest in a co-ordinated fashion.

On the whole, the objection to this view at the time, raised most markedly by opponents of Hobbes, Hume and Rousseau, but still levelled at Bentham and his successors, was not that it was incoherent or rested on a mistaken idea of instrumental rationality; it was rather that by stressing the instrumental and conventional character of most social practices and moral norms, these writers undermined the force of all existing institutions, which came to be seen as amenable to radical change if our underlying interests required it. Hume, in particular, had an answer to this charge, in that he was very conscious of the complexity of conventions and the difficulty of altering them, but of course Bentham and his followers proudly espoused the cause of radical innovation in social life. Along with Rousseau, the early utilitarians were partly able to put forward a much more radical programme than Hume because they had joined their general theory of instrumentally rational politics with a specific theory of democracy, in which the fundamental political commitment was to secure a common life through an acceptance of majoritarianism;[1] but this presupposed the rationality of participation in an electoral process, and is an additional illustration of the fact that collaboration in very large groups did not present itself to them as a fundamental theoretical problem (though again, they were all fully aware of the potential failure of reasoning on the part of some members of the electorate).

It is worth stressing that the actual numbers of people with which they were concerned were already large, as it is sometimes said that the problem of co-operation in large groups is a specifically modern problem, engendered by the rise of mass democracy in the late nineteenth century. The old electoral system of England with which Hobbes (for instance) was familiar was much more inclusive than is often realised; about a third of the male population may have had the vote in 1640 (along with some women), out of a total population of some four and a half million.[2] And Bentham advocated a near-universal franchise, including votes for women. While Rousseau famously thought that ideally the large existing states of Europe should be broken up into smaller units, his enthusiasm for the Roman Republic as a democratic model suggests that the numbers involved might still be very large (for, as I remarked earlier, the republic may have had a million citizens). Even Hume, though he was not so interested in democratic mecha-

---

1. I have argued elsewhere, though somewhat controversially, that the same was true of Hobbes. See my 'Hobbes and Democracy', in *Rethinking the Foundations of Modern Political Thought*, ed. Annabel Brett (Cambridge: Cambridge University Press, 2006).

2. See Derek Hirst, *The Representative of the People* (Cambridge: Cambridge University Press, 1975), p. 105, and pp. 18–19 for women.

nisms, recognised that politics was now conducted perfectly effectively in very large states; this was part of the point of his famous essay 'On the Populousness of Ancient Nations', in which he demonstrated that modern states had far outstripped in size those of antiquity.

Moreover, acceptance of the rationality of large-scale collaboration continued all through the heyday of mass politics in the nineteenth century; indeed, the sight of mass revolutionary action, or prolonged and bitter strikes by trades unionists, was a powerful vindication of the theory. As we have seen, J. S. Mill still shared the commitment of his father's generation to collective action, and even Edgeworth, as I showed in Chapter Five, contrary to the popular impression of his work, believed that collaboration among agents such as trades unionists made perfectly good sense. The difficult issue with which these philosophers, including most notably Sidgwick, grappled was the question not of collaboration but of *universal* participation. They assumed on the whole (I would say rightly) something like a threshold in co-operative activity, after which there is not the same reason to contribute as there had been before; they also assumed (again I would say rightly) that an individual has a reason to contribute only if enough other people do likewise.

It is clear that these two assumptions make an ethics based on this kind of theory in principle very different from a conventional ethical theory, in which we have a *moral* reason to act, independently (often) of what other people do; though it is not so clear that they make it different in practice, as it might well be that the most effective way of co-ordinating our activities is to create structures in which the participants are not called upon to make these kinds of calculations. It might also be the case that (for the reasons I outlined in Part I) the participants would want to contribute to the common enterprise even when they knew that enough other people were going to do so, as they might thereby be able to claim some role in bringing it about. For example, I might wish on instrumental grounds to keep my word, even though I know that promise-keeping is such a widespread practice that my defection from it is not going to weaken it, because my action has a reasonable chance of being part of the set of actions which do serve to maintain the practice. But even with these provisos, a utilitarian theory of this kind cannot put the same weight on universal compliance as a more familiar ethical theory would. This was indeed what chiefly troubled the twentieth-century inventors of 'rule' utilitarianism; in many ways their idea was a revival of the original attack on instrumental ways of thinking, in which instrumentalism was accused of undermining or contradicting quite central and familiar features of our ethical life.

There is a real argument here. I think that it is indeed impossible to justify (within the instrumental view) universal co-operation as a fundamental principle, and if one feels strongly that no exceptions to a collaborative practice can be legitimate, then one cannot in the end base one's belief on the instrumental view. But this is quite different from saying that there is an internal incoherence in the instrumental approach. What I have been arguing in this book is that it is at least theoretically possible to treat all collaborative enterprises as if they contain appropriate thresholds for participation, and that if those thresholds can be reached (or be presumed to have been reached), then collaboration up to that point makes sense for the individuals concerned. The rule utilitarians of the mid-twentieth century, however, tended to confuse these two issues, and sometimes wrote as if an answer to the question of why we should collaborate in large groups would allow the utilitarian to put forward a moral theory broadly identical to the conventional alternative; this was true, as we saw in Part I, even of David Lyons, who up to that point in his book had provided the most profound analysis of the problem.

Even more surprising, perhaps, than the story I have told about utilitarianism is the story I have told about modern economics. If my account in Chapter Five is correct, the modern idea that numbers (or, more properly, the relative size of one's contribution) are critical to the question of whether economic agents will collaborate or not did not appear clearly and unequivocally until the 1920s. Indeed, it seems that the appearance of the word 'oligopoly', coined by Chamberlin in 1927,[3] was more or less coeval with the invention of the idea. This should not surprise us: the essence of the idea is a contrast between insignificant contributions, under perfectly competitive

3. The date of his Ph.D. dissertation. The word was eliminated from the first appearance in print of Chamberlin's argument, his article 'Duopoly: Value Where Sellers are Few'(*Quarterly Journal of Economics* 44 [1929]: 63–100), on the grounds that F. W. Taussig, the editor of the journal, thought the word a monstrosity. As Chamberlin subsequently discovered, the word 'oligopolium' had in fact been invented in More's *Utopia*: '*Si monopolium appellari non potest quod non unus vendit, certe oligopolium est*'!; *The Complete Works of St. Thomas More*, vol. 4, ed. Edward Surtz and J. H. Hexter (New Haven, Conn.: Yale University Press, 1965), p. 68. See Chamberlin's 'On the Origin of Oligopoly', *Economic Journal* 67 (1957): 211–218.

conditions, and significant ones, and some term was immediately needed to describe the state of affairs where an individual's contribution, however small, still makes an appreciable difference to the outcome. As I stressed, the original idea of unrestricted competition was that there should be no artificial barriers to entry—it was part of the same campaign against partial associations which was central to the work of Hume, Smith and Bentham. The relative size of the producer's enterprise was not an important aspect of the theory, except insofar as many producers who were widely dispersed might find it hard in practice to co-ordinate their activities and to conspire against the public. Again, there are many qualifications to be made to this generalisation, and some writers (for example, Wicksell) came quite close to the modern formulation, but in virtually every instance they shied away at the last moment and concluded that collaboration even in large groups could be rational. Given the power and ubiquity of cartels, both formal and informal, in the world before the First World War, and given the passion behind organised working-class movements, it would have been ridiculous to call this into question.

But if this is the history of the modern idea of perfect competition and oligopoly, the obvious question is, why did it take this shape? What happened in the first decades of the twentieth century to make an argument plausible which had virtually never occurred to anyone before as a good argument on which to base a theory of human behaviour? It seems to me that a number of things converged to allow the theory to be put forward. First, the techniques of marginalist economics themselves encouraged an approach of this kind. If we are primarily interested in small shifts by an economic agent away from an existing position, this in a sense builds into our analysis a concentration on the short-term and immediate benefit to the agent, rather than the long-term and rather remote benefit. This is, of course, not a *necessary* feature of the techniques, since it is quite possible to specify the options among which the agent is choosing in such a way as to build in long-term benefits, but in practice many arguments couched in marginalist terms did not do this. We have seen repeatedly that a failure to collaborate even in large groups was usually viewed by the classical political economists, and the philosophers who influenced them, as a failure of reasoning produced by the irrational (though understandable) inclination to be misled by short-term interests, and this attitude to the question was to some degree discouraged by the practice of marginalism.

But more important, I think, was the fact that, as we saw in the case of

Clark and Knight (not to mention the 'increasing returns' theorists in England, such as Harrod), economists in the 1920s and 1930s remained impressed by the power of combinations and the relative deficiencies of traditional competitive markets, and realised that the old idea that freedom of entry would guarantee a competitive result had turned out to be false. Formal freedom—that is, the absence of legal privilege—had proved wholly inadequate in securing competitive behaviour, and the enormous range of informal barriers suggested that it would be useless to depend on free entry to combat the power of combinations or monopolies. One of Chamberlin's own objectives was precisely to call into question freedom of entry as either a sufficient or a necessary condition for a competitive market, and many of his contemporaries on both the right and the left agreed with him.[4] But the absence of this prospect meant that unless there could be a justification of competitive behaviour *within an existing group of producers*, there would be no hope of securing a desirable distributive outcome through competitive behaviour. This was particularly troubling as by the 1920s it was widely believed that socialism offered a much more effective means of securing this goal than a competitive market could do, precisely because competition would always be undermined by cartelisation and monopoly; only a centrally planned economy could be the ideal form of capitalism.

This is an important and now rather neglected aspect of twentieth-century history: as central planning has receded from the political agenda of both Western and Eastern societies, its intellectual characteristics have largely been forgotten. But it played a very important role in the formation of the modern theory of competition. To understand the issues, we should remember that (as we saw in Chapter Five) for the generation of Sidgwick and Edgeworth, a competitive market went along with utilitarian social policy: by itself, competition would simply degenerate into a war of combinations, and political intervention of some kind would be required to secure a utilitarian outcome from market behaviour. This model, which I described in Chapter Five as embodying a lexical ordering, in which a social policy was to choose the utilitarian optimum from the set of Pareto-superior allocations which might be generated by market bargaining, became the basis for the so-called old welfare economics of early twentieth-century English writers such as A. C. Pigou, who continued to subscribe to a form of utilitarianism

---

4. See his remarks agreeing (in this instance) with Joan Robinson, in a chapter which he added to *The Theory of Monopolistic Competition* in its fifth edition (Cambridge, Mass.: Harvard University Press, 1947), pp. 199–200.

as the basis for welfare calculations.[5] But among economists, utilitarianism increasingly came to seem to be an unreliable, contentious and 'unscientific' principle upon which to base political decisions which—among other things—deprived people of their liberty in various ways. Because, as I said in Chapter Five, the competitive equilibrium could be viewed as non-contentiously superior to other allocations in the sense that anyone could in principle be adequately compensated for losses incurred in moving to that allocation, the equilibrium emerged as a prime goal of social policy—despite the obvious objection that compensation would actually have to be paid if the equilibrium was to be superior to previous states, and that such payments very seldom happened.

Though the equilibrium could be represented as if it were the result of unconstrained bargaining among lots of producers and consumers, as indeed it had been by Edgeworth, there was still no good reason to suppose that it would actually be generated simply by free market behaviour. As long as it seemed rational that producers would collaborate to set a quasi-monopolistic price, the competitive equilibrium might have to be enforced by the same kind of political action which would have been employed to enforce the utilitarian optimum. This was exactly what Pareto himself envisaged: he consistently wanted socialism if he could not have a genuinely competitive market, as he thought that the socialist bureaucrats would arrange the allocation of goods in the society in such a way as to ensure the equivalent of the competitive equilibrium. 'Pure economics does not give us a truly decisive criterion for choosing between an organization of society based on private property and a socialist organization.'[6] As early as 1908, Pareto's follower Enrico Barone set out a systematic account of how a ministry of production in a collectivist society might ideally do the calculations in such a way that a Paretian allocation was secured: 'the system of the equations of the collectivist equilibrium is no other than that of the free competition.' Barone even asserted that this was 'at bottom, Marx's theory of value'[7]—the

5. See Pigou, *Wealth and Welfare* (London: Macmillan, 1912), 2d ed., entitled *The Economics of Welfare* (London: Macmillan, 1920).

6. Vilfredo Pareto, *Manual of Political Economy*, trans. Ann S. Schwier (London: Macmillan, 1972), p. 269; see his general discussion of the ministry of production, pp. 267–269.

7. Barone, 'The Ministry of Production in the Collectivist State', translated and reprinted in *Collectivist Economic Planning*, ed. F. A. von Hayek (London: Routledge, 1935), pp. 274, 275.

ideas that Marxism was 'scientific' and that modern Paretian economics was 'scientific' had coalesced in a single principle of distribution.

Socialists, particularly in Central Europe, quickly picked up this idea. The most prominent instance in the second decade of the century was the Austrian Otto Neurath, more famous later for his membership in the Vienna Circle, but during the First World War one of a group of economists employed by the Austrian government to manage the war economy; after the war he was also briefly an official in the two short-lived Bavarian soviet republics. Neurath wrote extensively on the principles involved in central planning, and his writings may have contributed to the formation of the Soviet Union's centrally planned economy. He consistently argued that the Pareto principle should be the basis for the planned economy:

> [T]he administrative economy [Neurath's term for the planned economy, as distinct from the market economy] can, by rewards and penalties, prompt the individuals to do things which they would not have done in an economy characterised by exchange, because without these rewards and penalties the consequences would have been different. For example, the administrative economy could enforce a transfer, the completion of which would not mean a lower quality of life for anybody, but a higher one for one individual. Such a transfer of course would not have taken place in the market economy.

The 'general principle of exchange' in an administrative economy, he wrote, was that 'those transfers will be executed which produce a higher quality of life for some and do not lower that of anybody else'.[8] In turn, Neurath was the chief target when Hayek put together his famous volume on *Collectivist Economic Planning* in 1935, in which he argued that the kinds of calculation presupposed in this form of socialism were impossible: only the actual functioning of a competitive market could yield the sort of information which the Neurathian administrative economy would need in order to produce the

---

8. These quotations are from an essay of 1917 entitled 'The Conceptual Structure of Economic Theory and Its Foundations' ('Das Begriffsgebäube der Wirtschaftslehre und seine Grundlagen'), *Zeitschrift für die gesamte Staatswissenschaft* 73 (1917): 484–520, translated in Neurath, *Economic Writings: Selections 1904–1945*, ed. Thomas E. Uebel and Robert S. Cohen, Vienna Circle Collection vol. 23 (Dordrecht: Kluwer, 2004), p. 321. For Neurath's role in the Austrian war economy and in the Bavarian soviets, see Uebel's introduction to this volume, pp. 26 and 40. For an account of the possible links between Neurath's work and the Soviet Union's command economy, see ibid., p. 82 n. 99.

equivalent of a competitive equilibrium. But views like Neurath's continued, and to some degree formed the basis of the 'new' welfare economics of the 1930s, in which the Pareto principle displaced utilitarianism as the guide to social policy.

So socialism in the first three decades of the twentieth century challenged the old principles of a free competitive market *from within:* it announced itself as the only method by which the distributive consequences of free competition could in fact be realised. The rational propensity of people to take collective action in their own interests had led to the creation of monopolies and cartels and to a failure to secure the benefits of free competition; but that same propensity could in turn be harnessed to achieve the benefits, if an entire community were to act together to implement the distributive equivalent of a competitive equilibrium through central planning. This was at bottom a very simple idea, and it could be countered by an equally simple idea: that collective action of this kind was in fact against the interests of the participants, whether the action took place at the level of the state or at the level of the industry. If competitive behaviour, at least in a situation of perfect competition, was in fact rational and (assuming no distorting circumstances) would therefore be self-sustaining, this brand of socialism would be circumvented and a free capitalist economy would continue to be the means by which the desirable social outcome could be achieved.

An additional factor in the appearance of the new theory of competitive behaviour in the 1930s, and its triumph in the 1950s and 1960s, may have been that the artificial character of the Sherman Act, and of similar restrictions on cartels in other countries, had come to be forgotten, or at least was not so vivid as it had still been to economists of Knight's generation. Behaviour induced by the act increasingly seemed to be normal and unconstrained; the maintenance of effective cartels appeared to be much more difficult than it had seemed to be half a century earlier, and the model of rational competitive behaviour seemed to be vindicated by events. The fact that modern competitive economies actually operate against a background of threatened state action, in which collective action of certain kinds will be prevented or punished, tended to be forgotten, or was treated only as providing an environment in which people were encouraged to act rationally.

For Olson and his successors, the model had been validated by modern circumstances, and it was entirely appropriate to begin to extend it from the narrow domain of economics into social and political science as a whole. They did not foresee the danger that what they were doing was producing a *reductio ad absurdum* of the theory, which would in time rebound upon its original formulation and call into question the modern account of competitive behaviour itself; for whereas the claim might have seemed plausible in the special circumstances of post-war economics, it seemed much less plausible when extended to all areas of human social life. There has been much more (so to speak) visceral objection to the idea of free riding as rational in political science than to the theory of perfect competition in economics, despite the fact that the theories are in fact the same.

If the arguments advanced in Part I are correct, what are the implications for the actual practice of modern economics? From one point of view, there are few implications: if there is a tendency for people not to co-operate when their contribution would be negligible compared to the size of the common good, then that is a fact about their behaviour, even if on my account it is irrational, and economic analysis can simply take it as such. Economists today are anyway rather less anxious than their predecessors about systematic incoherences in people's preferences, as judged by the austere criteria of rational choice theory; so-called experimental economics, not to mention the currently fashionable 'neuro-economics', takes for granted that people may not act as straightforward maximisers. On the other hand, as we have seen in Part II, for economists down to the 1930s the obvious 'fact' about economic behaviour was that people *did* co-operate in order to produce cartels and trades unions, and that such co-operation was indeed the most obvious feature of the modern world. It would be hard to argue that even if there is a propensity at the moment for people not to co-operate, the propensity is a fundamental and consistent feature of human action; after all, the whole point of labelling non-co-operation rational was (I have argued) to give non-co-operation a special salience for us in the face of the clear evidence that people do, as a matter of fact, combine reasonably successfully. If we cease to label it in this way, we will presumably begin to take seriously again the possibility that perfectly competitive markets cannot exist without constant political intervention.

The appropriate way to think about behaviour in a broadly competitive market would then be along one or another of the routes taken by economists in the nineteenth century. As we have seen, many possibilities were explored by theorists during that period, ranging from the pure (though I would say vague) utilitarianism of the Benthamites, through to what one might term the 'lexical utilitarianism' of Edgeworth and the old welfare economics, down to the centrally planned Paretianism of the 1920s and 1930s.

All had in common a much more realistic sense of rational conduct than was possessed by their successors, and also a much clearer sense of the fact that distributive questions require some sort of *moral* answer, even if the moral answer is intended (as with Pareto) to be as thin and universal as it can possibly be. Practically speaking, on this view the best way of thinking about competitive behaviour will be along the lines of the modern theory of oligopoly, with its acceptance that strategic interaction among broadly self-interested agents is extremely complex and that there are few general conclusions which can be drawn; in Edgeworth's phrase, competition will inevitably be marked by 'dissimulation and objectionable arts of higgling'. As everyone recognises, oligopolistic markets will not by themselves necessarily deliver acceptable distributive results, and so a competitive analysis which restricts itself to oligopoly and treats perfect competition as a fantasy will have to accept that (so to speak) the distributional decisions will be made at a different level from the economic analysis. If that means that we recognise once again that we all have to make these decisions ourselves through our political processes, and cannot rely on a chimera to do our moral and political work for us, then that is all to the good.

Index